"BRIDGE is a must-read for educators and activists looking for practical approaches to discussing immigrant rights and building strong movements for social change."

— Nadine Naber
Assistant Professor of Arab American Studies and Gender Studies, University of Michigan, Ann Arbor

"Our undying thanks to NNIRR for contributing this incredible workbook to the struggle for immigrant rights and human dignity. We're already putting it to good use!"

— Tarso Ramos
Western States Center, Portland, OR

"The BRIDGE Project workbook reflects a wonderful combination of commitment and practicality that will help meet a need that is greater than ever in today's society. We have see how changing demographics, increasing global poverty, a declining U.S. economy with ever shrinking human rights make it vital to find new approaches for defending and advancing immigrant rights. The entire BRIDGE Project and this workbook in particular are rooted in creativity and dedication of people with long experience in different immigrant communities and building understanding between them. The workbook's modules are realistic, imaginative, and even fun to utilize. They can be used to make a serious difference in overcoming the difficulties and hardship faced by so many immigrants today. Try them and see!"

— Elizabeth (Betita) Martínez
Director, Institute for MultiRacial Justice

"Based on their many years of experience, working in the immigrant community as activist practitioners, the authors raise issues so rarely discussed within the immigrant community and among immigrant advocate organizations and activists. The detailed, systematic, hands-on approach assembled in this workbook explores the complexity that is the immigrant community. The exercises found within, along with the teaching points, can be applied in community workshops, academic classrooms and workplace seminars. This book must be shared with colleagues, fellow activists and friends and will surely serve as a valuable resource for community-based organizations and classrooms!"

— Marta López-Garza
Associate Professor, Women's and Chicano/a Studies, California State University, Northridge

"This workbook will find a home in the hands of educators, organizers and activists looking for practical, and proven tools in the work of building the power of immigrant workers and communities. These flexible, fun exercises can be done anywhere- in union halls, church basements, university classrooms, and community forums- even on a moving bus! I wholeheartedly recommend BRIDGE."

— Dave Glaser
National Director, Immigrant Worker Freedom Rides

BRIDGE

Building a Race and Immigration Dialogue in the Global Economy

A Popular Education Resource for Immigrant & Refugee Community Organizers

by Eunice Hyunhye Cho,
Francisco Argüelles Paz y Puente,
Miriam Ching Yoon Louie, and Sasha Khokha

nnirr

national network for immigrant and refugee rights

www.nnirr.org

BRIDGE: Building a Race and Immigration Dialogue in the Global Economy
A Popular Education Resource for Immigrant and Refugee Community Organizers

Edited by Eunice Hyunhye Cho
Written by Eunice Hyunhye Cho, Francisco Argüelles Paz y Puente, Miriam Ching Yoon Louie, and Sasha Khokha

Published by the National Network for Immigrant and Refugee Rights
310 8th St. Suite 303, Oakland, CA 94607, USA
Tel: 510-465-1984   Fax: 510-465-1885
www.nnirr.org
nnirr@nnirr.org

The National Network for Immigrant and Refugee Rights (NNIRR) is a national organization composed of local coalitions and immigrant, refugee, community, religious, civil rights and labor organizations and activists. It serves as a forum to share information and analysis, to educate communities and the general public, and to develop and coordinate plans of action on important immigrant and refugee issues.

We work to promote a just immigration and refugee policy in the United States and to defend and expand the rights of all immigrants and refugees, regardless of immigration status. The National Network bases its efforts in the principles of equality and justice, and seeks the enfranchisement of all immigrant and refugee communities in the United States through organizing and advocating for their full labor, environmental, civil and human rights. We further recognize the unparalleled change in global, political and economic structures which has exacerbated regional, national and international patterns of migration, and emphasize the need to build international support and cooperation to strengthen the rights, welfare and safety of migrants and refugees.

Copyright © 2004 by National Network for Immigrant and Refugee Rights
All rights reserved.

Front cover art © Christine Wong, 2004
Design by Guillermo Prado, 8.2 design, Berkeley, CA
Printed by Inkworks Press, Berkeley, CA with union labor
ISBN 0-9752973-0-9

Table of Contents

Table of Contents ... iii
Acknowledgements ... vi

Section One: Framing Tools
Introduction ... 1
What's In this Book? ... 3
How to use BRIDGE ... 6
    Our Methodology ... 9
    Tips on Facilitation ... 13
    Checklist for Training ... 15
    Ground Rules ... 17
    Evaluation ... 20
    Interpretation and Translation:
    Strategies for Sharing Power in Our Multilingual Movement, by Alice Johnson ... 22

Section Two: BRIDGE Modules
    Module 1: History of Immigration 101 ... 38
        Overview, Backgrounder, Summary Points, and Workshop Menu ... 39
        *Opening: Our Names, Our Stories ... 42
        *Immigration Timeline: Where Do We Fit Into Immigration History? ... 43
        Variation 1: Longer Workshop Setting ... 44
        Variation 2: Quicker Workshop Setting ... 47
        Variation 3: Quicker Conference Setting ... 48
        Variation 4: BRIDGE on the Bus! ... 50
        History Under the Magnifying Glass ... 53
        Closing: Another Look at Our Names, Our Stories ... 60
        Fact Sheet: U.S. Immigration History ... 62
        Facilitator's Overview: U.S. immigration History ... 66
        BRIDGE Immigration History Timeline in Pictures ... 75
        Suggested Readings ... 112

    Module 2: Globalization, Migration, and Workers' Rights ... 114
        Overview, Backgrounder, Summary Points, and Workshop Menu ... 115
        Opening: Let's Move! A Miming Introduction ... 118
        Opening: The Most Unusual Job ... 120
        Immigration and Globalization Quiz ... 121

Table of Contents

  *Screening and discussion of video:
    Uprooted: Refugees of the Global Economy   126
  Closing: Another World is Possible   129
  Resources   130

Module 3: Introduction to Race, Migration, and Multiple Oppressions   132
  Overview, Backgrounder, Summary Points, and Workshop Menu   133
  Opening: Circle of Strength   137
  *How Strong Beats My Heart? Looking at Our Individual Oppressions
    and Privileges   138
  *Exploring Stereotypes We Face   140
  *What's Behind These Stereotypes?   143
  The Multiple Jeopardy Conga Line: Our Intersecting Identities   146
  Closing: Spider's Web Exercise   148
  Resources   149

Module 4: Migrant Rights are Human Rights!   150
  Overview, Backgrounder, Summary Points, and Workshop Menu   151
  *Opening: Three Questions—Talking about Human Rights in Our Lives   154
  *The Human Rights Circle: Human Rights in our Communities   156
  Organizing for Human Rights: Discussing Case Studies   162
  Closing: Poetic Vision of Human Rights   169
  Fact Sheet: Migrant Rights Are Human Rights   171
  Resources   174
  Universal Declaration of Human Rights   176
  UN Convention on the Protection of Rights For All Migrant Workers
    and Members of Their Families   180

Module 5: Immigrant Rights and LGBT Rights   186
  Overview, Backgrounder, Summary Points, and Workshop Menu   187
  Notes for Facilitators   190
  Opening: Our Shared Circle   192
  *Act Like a Lady, Act Like a Man   193
  Who's In, Who's Out?   197
  Xenophobia, Homophobia, and More   200
  *Making the Stories Fit: Testimonies of LGBT Immigrants   202
  Closing: Head, Heart, Feet   209
  Fact Sheet: Glossary of Terms   210
  Fact Sheet: Historical Exclusion of LGBT Immigrants to the U.S.   212
  Resources   213

Table of Contents

Module 6: Immigrant Women's Leadership 214
    Overview, Backgrounder, Summary Points, and Workshop Menu 215
    Opening: Honoring Women in Our Lives 218
    *Our Roots and Branches: Three Generations of Women In Our Family 219
    *Step In, Step Out 222
    Focus on Immigrant Women's Rights 227
    *Dismantling Gender Inequality in Organizing 230
    Closing: Postcards to Ourselves 233
    Resources 234

Module 7: Finding Common Ground: The Changing Demographics of Race and Migration
    Overview, Backgrounder, Summary Points, and Workshop Menu 237
    Opening: Share Squares 239
    *Mapping Our Community 242
    *Identifying and Discussing Tensions in Our Community 245
    The Ten Chairs: Race, Migration, and Wealth in U.S. History 247
    *Building on Success Stories 254
    Closing: Our Common Circle 261
    Resources 262

Module 8: Conflict Transformation In Community Organizing 264
    Overview, Backgrounder, Summary Points, and Workshop Menu 265
    *Opening: Naming Conflict 269
    *Visualizing Personal Experiences of Conflict 271
    Changing the Script: Visualizing Solutions to Conflict 276
    Closing: Naming Conflict Transformation 278
    Fact Sheet: Tips for Conflict Transformation In Our Communities 279
    Resources 282

Section Three: Additional Resources
  Additional Resources 285
  Organizational Contacts 288
  BRIDGE Glossary 292
  About the Authors 302
  Order Forms 304

* core exercises

Acknowledgements

The BRIDGE Project workbook is the result of a collective process that builds on the wisdom and experience of many people. We give our thanks to everyone who generously gave us their energy, time, expertise, wisdom, and enthusiasm on our long journey to the publication of BRIDGE. We build on the many lessons that were shared with us and that we learned on our way; we offer BRIDGE as an addition to the rich tradition of popular education, freedom fighting, and the vision for a better world.

Many thanks to our **BRIDGE Advisory Board** members, who gave us their humor, wisdom and experience, as well as critical feedback that gave shape to much of BRIDGE: Tomás Aguilar; Jennifer Allen, *Border Action Network*; Susan Alva, *Migration Policy and Resource Center*, Occidental College; Pablo Alvarado, *National Day Labor Organizing Network*; Sung E Bai, *CAAAV: Organizing Asian Communities*; Amy Casso, *National Organizers Alliance*; Jung Hee Choi, *Women of Color Resource Center*; Trishala Deb, *Audre Lorde Project*; Eman Desouky, *Arab Women's Solidarity Association*; Leah Grundy, *UC Berkeley Labor Center*; Mónica Hernández, *Highlander Center*; Stacy Kono, *Asian Immigrant Women Advocates*; Alma Maquitico, *Border Network for Human Rights*; Victor Narro, *UCLA Labor Center*; Lisa Moore, *Mujeres Unidas y Activas*; Rosa Perea, *Centro Juan Diego*; Katie Quan, *UC Berkeley Center for Labor Research and Education*; Tarso Ramos, *Western States Center*; Ninaj Raoul, *Haitian Women for Haitian Refugees*; Loretta Ross, *National Center for Human Rights Education*; Jerome Scott, *Project South*, Atlanta, GA; and Mangala Sharma, *Refugee Women's Network*.

Gracias to all the talented organizers and groups who tested out the BRIDGE modules around the country, giving us their thoughtful evaluation and suggestions to make it work! Special thanks to Tomás Aguilar, Josefina Castillo, and Yvonne Montejano for helping to organize pilot testing in Boston and San Marcos, TX. Thanks to our **Bay Area Community Organizers**: Brenda Anibarro, *Datacenter*; Maya Anderson, *AFSC/Project Voice*; Martha Benitez, *EBASE*; Mariana Bustamante, *ACLU Immigrant Rights Project*; Marta Donayre, *National Center for Lesbian Rights*; Sister Cecilia Calva, *Interfaith Coalition for Immigrant Rights*; Jung Hee Choi, *Women of Color Resource Center*; Conte Davis, Hillary Ronen, and Jill Shenker, *La Raza Centro Legal/Day Labor Program*; Leslie Bulbuk, *Love Sees No Borders*; Dae Han Kim, *Korean Community Center of the East Bay*; Lisa Macapinlac and Ed Vallardares, *Filipinos for Affirmative Action*; Kai-Yuan Tan, *API-FORCE*. Thanks to our **Boston Area Community Organizers**: Marcony Almeida, *Brazilian Immigrant Center*; Ana Amaral, *Jobs with Justice*; Nikhil Aziz and Palak Shah, *Political Research Associates*; Gabriel Camacho and Mario Dávila, *AFSC/Project Voice*; Yee Won Chong and Kwah Waadabi,

Acknowledgements

Haymarket People's Fund; Kate Driscoll, *Voices In Action*; Isaac Hodes and Corey Kurtz, *Irish Immigration Center*; Lawrence Joe and Karlo Ng, *Chinese Progressive Association*; Sophia Kim, *Coalition for Asian Pacific American Youth*; Sandy Lin, *National Immigration Project of the NLG*; Minsu Longiaru, *Greater Boston Legal Services*; Suren Modoliar, *North American Alliance for Fair Employment*; Jason Pramas, *Campaign on Contingent Work*; Michele Rudy, *MIRA*; Basav Sen, *Center for Economic Justice*. Thanks to our **Austin/Houston/San Antonio, TX Area Community Organizers:** Viola Casares, Gabriela Gutiérrez, and Petra Mata, *Fuerza Unida*; Amy Casso, *NOA*; Josefina Castillo and Yvonne Montejano, *AFSC*; Luz Marina Díaz, *Clean Water Action*; Erika González, *PODER*; Anita Grabowski, Julien Ross, *Equal Justice Center*; Sarah Henkel, *Manos de Cristo*; Rose Hernández, Eduardo Montiel, *Texas Council on Family Violence*; Concepción Miranda, *Houston Area Women's Center*; Briana Mohan, *Our Lady of Guadalupe Church*; Iracema Mastroleo, Sandra Molinari, Sandra Rangel, Claudia Thompson, Yasmin Turk, *Safe Place*; Elizabeth Walsh, *Casa Marianella*; Anna Nuñez, *Pacifica Radio*. We also appreciate the opportunity to have seen BRIDGE materials used in action. We thank the **groups that showcased BRIDGE on the way:** Cheers to the *Immigrant Workers Freedom Ride*—and all of the Freedom Ride Education Coordinators who used BRIDGE activities on the bus as they braved popular education, cross-country style, and a special thanks to all of the Houston and San Francisco Bay Area Freedom riders, whose friendship and inspiration supported our work. Many thanks to the *Refugee Women's Network* and the *Bay Area Immigrant Rights Coalition* for giving us the chance to present and promote BRIDGE. Thanks also to the SEIU Western Region for their feedback and for their adaptation of BRIDGE materials in their Citizenship, Race, and Immigration curriculum training sessions.

We couldn't have done it without other **curriculum developers and educators** that inspired us, who generously shared their ideas and work with us to enrich this curriculum. Many thanks to Moira Bowman, *Western States Center*; Linda Burnham, *Women of Color Resource Center*; Leah Grundy, *UC Berkeley Labor Center*; Alice Johnson, *Highlander Center*; Joanne Kim, *Community Coalition of LA*; the Women of Color Resource Center's curriculum, *WEDGE: Women's Education in the Global Economy*; to Project South's *Popular Education for Movement Building*, to the Todos Institute, and to Bev Burke, Jojo Geronimo, D'Arcy Martin, Barb Thomas, and Carol Wall for letting us adapt material from their fantastic book, *Education for Changing Unions*.

Many thanks to Dena al-Adeeb, Nahar Alam, Hatem Bazien, Youmna Chlala, Jane Chung, Eunsook Lee, Nadine Naber, Elizabeth Martínez, Shaily Matani, Vivek Mittal,

Acknowledgements

Betsy Raasch-Gilman, Thenmozhi Soundararajan, Andrea Smith, and Laura Valdez for answering our calls and providing us with information, analysis and answers when we needed it! Thanks also to Loan Dao and the Asian American Studies 126 class at UC Berkeley for their valuable help.

NNIRR staff members were the back-up team for BRIDGE: Arnoldo García, Claudia Gómez, Colin Rajah, and Catherine Tactaquin helped shape the project in every way, and gave critical feedback and support. Thanks to NNIRR interns who have worked on BRIDGE over the years: Diana Bernal, Tzong Chang, Christina Charuhas, Evonne Lai, David Menninger, Betty Marin, Shea Rao, and Michelle Yamashita. It most definitely would not have happened without you.

Thanks to our designers and artists: Juan Fuentes, Belvin Louie, John Minardi, Guillermo Prado and 8.2 design, and Christine Wong for their beautiful work. Thanks to our printers, at Inkworks Press, who always do a great job! Special thanks to: Hyung-Yul and Sunsook Cho, Christine Kovic, John Minardi, JP Pluecker, and Belvin Louie.

Thanks to Lori Villarosa for her continued support of BRIDGE, and many thanks to the C.S. Mott Foundation for their generous support of the BRIDGE Project.

Thank you for your work in building an immigrant rights movement that goes beyond all borders!

Eunice Hyunhye Cho,
Francisco "Pancho" Argüelles Paz y Puente,
Miriam Ching Yoon Louie,
and Sasha Khokha

Michelle Yamashita

BRIDGE: Building a Race and Immigration Dialogue in the Global Economy
www.nnirr.org

section one
framing tools

Introduction

TOOL FOR ORGANIZERS

BRIDGE **Building a Race and Immigration Dialogue in the Global Economy** is a tool for all organizers, community groups, educators, activists, advocates, and leaders—anyone committed to supporting the rights of immigrants, refugees, and the communities where we all live.

Who and what does this "bridge" connect? This workbook contains tools for organizers working with immigrant communities to build alliances and find common ground for action with others fighting for economic, social, and racial justice, and to envision alternatives and resistance in these times of global exclusion, racism, and human rights abuses. BRIDGE strives to place the current work of the immigrant and refugee rights movement in larger historic and global contexts, and to promote the human rights of all migrants and refugees.

The BRIDGE Project workbook is a "toolbox" of training materials, tips, and resources based on a popular education framework. We see this collection as part of a wider strategy of analyzing and transforming power and relationships—including power dynamics of teaching and education—in the learning experience. We believe that a popular education curriculum is not merely a pile of issues, techniques and information to be repeated in a classroom, but that it is part of an organizational commitment to a process of dialogue, learning, and building community.

BRIDGE is also a set of tools to more closely examine the dynamics of privilege and oppression, inclusion and exclusion in our own lives and work, including racism, sexism, homophobia, and other forms of oppression within our own communities. These discussions can only help us to more closely analyze and understand power, and to develop better tactics, strategies and organizing models for change.

How Did We Get Here?

The BRIDGE Project is a political education project of the National Network for Immigrant and Refugee Rights to build and sustain alliances between immigrant and non-immigrant communities and institutions. NNIRR first launched the BRIDGE Project in 1998 to bring together diverse communities and institutions in local areas to explore how immigrant communities related to critical issues of racism and race relations, globalization, human rights, and other key topics. The events of September 11, 2001 and the resulting attacks against immigrant and refugee rights in the U.S. and around the world further underscored the importance of developing educational tools. These dynamics shaped this resulting workbook in many ways. The BRIDGE workbook is the result of a shared process of many discussions,

Introduction

dialogues, meetings, requests for materials, and test-runs with community groups around the U.S. from 2002-2004. While many of the materials in this book were developed within a U.S.-based immigrant and refugee rights context, we hope that they can be useful to others in a wider, global context.

We hope that BRIDGE provides practical and realistic tools for communities to engage around difficult issues and to build allies. We hope that it helps to build spaces for different communities to dialogue, share experiences, and learn from each other. As with any set of tools, some will be more useful than others, depending on local situations. We hope that these tools can also help to strengthen initiatives and commitments to building processes of dialogue, shared education, and political agreements for common action. We hope that the ideas and information in BRIDGE can be adapted to support the local efforts of political and educational work in different communities.

These modules in no way present a comprehensive look at topics that relate to the broad topics of immigration, race, globalization, and the complexities of building sustainable communities and movements for social justice. There are many topics that we did not cover and perspectives that we could not adequately include in this workbook, including those of community members with disabilities. However, we hope that this workbook can serve as a useful resource to begin these discussions, and to stimulate more discussions on these critical issues.

A few words on translation: this workbook is written in English, which will not meet the needs of communities in our multilingual immigrant rights movement. As we developed this workbook, we continually grappled with this question—how could we best use our limited resources to develop this tool? Our decision was ultimately to finish a complete version of this workbook in English as quickly as possible, and to find resources to support the critical work of translation after its completion. We will, at minimum, place translations of BRIDGE in multiple languages as we complete the translation. We ask for your support as well—if you are interested in supporting translation work with a donation, or if you develop high quality translations from BRIDGE in the course of your work that you would be willing to share with other organizers, please let us know.

The letter "D" in BRIDGE stands for dialogue—which we want to continue with you as you use this workbook. Please keep in touch with us—we are excited to hear how you have been able to use, adapt, and build on the materials in this workbook. NNIRR is also available to help host training sessions, develop other curriculum materials, and to support you as you build more "bridges."

what's in the book

BRIDGE: Building A Race and Immigration Dialogue in the Global Economy is composed of three sections, each highlighting different tools for popular education around issues of immigration.

> **Section One** highlights what we call "framing tools," a collection of articles, tips, and activities to help provide effective facilitation. This section includes articles on the importance of translation and interpretation on creating multilingual spaces—an issue of critical importance in the immigrant rights movement; popular education methodology, tips for facilitation, energizers and activities for facilitators, evaluation forms, and more.
>
> **Section Two** consists of eight BRIDGE workshop modules, the core of this workbook. Each module includes a series of activities, exercises, and discussion questions grouped thematically around a particular subject area. Each module also includes a short background article on the theme of the workshop, as well as fact sheets and resource lists for more information on the topic.

The modules in this workbook include:

> **Module 1:** *Immigration History 101* is one of the cornerstones of the BRIDGE Project, and one of the most flexible modules in the whole curriculum. This module is excellent to use as an introductory level orientation to immigrant rights and racial justice, and we recommend that it be one of the first modules that you conduct when using the BRIDGE Project. Participants will become familiar with the history of immigration to the United States, their own migration history, and discuss some of the key issues that intersect with immigration, such as labor, institutionalized racism and the formation of race, liberation struggles and social movements. This module features the BRIDGE Immigration History Timeline in Pictures, with historical photos to illustrate key dates in U.S. immigration history.
>
> **Module 2:** *Globalization, Migration, and Workers Rights* highlights NNIRR's award-winning video, *Uprooted: Refugees of the Global Economy,* which examines globalization as a force that impoverishes and displaces communities, while erecting borders to migration and allowing corporations free economic access to economies in the Global South. Participants will examine corporate globalization and its impact on migration and communities throughout the world.

what's in the book

Module 3: *Introduction to Our Multiple Oppressions, Multiple Privileges* underscores one of the key themes of BRIDGE: the complexity of privileges and oppressions that every individual experiences in society. Participants will explore how all parts of their identities—which include race, immigration status, gender, sexual orientation, class, and others—shape their experiences with different forms of oppression and resistance. This module is a useful starting point for facilitators who plan to use the BRIDGE curriculum in a long-term process, as it builds a framework for all the other exercises.

Module 4: *Migrant Rights are Human Rights* links immigrant and refugee rights organizing to the human rights framework. Participants will gain a basic introduction to human rights in this module, as they explore the role of human rights in their lives, assess the condition of human rights in their communities, and discuss how different community organizations have organized and strengthened their communities by using human rights tools. This module also includes fact sheets and supplementary materials on key human rights documents that relate to migration.

Module 5: *Immigrant Rights and Lesbian, Gay, Bisexual, and Transgender (LGBT) Rights* provides a tool to address homophobia and heterosexism within the immigrant rights movement and other social justice movements. Participants will explore the connections between immigrant rights and the rights of LGBT people, examine how homophobic messages about gender and sexual orientation are shaped very early on from our cultures, families, and communities, and discuss some of the ways immigration policies affect LGBT people. This module works best with groups that are largely unfamiliar with LGBT issues, but who may have more familiarity with immigrant rights issues.

Module 6: *Immigrant Women's Leadership* celebrates the leadership of migrant and refugee women. Participants will honor important women in their lives, examine the impact of migration on women's lives and families, discuss the specific impact of immigration policy on women, and explore ways that social justice organizations can better support the leadership of immigrant women. This module is designed for mixed-gender audiences, although it is also effective with single-gender groups. It is primarily intended for groups whose primary focus is immigrant and refugee rights, and have less experience addressing gender or women's leadership.

what's in the book

Module 7: *Finding Common Ground I: The Changing Demographics of Race and Migration* explores the intersection between immigrant rights and a movement for racial justice. Participants will examine the racial and ethnic makeup of their communities, place demographic changes and tensions within a broader political context, and examine ways that different communities have interpreted these changes as opportunities for new learning, organizing, and alliance-building. This module works best with groups where participants have a shared context and are engaged in a process of building a relationship, such as a workplace, neighborhood, campaign, organizing drive. Because this module addresses divisions and conflicts within communities, we strongly advise facilitators and participants to first use some of the earlier modules before this one.

Module 8: *Finding Common Ground II: Transforming Conflict in Community Organizing* opens a discussion of participants' conceptions and styles of handling conflict. Together, participants will examine different conceptions and styles of conflict, and identify how different approaches to conflict can be put in a wider context. The module also includes background material that further explores different approaches to conflict resolution in communities for facilitators.

Section Three includes additional resources, including a glossary of terms, a list of resources on immigration and popular education, and organizational contacts.

how to use BRIDGE

Using the Toolbox: BRIDGE Workshop Modules

BRIDGE workshop modules cover a variety of topics related to immigration. In each workshop, participants will engage in activities and discussions, drawing on their own experiences and the information provided in workshop materials.

Each of the workshop modules includes:
- Overview of goals, stated as statements and as framing questions;
- Brief background article on the topic;
- A summary of the workshop's main teaching points;
- A menu of workshop activities;
- Tips and notes for facilitators;
- Directions for each workshop activity, including goals, time, list of materials needed, facilitator preparation, the source of the exercise, and often teaching points, variations, and a few words on challenges to watch for during the activity;
- Supplementary resource materials, including fact sheets and organizational contact information.

Organization of the Modules

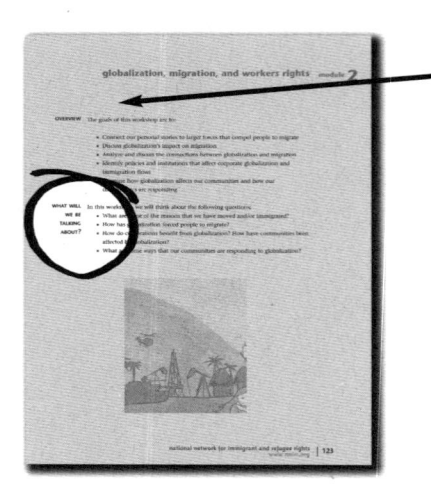

Overview: Describes the goals of the workshop for the facilitator

how to use BRIDGE

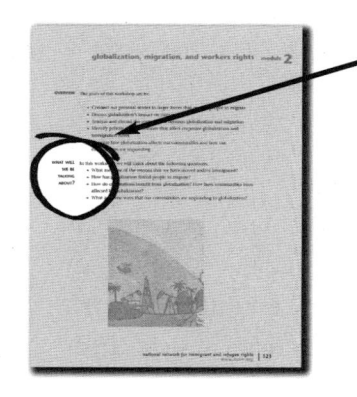

What will we be talking about? This part of the facilitator's guide states the goals of the workshops in question form, which we have found is a more effective way to convey goals to participants. You may want to review these questions with participants at the start of the module.

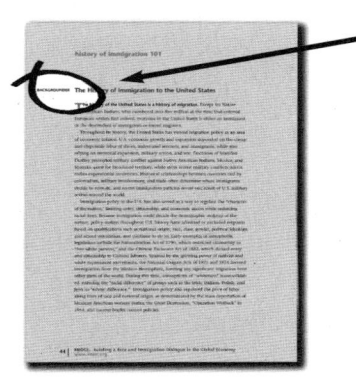

Backgrounder: This is a short article that provides you, the facilitator, with a short background on the topic covered by the module.

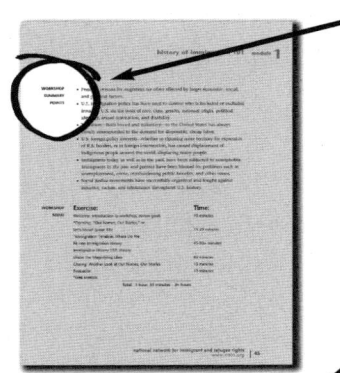

Summary Points: A summary of teaching points that underline activities in the module. You may choose to review these points with participants before or after the module.

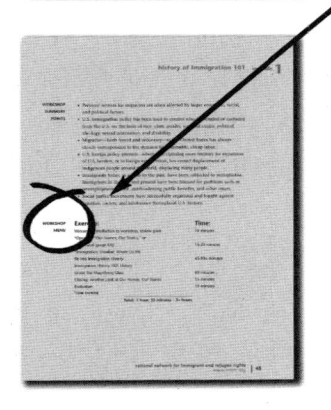

Workshop Menu: A list of activities and the time it takes to conduct activities in the module. Many of the activities, such as the openings and closings, can easily be interchanged from module to module. Core exercises, marked with an asterisk *, are the activities that we feel have been the most effective and important in conveying the teaching points in the modules. Although the rhythm of a workshop is best with the full range of activities, if you don't have enough time for the whole workshop or if you are running short on time, the core exercises are the ones to prioritize as you conduct the module.

national network for immigrant and refugee rights
www.nnirr.org

how to use BRIDGE

Workshop Activities:

Each module is structured around the following moments:

Framing and Opening: The beginning of a workshop is often the most important component of a successful workshop—if you have a strong start, participants will be more willing to work with you, even at rocky moments. This is a time when facilitators can introduce themselves with the group, establish rapport, review the workshop's goals and establish ground rules to create a respectful environment in the group. Opening exercises can bring participants to become more comfortable with one another, and also provides an opportunity to begin connecting personal experiences with the information and issues presented in the workshop.

Issues and Information: The workshop develops with a series of exercises and activities that introduce the issue, and connect with the personal experience of participants through a process of reflection, discussion, and analysis. The group will often arrive at shared conclusions, visions, and strategies for action.

Closing: Closing exercises provide a way for the group to synthesize the discussions, ideas, and action developed during the workshop, and sometimes can set next steps for action.

Evaluation: In some cases, the evaluation can occur with the closing activity, and in other cases, can take place after the end of the workshop. Evaluation is important to build accountability, and it also provides critical feedback for facilitators, and creates a method of documenting your work and performance.

our methodology

Where Are We Coming From?
A Few Words on Our Popular Education Model

BRIDGE is based on a popular education approach. In a few words, we believe that education should be participatory, develop critical thinking and engagement about relations of power, and should support people in organizing to change their lives.

What do we believe is popular education? We believe that:

- Popular education **draws on the direct lived experiences** and knowledge of everyone involved—including participants and facilitators.
- Popular education encourages **active participation** to engage people in dialogues, fun and creative activities, and draws on the strength of our diverse cultures. We learn in many ways—by seeing, hearing, talking, doing, creating, or a combination of these modes. We include dialogues and learning experiences that engage all of our senses, emotions, perceptions, and beliefs.
- Popular education draws on these **multiple modes** of learning: discussion, drawing, writing songs, making sculptures or acting out a skit gives us tools to express ourselves and communicate at all levels of our human experience.
- Popular education creates spaces for **trust and participation**. All education takes place within a larger context of behaviors, attitudes, and values. The ways in which we feel "safe" in a space depends on our own circumstances—our class, our race, gender, sexual orientation, age, immigration status, disability, and many other variables. As facilitators, we cannot remove these differences, but we can acknowledge their existence in order to open a space of more direct dialogue.
- Popular education is clear about its **agenda**. All education reproduces a set of values, ideologies, and attitudes. Popular education is not neutral, but holds a commitment to liberation from oppression at its ethical core.
- Popular education is **accessible** to all participants, and actively works to explore and challenge ways that create unequal access to participation, such as language barriers, disability, and group dynamics.
- Popular education **connects our lived experiences to historical, economic, social, and political structures of power.** When our personal experiences are placed in larger contexts and patterns of power, our personal realities are transformed.
- Popular education **explores our multiple identities and experiences** of inclusion and exclusion, oppression and privilege. The underlying truth of

popular education is of the existence of oppression: racism, classism, sexism, homophobia, heterosexism, transphobia, etc. is a reality in all of our lives. Popular education is not about building tolerance, but about building respect, acceptance, equality, and solidarity.

- Popular education **empowers individuals and groups to develop long-term strategies** to transform structures of power and to build a more just society. Popular education and organizing should not be reduced to short-term campaigns, mobilizations, or events, but rather, a democratic process based on values, connected and accountable to concrete needs of a community.
- Popular education **develops new community leaders** to build movements for social change. Popular education is a way to develop new leaders, who will in turn, develop other leaders. This kind of leadership will be based upon concrete experiences of collective action and organizing.
- Popular education **results in action** that challenges oppression, and help develop political spaces that are democratic and equal.
- Popular education **affirms the dignity** of every human being.

Developing Popular Education in Our Work: *Is It Hot?* Some Critical Questions

As we "cooked up" BRIDGE, we asked ourselves—is it *picoso* (Spanish for spicy or hot)? These are some questions to consider when integrating popular education into your work:

Participatory
Integrated into group needs
Critical thinking/Creativity/Constructive Criticism
Organizing
Symbolic Power
Operational Capacity

Participatory
In the workshop: Are we engaging all participants in the learning process? Do our activities and exercises encourage equal participation?

Outside the workshop: Who is participating in supporting the education process?

On a larger scale: How do people participate in an organization's decision-making process? Are we democratic? Who defines the agenda, establish goals, and controls resources?

Integrated into group needs
In the workshop: Are we integrating the experience, knowledge, and skills of the participants? Is the content relevant to the realities and needs of the participants?

Outside the workshop: Have we included everyone in the group? Who is included, and who is missing?

On a larger scale: Are we connecting the educational topics with the short and long-term needs and goals of the group? Is education integrated into the political work of the group?

Critical thinking/Creativity/Constructive Criticism
In the workshop: Are we raising critical questions of power in our workshops? Are we making space for creativity in our workshops? Do we have mechanisms for feedback?

Outside the workshop: How are we reacting to feedback (personally and as a team)?

On a larger scale: Is our work addressing the root causes of a problem or only the visible symptoms?

our methodology

Organizing
In the workshop: Are we creating space for participants to connect knowledge to action and organizing?
Outside the workshop: Is our education work connected to organizing work?
On a larger scale: Are we creating and strengthening organizations and groups, or are we carrying out events and mobilizing?

Symbolic Power
In the workshop: Are we incorporating the strengths of our many cultures and faiths into education?
Outside the workshop: Are we incorporating art and culture as part of our organizing strategies?
On a larger scale: What kind of power are we using and creating in our work? Are we clear about who we are? Are we using the tools and language of our oppressors, or are we drawing from our own strengths?

Operational Capacity
In the workshop: Is the process and content of our education work helping to build the capacity of participants and the organization?
Outside the workshop: Is our education work helping to address and develop solutions to concrete issues in the group/organization?
On a larger scale: Are we responding to concrete needs of the community. Are our operations efficient? What are we doing right? How can we improve?

Adapted from the *PICOSO Guide for Participatory Planning*, developed by Pancho Argüelles, Universidad Campesina, Estelí Nicaragua, 1991.

Tips for Effective Facilitation

Facilitators play a key role in creating a positive and respectful learning environment for participants, and for making sure that a workshop creates and develops new learning and knowledge for participants through activities and discussions. Here are some tips on effective facilitation:

- Listen to your group, and flow with how they are feeling. Good listening includes checking for non-verbal cues, such as body language, which may suggest more about how participants are feeling than what they are saying.
- Develop ground rules as a group. Ground rules can be an effective way to develop an atmosphere of trust and respect; you can refer to them later in the workshop when needed.
- Equalize participation throughout the group. Encourage a variety of participants to report back from discussions and in large group discussions. (Remind participants of the "Step up, step back!" ground rule). Ensure that you create small group discussion spaces to allow participants to share their perspectives in closer settings.
- Watch for power imbalances between individuals and groups of participants—and point them out (for example, if men are overshadowing women in the discussion.)
- Be flexible with your agenda—there may be moments where an activity goes on for too long or that may not be working for the participants. There are many ways to meet different goals, even if you have to cut an activity. The resulting activities will be stronger, especially if you don't rush through them to fit the whole agenda into the day.
- Do everything possible to ensure that logistics—such as meals, location, etc. are taken care of well before the workshop, so they don't disrupt the flow of the agenda. If possible, try and find another person who is not facilitating to handle logistics so that you don't break the flow of the workshop while setting up lunch, for example.
- Challenge discrimination when it happens, without attacking the person.
- Take breaks when needed, or use energizing activities. If you don't schedule breaks when they are needed, participants will often "take breaks" themselves, either by disengaging in the conversation, or leaving the room for the restroom. Breaks can also be useful in discussions that are particularly tense or have reached an impasse—they can allow participants to relax a bit, and for you to discuss ways with co-facilitators or with specific participants on ways to address the problem.
- Encourage participants to actively engage in the exercises and discussion by

national network for immigrant and refugee rights
www.nnirr.org

Tips for Facilitators

asking open-ended and clarifying questions, creating space for participants to speak up.
- Give everyone the benefit of the doubt, and avoid making assumptions about what participants will say.
- Summarize key points and highlight points of agreement. You can repeat a statement back to a participant to clarify what s/he has said; connect points of agreement between participants to demonstrate a common thread developed by the group, but only after it has been stated by participants.
- Don't fish for the "right answers;" if there are important points that you want to make through a discussion, be sure to state it, instead of trying to lead participants into giving you the right answer. For example, if you would like to draw out the "teaching points" from a discussion, use discussion questions to develop some of the points—and chart out the different points raised by participants on easel paper. After the discussion is finished, highlight the points raised, and if all the teaching points have not been covered, add them to the list.
- If you are charting responses to a discussion on easel paper, be sure to record all statements made by participants—if you are selective about what you record, it implies that their point is not important.
- Allow participants to "pass" on an activity. Some participants may be uncomfortable with certain modes of activity, or may be emotionally triggered by an activity. Giving participants the option to pass conveys a message of respect for participants to choose their level of involvement.
- Expose yourself as a learner, particularly after you have established rapport with a group. Don't be afraid to say "I don't know," but instead, use it as a moment for the group to figure out what new information they need to discover. If a participant raises a point that is new to you, say so; it communicates to participants that what they have to share is valuable and important.
- Take care of yourself: if you are too exhausted or burned out, your capacity as a facilitator will also be affected. Work with a team, and take time out if you need!
- Be forgiving to yourself when you make mistakes. It's human nature, and only presents you with a learning opportunity for the future.
- Expect frustration! Expect joy! They are both elements of education.
- Remember: Good things happen when good people come together!

Many of the points in this list is adapted with permission from the excellent discussion in *Education for Changing Unions*, by Bev Burke, Jojo Geronimo, D'Arcy Martin, Barb Thomas, and Carol Wall, which explores this topic in much greater depth.

Checklist for training

Before your workshop....

- Consider your audience. Who will be participating in the workshop? What are their backgrounds? What is their previous experience with the topic of the workshop? What are the organizational goals of conducting this workshop?
- Consider the space. Is the space where you will be holding the workshop accessible to all participants? Is it wheelchair accessible? Is it large enough? Do you need additional equipment (i.e. TV/VCR, easel stand, chairs, tables, etc.)? Can you rearrange the furniture in the room? Are there restrooms nearby?
- Finalize interpretation and translation arrangements. What languages do your participants speak? What interpretation and translation support will you need to provide?
- Refreshments and meals. What are your participants' dietary needs? Can you serve food and refreshments?
- Outreach. Are your outreach tools relevant and in the language of your participants? Are you conducting outreach to participants to ensure diversity and representation of all people in your community?
- Facilitation. Consider co-facilitating your workshop with someone else. Co-facilitation can be an effective way to share the workload, develop new educators, and to ensure diversity within a facilitation team.
- Prepare the workshop content. Spend a few hours before the workshop to familiarize yourself with the training. How much time do you have? What activities are you going to do? Why are you going to do specific activities? Who will facilitate each section?
- Gather materials and equipment; prepare copies of handouts. We've included a list of "materials needed" and "facilitator prep" for each BRIDGE activity.
- Write down an agenda and session objectives on easel paper for your workshop.
- Circulate a "sign-in sheet" to gather contact information of participants. Be sure to ask permission from participants if you can circulate their contact information.

Tips for Facilitators

Checklist for training

After the workshop:
- De-brief with your co-facilitator on the strengths and improvements needed for the workshop.
- Review the evaluations, and consider changes that you can make to the workshop while your memory is still fresh.
- Review any commitments for follow-up made during the workshop, and be sure to follow-up!
- Send participants a summary of the workshop evaluations, a contact list of participants, and any news on follow-up steps.
- Email us! We'd love to know how you have been able to use BRIDGE in your work.

Setting the Agenda: Reviewing Goals and Establishing Ground Rules

Each BRIDGE module begins with a session of reviewing goals and establishing ground rules for the workshop. The beginning of a popular education session is one of the most important moments—it is the time when you can establish a respectful and open tone with the group; develop rapport with participants; expose yourself as an equal and as a learner; and clarify goals for the workshop. A good opening moment can create a lot of positive mileage for facilitators—chances are that even if you hit some difficult moments later in the workshop, participants will be willing to give more, and remain more engaged in the process.

Why Do It?
- To establish trust and agreement within the group before starting the workshop.

Time Needed
- 10-15 minutes, depending on style and time limits

Materials needed:
- Easel paper, markers, tape

Facilitator Prep
- Write out the agenda and the workshop objectives on butcher paper before the start of the workshop

Directions
(order can be switched, according to your individual style and time limitations):

1. Introduce yourself to the group, and have participants introduce themselves.

2. Familiarize participants with agenda and workshop objectives. Provide some background information on the workshop: what is the reason for this workshop? Read the agenda and workshop agenda out loud (posted for the participants). This is also the time to clarify any questions about the agenda. It is often useful to review the goals that are stated as questions ("What will we be talking about?") for clarity, and get feedback from participants about their goals—and how they will be met in the workshop.

3. Clarify any logistical details: Where is the restroom? When will there be breaks or meals?

Setting the Agenda: Reviewing Goals and Establishing Ground Rules

4. Develop ground rules as a group: If you are facilitating a module in an ongoing series, participants may have already developed ground rules and you may have written them up before the session. In this case, ask a participant to read them out loud. Ground rules are particularly helpful to establish an environment of mutual accountability, respect, and trust.

Ask participants to list some ground rules for the workshop.

Here are some ground rules that we've heard:
- Respect yourself and others.
- Honor confidentiality: Nothing shared in the workshop is to be repeated without permission of the person(s) involved, even to the person who shared it outside this space.
- Challenge your limits and take responsibility for your own learning: If someone goes too fast or is unclear, ask him/her to slow down and explain the points you don't understand.
- Affirm each other: We are creating a supportive learning space for each other.
- It's ok to challenge each other respectfully: These can be the biggest opportunities for the whole group to learn from one another.
- Step Up, Step Back: If you like to talk, try to "step back" to give others a chance to participate; if you're a quiet person, try to "step up" and contribute to the group.
- Listen to each other: Have only one person talk at a time, with others giving their full attention.
- Speak for yourself: Each person has much to contribute. Say "I think" or "I feel" or "I believe" rather than "women think" or "middle class people think."
- Don't be afraid to call time out when dealing with tough issues Sometime taking a break really helps you create the space and extra awareness needed to make it through hard patches. The hard stuff sometimes yields the richest mines for learning.
- Expect unfinished business. We can only make a start on these issues. Expect that there may be things that you will want to know more about, and intense feelings that will surface that you will want to explore in the future.

Setting the Agenda: Reviewing Goals and Establishing Ground Rules

Challenges
- If you rush through ground rules or generate the list without involving participants, ground rules can lose their legitimacy within the group. Establishing ground rules is one of the first chances to set a respectful tone for the workshop.

Source

Authors; Ground rules adapted from Nationwide Women's Program, American Friends Service Committee, *Facilitator's Guide for Women's Workshops on Women, Poverty & Economic Power* (Philadelphia: AFSC, 1990) 2-3; and from Miriam Ching Louie and Linda Burnham, "Ground Rules to Facilitate Participation," *Women's Education in the Global Economy: A Workbook of Activities, Games, Skits and Strategies for Activists, Organizers, Rebels and Hell Raisers,"* (Berkeley: Women of Color Resource Center, 2000) 20.

Conducting Evaluations

Conducting evaluations at the end of a workshop session is a powerful way to bring closure to the day's activities, gather feedback to improve the workshop and your facilitation, and to document the benefits of your work. Evaluations can be conducted in a number of ways, including oral evaluations that can range from quick to lengthy discussions; interactive exercises; or written evaluations.

Oral evaluations are an effective way for the group as a whole to process and share what they learned and experienced collectively, and can provide some closure for a group. A quick way to evaluate a day's activities is to ask participants to name one thing that they learned during the day or to quickly describe one experience that they will take home with them. A more comprehensive oral evaluation can ask participants to collectively list the strong and weak points of the workshop, as well as things that they would change about the workshop. Facilitators can choose to chart these responses on easel paper.

Many of the "closing" exercises in the BRIDGE curriculum provide places for group evaluation to occur, including the "Head, Heart, Feet," exercise in the LGBT/Immigrant Rights module; the "Another World is Possible" closing in the Globalization, Migration, and Workers' Rights module; "Postcards to Ourselves" activity in the Women's Leadership module; and the "Spider's Web" exercise in the Introduction to Multiple Oppressions module.

Written evaluations can be a valuable way to document the impact of your educational work, especially if you have used BRIDGE closing exercises to allow participants to process the workshop with the rest of a group at a creative and even emotional level. The results of written evaluation forms can allow participants to share information about the workshop with you, suggest improvements, and give you feedback on your strong points. We have included a sample written evaluation form on the next page for your use; if possible, we would love to see any summation notes or evaluations from workshops that you conduct using BRIDGE, to hear what is working well, and for suggestions for change.

BRIDGE: Building a Race and Immigration Dialogue in the Global Economy
EVALUATION FORM

What were your expectations for the day?

What was most useful about today?

What needs improvement?

Evaluate your participation:

Did you feel like you were able to participate in today's activities? ❑ Yes ❑ No

Do you feel like you learned from others participating in the activities? ❑ Yes ❑ No

Any other comments?

Logistics

Did you receive logistical information in a satisfactory manner? ❑ Yes ❑ No

Was the meeting location satisfactory for your needs? ❑ Yes ❑ No

Were translation and interpretation of high quality? ❑ Yes ❑ No

BRIDGE Workshop title:_____

Your Name (optional):_____

Your Organization (optional): _____

Today's Date: _____

national network for immigrant and refugee rights
www.nnirr.org

Interpretation and Translation: Strategies for Sharing Power in Our Multilingual Movement
By Alice Johnson, Highlander Center

This article is adapted from "Interpretation and Translation: Power Tools for Sharing Power in Grassroots Leadership Development," by Alice Johnson for El Centro Hispano, 2002, supported by the Mary Reynolds Babcock Foundation. The original article can be found online at: www.mrbf.org.

Why Is A Commitment to Multilingual Organizing Important?

A community's strength depends in large part on the strength of its culture, and language is an essential aspect of one's culture, in terms of cultural transmission, regeneration, and collective power. Translation and interpretation are language tools that can be wielded to achieve different political goals. They can be used to marginalize the power, culture, and voice of a community in ways that maintain the status quo of power, privilege, and oppression between peoples, or they can be used to create space for new community voices and strength in ways that transform race relationships and empower marginalized groups. As a multilingual movement, immigrants, refugees, and allies can use the tools of translation and interpretation to create bridges of communication, to strengthen the voices of traditionally excluded groups, to deeply promote cross-racial, cross-cultural, broad-based community participation, and to create political power for change.

The following article is based on the experience of El Centro Hispano, a Latino community organization based in Durham, NC. This information is presented here to encourage others to explore the potential of using interpretation and translation as a critical tool for social change. This article will explore several different modes of interpretation, translation, and provide some best practices and logistical tips on integrating interpretation, translation, and multi-lingual spaces into our work. Interpretation refers to verbal communication, while translation applies to written documents. For the purpose of this article, we assume that English is the primary, dominant language, since we are writing from a U.S.-based perspective, although that is not always the case.

Types of Interpretation:
- Consecutive interpretation
- Simultaneous Interpretation: One-way
- Simultaneous interpretation: Bi-Directional
- Simultaneous Interpretation: Multi-Directional

Other Topics:
- Comprehensive Written Translation
- Creating a Multilingual Space in Organizing
- Some Tips for Successful Interpretation at Meetings and Events

Consecutive Interpretation:

What Is It?

Consecutive interpretation is a mode of interpretation where a speaker speaks a few sentences and then pauses to allow the interpreter to repeat them in the other language. The speaker and interpreter alternate turns talking. This method requires interpreters with good memory retention skills, but does not require any special audio equipment.

When it's OK to Use:
- Most useful with very big crowds and for limited periods of time, hopefully not more than 5-10 minutes. It is best for speeches to an audience rather than for a more intimate interactive discussion.
- Using consecutive interpreting for a day-long workshop is frustrating and could easily give grassroots leaders a negative attitude toward cross-language work.

How It Works:
- Speakers talk for a short segment and then pause for the interpreters to interpret the segment, and so alternate back and forth.

What You Need:
- No special audio interpreting equipment needed.
- Experienced interpreters who can manage a discussion that moves forward in short segments. Interpreters may serve an organization as a volunteer, or charge for their services.

The Upside:
- Everyone is able to participate more, in their language of choice.
- Both languages are more equally represented in the discussion.
- Requires no special equipment, and it can accommodate any number of participants.

The Downside:
- Repeating every comment sequentially makes the process take twice as long.
- Establishing a rhythm between speaker and interpreter can be tricky, so that neither one speaks for too long or too short.
- Participants usually listen when their language is being spoken, and may disengage when the other language is being spoken.
- Participants tend to look at the interpreter and not at each other, thus building relationships with the interpreter and not with each other.
- It is easy for the interpreter to "take control" of the meeting, basically assuming the role of moderator and sidelining the speaker.

Consecutive Interpretation

Contribution to Leadership Development:
- Allows monolingual immigrant leaders to speak up publicly and have their voices heard in an English-speaking public space, which can be very empowering for individual leaders.
- Can allow a group to share power and responsibility among participants: everyone gets to speak up in the language of their choice, and everyone has to wait for the interpreter in order to hear or be heard.
- Choppy stop-start discussion style is equally inconvenient to everyone.

Simultaneous Interpretation: An Overview

What Is It?

Simultaneous interpretation is a mode of interpretation where an interpreter interprets at the same time that the speaker is talking, without interrupting the flow of discussion. Special audio equipment is usually used. While a speaker is talking, the interpreter speaks quietly into a microphone that transmits to headphones worn by those listening to the interpretation.

There are three types of simultaneous interpretation, which we will discuss further:
- One-way interpretation: used when only a small number of listeners in the group don't understand a "majority" language
- Bi-directional interpretation: used in a group where two languages are spoken
- Multi-directional interpretation: used in a group where three or more languages are spoken

When It's OK To Use:
- Group events, such as meetings and workshops, where there are two or more languages spoken.

How It Works:
- Participants are given a set of headphones and a small walkman style "receiver," which are plastic, electronic boxes that have a volume control, sometimes a channel control, and headphones.
- Interpreters hold a "transmitter," and speak quietly into the transmitter's microphone. Their voices are heard through the receiver-headphones worn by the folks who need interpretation.
- The interpreter's job is to completely repeat the message of the speakers in the group, rendering it into the language of the listeners, and to do so at the same time that the speakers are talking.

Simultaneous Interpretation: An Overview

- Simultaneous interpreting has virtually no delay (not more than 2-4 seconds) in getting the message from one language to into the other. The speakers do not pause to wait for the interpreter, nor do they alternate turns talking between speaker and interpreter, as is done in consecutive interpreting.

What You Need:
- Audio equipment with transmitters and enough receivers for participants. These may be purchased, rented, or borrowed. When using the equipment, the organizers will need to arrange a table to put it on: a seemingly small detail, until you find yourself spreading electronic equipment all over the meeting room floor.
- Plenty of time: Good interpreters will want to be contacted at the beginning of the planning, so that they will have time to discuss with the organizers the special arrangements needed in a multilingual setting.
- A pair of talented interpreters: simultaneous interpretation is an intense job that requires high levels of mental concentration, and works best when interpreters can alternate every 20-30 minutes. Simultaneous interpreters must have special skills to work "simultaneously"— it is not enough to simply be bilingual. Most skilled simultaneous interpreters will work on contract for a fee.

One-way Simultaneous Interpretation

What is it?

One-way simultaneous interpretation is used when only a small number of listeners in the group don't understand the language of most of the participants, and only they wear headphones to listen to the interpreter. When those listeners want to speak to the group, they speak in their language and the interpreter interprets for them consecutively.

When It's OK To Use:
- Group events, such as meetings and workshops, where there are two languages spoken.
- Used when only a small number of listeners in the group don't understand a "dominant" language.
- When one-way simultaneous interpreting is the only option available.

One-way Simultaneous Interpretation

How it works:
- Same as simultaneous interpretation in general, but only participants who need interpretation from the "dominant" language are given a set of headphones and receiver.
- When those who are wearing headsets want to talk, the interpreter switches into consecutive interpretation, speaking out loud to the whole group.

What you need:
- Same as simultaneous interpretation in general.

The Upside:
- Best as a last resort when there are not enough listening receivers to hand out to all the folks in the group, or when there are so few people who require interpretation that bi-directional simultaneous interpretation will not work (i.e. a ratio of 1 Spanish-speaker for every 20 English-speakers.)
- This method, in the long-term, exposes all participants to the use of simultaneous interpretation and can result in better cross-cultural awareness and confidence.

The Downside:
- Giving headphones to only one group of participants allows them to listen to everything passively, but doesn't really allow them to speak up and join in the discussions in a spontaneous way. This method can keep some participants from integrating into the group and bonding equally with everyone else.
- This style constructs a dynamic where the group with headsets are seen by the other participants as passive listeners, rarely speaking up and connecting with the rest of the group. This does not challenge the social structure or dynamic in the group an can even have the effect of making one group appear to be the quiet folks, grateful to be invited but in no way affecting the way in which the group operates.

Contribution to Leadership Development:
- One-way, passive simultaneous interpreting allows monolingual community leaders some access to growth and training opportunities, but is limited in its ability to fully integrate community leaders into the larger grassroots leadership forum.

Bi-directional Interpretation

What is it?

Bi-directional interpretation is used in a group where two languages are spoken. In this setup, all those who do not understand both languages wear headphones. Everyone speaks in their language of choice, and the interpreter switches language directions, depending on what language is spoken at the given moment. Everyone who is not bilingual will at some point have to listen and understand through the interpretation.

When It's OK To Use:
- We believe that bi-directional, interactive interpreting should be used whenever possible in multilingual settings.
- Group events, such as meetings and workshops, where there are two languages spoken. It works best in groups that are small enough to facilitate such interaction—many would say that groups of less than 30 folks are ideal for this.
- Works best when there at least some balance between the numbers of speakers for both languages.

How It Works:
- Same as simultaneous interpretation in general, but any participant who does not understand both languages receives headphones.
- Everyone speaks in their language, and the interpreter will switch between the two languages.

What You Need:
- Same as simultaneous interpretation in general, although it is important to make sure that the interpreters will be able to switch back and forth seamlessly between both languages.
- Advance planning with the organizers, facilitators, and interpreters

The Upside:
- Virtually no "translation lag time," no matter what language is being spoken.
- All participants are free to join in spontaneously.
- There's no overtone that one language is a "handicap," both languages (i.e.: cultures and communities) are on more equal footing in the group.
- Participants look each other in the eye, bonding with each other and not the interpreter.
- Huge contributions to leadership development (see below.)

Bi-directional Interpretation

The Downside:
- Requires more concentration for all participants, as the listener has to decide to listen to the speaker or the earphone, and filter out the other voice when not needed. This may be a new experience, particularly for English-speakers.
- Resistance from participants new to interpretation can look like:
    - flatly refusing to put on the headset;
    - frequently removing the headset and consistently being unprepared for when interpretation is needed;
    - interrupting the interpreter to make her repeat everything because the participant wasn't listening or zoned out for a minute; or
    - interrupting the discussion because their receiver's battery got low (instead of quietly getting up and going to the designated battery-changing station in the room).
- On the flipside, non-English-speaking immigrant participants may have the opposite problem, never speaking up for their needs at all.

Contribution to Leadership Development:
- Offers real development opportunities for both mono-lingual immigrant leaders and their fellow English speaking grassroots leaders.
- Eliminates language barriers in group settings, and frees all participants to participate spontaneously, helping to de-stigmatize speaking languages other than English.
- The discomfort or resistance to bi-directional interpreting shown by English-speakers highlights the potential contribution to their leadership. Reflecting on this is in itself an experience in dismantling racism and examining internalized assumptions of language privilege.

Multi-directional Interpretation

What Is It?

Multi-directional interpretation is a mode of interpretation when there are three or more languages spoken in one setting. All participants who are not fluent in all represented languages will wear a headset, and all interpreters must have at least one language in common.

Multi-directional interpretation can be done in a variety of ways, from simple to complex. The simplest way we have come across is to designate one of the languages as the "Hub Language." All interpreters of the various languages represented would interpret in and out of the central hub language. In the U.S., English would likely be a common hub language for multi-directional interpreted events, though not necessarily.

Multi-directional Interpretation

When It's OK To Use:
- Group events, such as meetings and workshops, where there are three or more languages spoken and/or cultural communities represented.

How it works:
- Each language has a transmitter channel dedicated for interpreting into that language (for example: English will always be transmitted on Channel 1, Spanish always on Channel 2, Creole on Channel 3, and Hmong on Channel 4). If English is designated as the Hub Language, then each interpreter pair for Spanish, Creole, and Hmong must be able to interpret between English and their respective language, but they are not required to interpret between two non-English languages.

For instance, the Hmong interpreters are not expected to understand Creole, nor are Creole interpreters expected to understand Hmong. In such an instance, when Creole is spoken out loud, the Hmong interpreter herself listens to the English interpretation of the Creole, and then interprets THAT into Hmong. Thus the interpreters act like daisy-chains for each other, linking the message from Creole into Hmong via the English interpretation. When the hub language of English is spoken out loud, then all the interpreters just go straight into their respective other languages.

What you need:
- Same as simultaneous interpretation in general, and all participants who do not understand the "hub language" wear a headset, tuned to the language channel they want to listen in.
- Transmitters with separate channels for each language spoken.
- A pair of interpreters for each language combo with English; and the interpreters must be very skilled and experienced with conference-style simultaneous interpreting.
- Steadfast commitment to the conviction that Language = Power, plus a sense of adventure and good humor, because multi-directional simultaneous interpreting can be daunting for organizers and participants alike.

The Upside:
- Allows many more communities to participate and bring their cultural voice into the group space.
- Begins to reduce the barrier that permits immigrant communities to only come together across languages with English-speaking groups.
- Allows speakers of various languages/cultures to come together directly, without having English-speakers brokering the relationship-building between different immigrant groups.

The Downside:
- Because it is so complex to organize, there is a higher chance of things going wrong.
- It can be very expensive to pull together, and very difficult to find enough interpreters with the required conference simultaneous interpreting skills needed for an event.
- Groups wanting to do an event with multi-directional interpreting should first become accustomed to bi-directional interpreting in their events, before expanding.

Contribution to Leadership Development:
- Everyone who participates in an event with multi-directional interpreting will gain more skills in cross-cultural exposure and competence than they would through other kinds of interpreting in events.
- This is the beginning of multilingual, multicultural grassroots base-building in the U.S. that goes beyond the dualism of traditional U.S. English/one other language.
- This is a critical tool for authentically inclusive and empowering multiracial, multicultural, multi-issue movements for social change in the U.S.

Translation is the act of rendering written messages in one language into another language, without losing any of its content, meaning or intent. Translation applies to written documents, while interpretation refers to verbal communication.

Comprehensive Written Translation in Organizing

What is it?

Comprehensive written translation is simply the idea of collecting every single document that is related to a program or event, and producing it in both English and in all the languages of the participants. For example, it's fairly common practice for meetings in the U.S. for English-speaking participants to receive full packets of reading materials in their language. Often the only materials available for speakers of other languages are copies of the draft agenda and a one-page summary of the rest of the materials. Comprehensive translation efforts by grassroots groups in the U.S. are best used when they strive to generate original materials in both English and other languages, not only writing in English and then translating into other languages.

How it works:
- Be sure to establish a relationship with outside translators, so they know as much as possible about your work and the purpose of your translations. Each translation done by an outside contractor should be reviewed by a native speaker on staff; contractors are not immune from mistakes in terminology, tone, and meaning.

Comprehensive Written Translation in Organizing

- Make sure to ask permission to translate something not written by your group. The author may already have it ready in the other language, or may allow you to translate it under only certain conditions.
- Be sure to name the translator with the author's by-line, which helps other organizations locate skilled translators, and also keeps translators accountable for their work.

When It's OK To Use:
- At all times, in fact the more the better.

What you need:
- Time and effort for organizations to analyze the whole collection of their materials, and to plan a system for producing them in more than one language.
- Skilled translators: A good translator needs to be fully bilingual, think methodically, and have excellent writing skills. It is also preferable that the translator be a native speaker of the translation language. For example, a document translated into Spanish is best translated by a native-Spanish speaker/writer.
- Staff to coordinate translation through outside contractors, or qualified on-staff translators who are fairly compensated and have translation included in their job description.
- A budget for translation: both hiring outside contractors or staff time for translation needs financial support. A safe estimate for outside translation costs – as of 2002 – is approximately $50/page, though prices vary by language and content. Also, as more translators begin entering the profession, prices will likely go down. However, an organization with talented in-house translators has a treasure on their hands.

The Upside:
- Comprehensive translation makes it easier for all members of the community to access the organization and provides further transparency and empowerment.
- Producing all its documents in the languages of its grassroots constituents makes a political statement that everyone deserves access to the same information, and puts participants on more equal ground.

The Downside:
- Translation is costly and time-consuming, and can be tricky to do right. As one major translation journal noted, "everybody has something to say about your copy," even years after the document has been published.

- Poorly translated documents can seriously hurt a group's credibility and trust with an allied/immigrant community, and the printed document floating around can haunt them for years.

Contribution to Leadership Development:
- When all materials are available to everyone in the language of their choice, participants can more fully take part in the process, and makes everyone feel more welcomed and part of the whole group. Non-English speakers are better positioned to take on a leadership role within the multilingual group, as opposed to being passive listeners.

Multilingual Space

What is it?

A multilingual space is developed when there is a collective commitment by grassroots leaders who speak different languages with one another and share leadership roles, in both languages at all times. For example, the facilitators of a Spanish-English workshop might easily be Spanish-only speakers, or a combination of two trainers—one speaking only Spanish, and one speaking only English, who are able to jointly work together and lead the group through a workshop.

How it works:

It goes without saying that a multilingual space cannot happen without superb bi-directional / multi-directional simultaneous interpretation, yet this is not enough to make it a success. It also requires:
- A collective commitment by everyone in the group, the facilitators, and the organization, to fully bring both / all languages and cultures to a discussion.
- A shared political analysis of the way language and culture can be used to both empower and oppress, to include and exclude.
- Co-facilitation with bilingual and bicultural facilitators, who can lead the process in both languages, and who can draw out and reflect the group's different cultural reference points.
- Comprehensive written translation, so that every single thing on paper for the group is produced fully in all represented languages.

When It's OK To Use:
- Any setting where you would use simultaneous interpretation, such as community meetings and trainings.

Multilingual Space

What you need:

A multilingual space needs the same basic things needed for bi-directional simultaneous interpreting:

- Special interpreter equipment (with techies to manage it)
- Skilled and politically educated simultaneous interpreters
- Politically educated facilitators/trainers, preferably multilingual/multicultural
- Organizers committed to creating a multilingual space---from the get-go
- Preparation of all written materials in all languages, in advance
- Time for advance planning
- A budget to pay for the additional translation and interpretation costs

The Upside:

- Politically, multilingual space recognizes the imbalance of power and access between the speakers of the different languages in the group.
- Multilingual spaces uses language inclusion as a means to empower non-English speaking participants who are oppressed in our society, and to encourage the English-speaking participants to reflect on and alter the ways in which their language privilege makes them participants in this oppression.

The Downside:

- Very little: there is everything to be gained, and very little to lose.
- Some points to keep in mind in making it work:
- As important as it is to bring both Spanish and English to the table in multilingual space, it is also key to be conscious and intentional about including cultural references and norms from each participant group.
- Facilitators should anticipate the enormous diversity of experiences discussed in a multilingual space, and find ways for the group to make linkages between their unique backgrounds. Facilitators can gently remind participants to explain cultural or historical references in a group with vastly different backgrounds.

Contribution to Leadership Development:

- A multilingual space is where a non-English-speaking immigrant leader can most expansively use their leadership and cross-cultural skills.
- A multilingual space is inherently multicultural as well as multiracial: grassroots leaders of different races, cultures, and languages gain experience working together to build broad based alliances for social change.
- Undergoing the political education process for a multilingual space also helps groups recognize and integrate the diversity in the room, and can make the space more open for other marginalized and excluded groups.

Some Tips for Successful Interpretation at Meetings and Events

- Prepare your interpreter about terminology before the meeting. Be sure to check in with interpreters about the subject matter of the event and some background on the participants so they can familiarize themselves with relevant vocabulary. Make sure that the interpreter receives in advance copies of materials to be used in the meeting to review in preparation for interpreting. An ethical interpreter will also let you know immediately if the subject matter is out of their scope of knowledge.

- Interpreters should work in pairs. In the meeting itself, interpreters should be contracted to work in pairs, alternating every 20-30 minutes. This is part of what makes interpreting so costly, as each interpreter is paid an hourly or daily rate. Be advised that any knowledgeable and ethical interpreter will avoid, if not flatly refuse, an interpreting assignment without a co-interpreter.

- Conduct a brief interpretation orientation with participants before starting a meeting. The agenda should allow the interpreters to give a brief orientation covering how the interpreting will work, how the audio equipment works, where to go for technical difficulties, establish some hand signals for the interpreters to request folks to talk louder, or slow down, and answer any initial questions.

- Interpreters should never participate in the meeting! No matter how tense or chaotic the discussion, the interpreter must simply render what's being said into the other language, without interrupting, editing, or adding anything.

- Interpreters should honor the message of participants. When interpreting, interpreters render everything in the same voice as the speaker, in first person. In addition, interpreters must interpret absolutely everything that the speaker says. It can be useful to have a bilingual person monitoring the interpreter for completeness and accuracy.

- Be clear about fees and payment beforehand. Interpreters usually serve as independent contractors and will need to submit an invoice with their tax information. While interpreting costs may seem extremely expensive for a small organization, the success of a multilingual gathering will only be as good as its interpreters. Poor, or unskilled volunteer interpreters can ruin an otherwise well-planned event.

- Designate an "equipment techie" to monitor equipment used by the participants, facilitators, and interpreters. It is useful to have a "techie" to hand out and collect equipment for the session, and to observe the group and watch for folks who are fiddling with their equipment and looking "lost," then go offer them fresh receivers, etc.

Some Tips for Successful Interpretation at Meetings and Events

- Replace your batteries. Most interpretation equipment takes 9 Volt batteries, which last roughly 8-16 hours in the devices. A tip: the battery that needs changing most will often be the interpreter transmitter!
- Conduct an in-room sound check before the event. "Techies" should test the equipment to see if new batteries are needed, or to determine if the room has spots in the room where the transmission of the interpreting equipment does not work.
- Love and care for interpreters. Make sure that interpreters have access to water and snacks (and restrooms when possible). If they are to interpret through a "working lunch," time should be planned in for them to eat, too. In gatherings with overnight stays, it's a good idea to put the interpreters in single, quiet rooms as even mild sleep deprivation can significantly lower an interpreter's performance during the day and jeopardize the success of the meeting.

section two
modules

history of immigration 101

history of immigration 101   module 1

OVERVIEW   The goals of this workshop are to:
- Share our personal and family stories of migration
- Place our personal migration stories in relation to landmarks in U.S. immigration, labor, and racial justice history
- Examine how immigration policy has shaped the U.S. by including or excluding immigrants based on their race, class, gender, sexual orientation, national origin, and disability
- Discuss social, historical, and economic factors that cause migration—including forced migration and displacement
- Examine current examples of immigrant rights violations in a historical perspective, and discuss similarities between current immigrant rights violations and strategies for resistance

WHAT WILL WE BE TALKING ABOUT?   In this workshop, we will think about the following questions:
- What are our personal migration histories?
- What are some of the reasons that people have migrated to the U.S.?
- What groups have immigrated to the U.S. throughout history? How were they treated by people already here?
- How have immigration laws prevented certain groups of people from coming to the U.S.? Who did these laws exclude? Who did these laws allow to enter? Who influenced these laws, and why?

NOTE TO FACILITATORS   The History of Immigration 101 module is one of the cornerstones of the BRIDGE Project, and one of the most flexible modules in the whole curriculum. This module is excellent to use as an introductory level orientation to immigrant rights and racial justice, and we recommend that it be one of the first modules that you conduct when using the BRIDGE Project.

The timeline exercise has several variations, depending on the length of time and the number of participants. We've done this workshop in settings as varied as community organizing workshops with 20 participants; university classes; 45 minute conference presentations with 60 people; even on buses traveling cross-country!

history of immigration 101

BACKGROUNDER ## The History of Immigration to the United States

The history of the United States is a history of migration. Except for Native American Indians, who numbered over five million at the time that colonial European settlers first arrived, everyone in the United States is either an immigrant, or the descendent of immigrants or forced migrants.

Throughout its history, the United States has viewed migration policy as an area of economic interest. U.S. economic growth and expansion depended on the cheap and disposable labor of slaves, indentured servants, and immigrants, while also relying on territorial expansion, military action, and war. Historical relationships between countries tied by colonialism, military involvement, and trade often determine where immigrants decide to relocate, and recent immigration patterns often reflect U.S. military action around the world.

Immigration policy in the U.S. has also served as a way to regulate the "character of the nation," limiting entry, citizenship, and economic access while enforcing racial divides. Because immigration can influence the demographic makeup of the nation, policy makers throughout U.S. history have admitted or excluded migrants based on qualifications such as national origin, race, class, gender, political ideology, and sexual orientation. Early examples of xenophobic legislation include the Naturalization Act of 1790, which restricted citizenship to "free white persons," and the Chinese Exclusion Act of 1882, which denied entry and citizenship to Chinese laborers. Spurred by the growing power of nativist and white supremacist movements, the National Origins Acts of 1921 and 1924 favored immigration from the Western Hemisphere, limiting any significant migration from other parts of the world. During this time, conceptions of "whiteness" reconsolidated, reducing the "racial difference" of groups such as the Irish, Italians, Polish, and Jews to "ethnic difference." Immigration policy also regulated the price of labor along lines of race and national origin, as demonstrated by the mass deportation of Mexican American workers during the Great Depression, "Operation Wetback" in 1954, and current border control policies.

history of immigration 101 — module 1

WORKSHOP SUMMARY POINTS

- Personal reasons for migration are often affected by larger economic, social, and political factors.
- U.S. immigration policy has been used to control who is included or excluded from the U.S. on the basis of race, class, gender, national origin, political ideology, sexual orientation, and disability.
- Migration—both forced and voluntary—to the United States has always closely corresponded to the demand for disposable, cheap labor.
- U.S. foreign policy interests—whether in claiming more territory for expansion of U.S. borders, or in foreign intervention, has caused displacement of indigenous people around the world.
- Immigrants today, as well as in the past, have been subjected to xenophobia. They have been blamed for problems such as unemployment, crime, overburdening public benefits, and other issues.
- Social justice movements have successfully organized and fought against injustice, racism, and intolerance throughout U.S. history.

WORKSHOP MENU

Exercise:	Time:
Welcome, introduction to workshop, review goals	10 minutes
*Opening: "Our Names, Our Stories," or "Let's Move!" (in Module 2)	15-20 minutes
*Immigration Timeline: Where Do We Fit Into Immigration History	45-90+ minutes
History Under the Magnifying Glass	60 minutes
Closing: Another Look at Our Names, Our Stories	15 minutes
Evaluation	10 minutes

*CORE EXERCISE

Total: Between 1 hour, 35 minutes – 3+ hours

national network for immigrant and refugee rights
www.nnirr.org

history of immigration 101

Our Names, Our Stories

WHY DO IT?
- To use as an icebreaker and introduction
- To get participants moving around
- To form a personal connection to the topic of immigration
- To gauge how participants feel about the topic of immigration

TIME 20 minutes (more for groups larger than 20)

MATERIALS NEEDED
- Sheets of paper—one for each participant
- Markers or pens for all participants
- Tape
- Easel paper

DIRECTIONS

1. Hand out a piece of paper and a marker to each participant. Ask each participant to write her/his name in big letters vertically, going down the center of the page.
2. Ask participants to think about immigration for a few moments. Then ask participants to use each letter in their name to write a word that describes their views, feelings, or experiences with immigration. Participants can use the letters at the beginning, middle, or end of a word, in any language. For example:

coMmunity
trAnsition
fReedom
famIly
dignidAd

3. After participants finish, they should take their paper and tape it to their shirt, as if it were a "giant name tag." Ask participants to walk around the room, and to talk to other participants about the words that they wrote on their paper. (5 minutes)
4. When participants have been able to meet and talk to most or all of the other participants, bring the group back into a large circle. Ask each participant to introduce her/himself, and to name *one word* on their paper that they would like to share with the group. As participants name their words, write the words that the participants have named on a large sheet of easel paper.

SOURCE the authors

history of immigration 101 module 1

Immigration Time Line: Where Do We Fit Into Immigration History?

WHY DO IT?
- To share our personal and family stories of migration
- To place our personal migration stories in relation to landmarks in U.S. immigration, labor, and racial justice history
- To examine how immigration policy has shaped the U.S. by including or excluding immigrants based on their race, class, gender, sexual orientation, national origin, and disability
- To discuss social, historical, and economic factors that cause migration—including forced migration, displacement, and immigration

TIME Time: 45-90 minutes, depending on variation

VARIATIONS
1. Longer Workshop Setting (90+ minute version)
2. Quicker Workshop Setting (45 minute version)
3. Quicker Conference Setting (60 minute version)
4. On the Bus: Long Road Trip Setting (90+ minute version)

Michelle Yamashita

national network for immigrant and refugee rights | 43
www.nnirr.org

history of immigration 101

Immigration Time Line Variation 1: Longer Workshop Setting (90+ minute version)

This version works well in a traditional classroom/workshop setting, from 10-35 participants, and gives a chance to cover the timeline in a more comprehensive way.

TIME 90+ minutes

MATERIALS NEEDED
- Copy of the "Immigration History Timeline in Pictures" (at end of section)
- Tape
- Sheets of paper, cut in half (enough for each participant)
- Crayons, colored pencils, markers, other art supplies for all participants
- Extra blank sheets of paper
- Easel paper, markers

FACILITATOR PREP
- Review immigration history materials and dates before facilitating this module. Check the "Immigration History: Facilitator's Overview" at the end of the section. Select dates you may want to add/take out, depending on the experiences of participants.
- Post the "Immigration History Timeline in Pictures" on the wall of the room (this takes about 10 minutes). You can also pin them to a clothesline with pins and have participants add images to the clothesline as well.

DIRECTIONS

1. Introduce the exercise by reviewing the framing questions for the activity.
In this exercise, we will be thinking about the following questions:
- What are some of the reasons that people have migrated to the U.S.?
- What groups have immigrated to the U.S. throughout history? How were they treated by people already here?
- How have immigration laws prevented certain groups of people from coming to the U.S.? Whom did these laws exclude? Whom did these laws allow to enter? Who influenced these laws, and why?
- How have different groups challenged injustice? What can we learn from their experiences to help us today?

2. Distribute a half sheet of paper and crayons/colored pencils/markers to all participants. Ask participants to think about the following questions:
- When did you/your family come to the U.S.?
- Where did you/your family come from?
- Why did you/your family move?

history of immigration 101 module 1

Immigration Time Line Variation 1

Ask participants to write the answers to the questions on their paper, and to draw a picture to illustrate their migration experience. (Some participants may want to do more than one drawing.) (5-10 minutes)

3. Ask participants to find a partner, preferably someone they don't know. (If there is an odd number of participants, form one group of three.) Ask participants to share their "personal migration history" with their partners. (10 minutes)

4. Participants should "tour" the timeline with their partners or their small groups. Distribute pieces of tape, so that participants can hang their personal history on the timeline as they walk through. Have extra sheets of paper available so that participants can add key dates that are not on the timeline. (10 minutes)

5. After participants have walked through the timeline, ask for 3-4 participants to share their personal migration story with the rest of the large group. (10-15 minutes) If you have more time, you can review each participant's personal migration story in the next step (this usually requires at least 30-45 more minutes.) Explain that our individual stories connect to historical patterns in immigration history.

6. Review the timeline from 1492 to the present with the large group. For each period in history, ask for participants' input on the larger economic, social, and political forces: What were some of the larger historical events happening during this time? (For reference, check the **Immigration History Facilitator Overview**, included at the end of this module.)
As you walk through the timeline, recognize any additional dates that participants have put up, and ask them to explain their reasons for adding it to the timeline. Recognize each participant's migration story as you review the timeline. (30 minutes)

7. Process the activity with the group. Ask:
- Did anything surprise you about this activity? If so, what?
- What similarities do you see in the reasons that lead people to migrate?
- How have immigration laws prevented certain groups of people from coming to the U.S.? Whom did these laws exclude? Whom did these laws allow to enter? Who influenced these laws, and why?
- How have immigration regulations and legislation affected immigration? How do you think they have affected the lives of immigrants?

national network for immigrant and refugee rights
www.nnirr.org

history of immigration 101

Immigration Time Line Variation 1

- What challenges and injustices do you think immigrants have faced throughout history? How have these challenges and injustices changed or remained the same over time?
- How have different groups challenged injustice? What can we learn from their experiences to help us today?

TEACHING POINTS

8. Review the teaching points with the group.

- Everyone who is not a Native American Indian in the U.S. has a history of migration—whether it is forced displacement, economic, or other reasons.
- Immigration and refugee policy has and continues to control who is included or excluded from the U.S. on the basis of race, national origin, class, gender, and sexual orientation.
- Migration to the U.S. has always been closely linked to labor needs within the U.S.
- U.S. foreign policy interests—whether claiming more territory for expansion of U.S. borders, or foreign intervention, has caused displacement of indigenous people around the world.
- Immigrants today, as well as in the past, have been subjected to xenophobia. Throughout history, immigrants have been blamed for problems such as unemployment, crime, overburdening public benefits, and other issues.
- Social justice movements have successfully organized and fought against injustice, racism, and intolerance throughout U.S. history.

Michelle Yamashita

history of immigration 101 module 1

Immigration Time Line Variation 2: Quicker Workshop Setting (45 minutes)

This version works well in a traditional classroom/workshop setting, and anywhere from 10-35 participants when you have a more limited schedule.

TIME 45+ minutes

MATERIALS NEEDED
- Same as Immigration Time Line Variation 1

FACILITATOR PREP
- Same as Immigration Time Line Variation 1

DIRECTIONS

1. Introduce the exercise by reviewing the framing questions for the activity. (See Variation 1)

2. Distribute a half sheet of paper and crayons/colored pencils/markers to all participants. Ask participants to think about the following questions:
   - When did you/your family come to the U.S.?
   - Where did you/your family come from?
   - Why did you/your family move?

   Ask participants to write the answers to the questions on their paper, and to draw a picture to illustrate their migration experience. (Some participants may want to do more than one drawing.) (5-10 minutes)

3. Ask participants to find a partner, preferably someone they don't know. (If there is an odd number of participants, form one group of three.) Ask participants to share their "personal migration history" with their partners. (10 minutes)

4. Participants should "tour" the timeline with their partners or their small groups. Distribute pieces of tape, so that participants can hang their personal history on the timeline as they walk through. Have extra sheets of paper available so that participants can add key dates that are not on the timeline. (10 minutes)

5. Process the activity with the group. Ask:
   - Did anything surprise you about this activity? If so, what?
   - What similarities do you see in the reasons that lead people to migrate?
   - How have immigration laws prevented certain groups of people from coming to the U.S.? Who influenced these laws, and why?
   - What challenges and injustices do you think immigrants have faced throughout history? How have they changed or remained the same?
   - How have different groups challenged injustice? What can we learn from their experiences to help us today?

6. Review teaching points with the group. (See Variation 1)

national network for immigrant and refugee rights

history of immigration 101

Immigration Time Line Variation 3: Quicker Conference Setting (60 minutes)

This version works well in a variety of settings: in classrooms/workshop settings with a large number of participants, or in medium-sized lecture settings (60-80+ participants).

TIME 60 minutes

MATERIALS NEEDED
- Copies of timeline dates, copied onto two different colors of paper
- Easel paper, markers, tape

FACILITATOR PREP
- Copy timeline dates and pictures onto two different colors of paper, according to whether the date signifies restrictive policies/discrimination, or whether the date signifies openings in policy/resistance. (More details on these policies can be found in the **Immigration History Facilitator's Overview**, at the end of this module.

Some examples of restrictive policies/discrimination include:
- 1790 and 1798: Naturalization Act and Alien and Sedition Act
- 1830: Indian Removal Act
- 1846-1848: Mexican-American War
- 1850: Fugitive Slave Act
- 1882: Chinese Exclusion Act
- 1907: "Gentlemen's Agreement"
- 1917: Literacy Requirement
- 1919: Palmer Raids
- 1921 and 1924: National Quota Acts
- 1934: Tydings McDuffie Act
- 1942: Japanese Internment
- 1954: Operation Wetback
- 1986: Immigration Reform and Control Act
- 1993: Border blockade strategies
- 1995: Proposition 187
- 1996: Anti-immigrant legislation
- 2001: PATRIOT Act, Special Registration, Secret Detention

Some examples of openings in policy/resistance include:
- 1807: Congress bans importation of slaves
- 1831-1861: Underground Railroad
- 1865-1870: 13th, 14th, and 15th Amendments outlaws slavery, grants equal

history of immigration 101 module 1

Immigration Time Line Variation 3

   protection, and gives African American males right to vote
- 1920: 20th Amendment gives women the right to vote
- 1943: Chinese Exclusion Act repealed
- 1945: War Brides Act
- 1954-1964: Civil Rights Movement
- 1965: Immigration and Nationality Act
- 1975: Indochina Migration and Refugee Assistance Act
- 1997: NACARA
- 2000: LIFE

DIRECTIONS

1. Frame the discussion by presenting the framing questions, as well as the teaching points. (10-15 minutes)

2. Distribute the timeline dates randomly to participants.

3. Explain to participants that they will participate in a collective presentation of the Immigration History Timeline. Starting with the first date, and reading the dates in order, ask participants who are holding timeline dates to read them aloud. After a participant has read their date, ask them to hang the date against the wall, in order. (It may help if you have a master list of dates, so you can anticipate the next date, and prompt the person holding the next date to read aloud.)

4. Briefly process the exercise with the large group. Ask:
   - Did anything surprise you about this activity? What did you notice?
   - What is the difference between the dates on the two different colors of paper?
   - What challenges and injustices do you think immigrants faced throughout history? How have these challenges and injustices changed or remained the same over time?
   - How have different groups challenged injustice? What can we learn from their experiences to help us today?

5. Review the teaching points with the group. (See variation 1)

national network for immigrant and refugee rights

history of immigration 101

Immigration Time Line Variation 4: On the Bus!

Long road trips on a bus—on the way to a protest or meeting—or in our case, the 2003 Immigrant Worker Freedom Rides, can be the perfect time to conduct popular education. This variation is adapted to the logistical challenges of holding workshops on a moving bus.

TIME 90+ minutes

MATERIALS NEEDED
- Copy of the "Immigration History Timeline in Pictures" (at end of section)
- Tape (very important!)
- Sheets of paper, cut in half (enough for each participant)
- Pens for participants
- Bullhorn, or a microphone that can be used throughout the length of a bus so participants can hear each other

FACILITATOR PREP
- Review immigration history materials and dates before facilitating this module, and select about 20 dates to copy. You may want to add/take out to highlight the experiences of participants.
- Familiarize yourself with the limitations of the bus. Establish a work center (seats at the front of the bus work best) to keep your supplies.

DIRECTIONS

1. Explain to participants that this exercise will examine the history of immigration to the U.S. Review the framing questions for the activity:
   - What are some of the reasons that people have migrated to the U.S.?
   - What groups have immigrated to the U.S. throughout history? How were they treated by people already here?
   - How have immigration laws prevented certain groups of people from coming to the U.S.? Whom did these laws exclude? Whom did these laws allow to enter? Who influenced these laws, and why?
   - How have different groups challenged injustice? What can we learn from their experiences to help us today?

2. Distribute a half sheet of paper and pens to all participants. Ask participants to think about the following questions:
   - When did you/your family come to the U.S.?
   - Where did you/your family come from?
   - Why did you/your family move?

Ask participants to write the answers to the questions on their paper, and to draw a picture to illustrate their migration experience.

history of immigration 101   module 1

Immigration Time Line Variation 4

3. Ask participants to turn to their partner (seated beside them), and share their "personal migration history" with their partners.

4. Distribute timeline dates and tape around the bus. Start with the first date in the first row on the right hand side of the bus, and work your way around until you have gone to the back of the bus, and up the left hand side of the bus.

5. Explain to participants that they will be creating an immigration history timeline with their personal histories and some significant dates in immigration history. Ask participant to read her/his timeline date out loud (preferably into a microphone or bullhorn, so everyone can hear). Then ask the participant to stick the timeline date to the window, so that everyone in the bus can see it. (It is very useful to have 1-2 assistants to help you in this stage of the exercise: one person to hold the microphone/bullhorn, and another to assist participants.)

6. Participants will proceed reading their timeline dates around the bus. As the timeline continues, ask participants to hold up their "personal migration history" drawing when the date of their migration approaches on the timeline, and tape their "personal migration history" to the window.

7. If there is time, and participants are still engaged, go around the bus once more, and have each participant share their "personal migration history" with the rest of the bus.

8. Briefly process the exercise with the participants. Ask:
   - Did anything surprise you about this activity? What did you notice?
   - What challenges and injustices do you think immigrants faced throughout history? How have these challenges and injustices changed or remained the same over time?
   - How have different groups challenged injustice? What can we learn from their experiences to help us today?

TEACHING POINTS
- Everyone who is not a Native American Indian in the U.S. has a history of migration—whether it is forced displacement or migration, or a history of immigration
- Immigration and refugee policy has and continues to control who is included or excluded from the U.S. on the basis of race, national origin, class, gender, and sexual orientation.
- Migration to the U.S. has always been closely linked to labor needs within the U.S.
- U.S. foreign policy interests—whether in claiming more territory for expansion of U.S. borders, or in foreign intervention, has caused

national network for immigrant and refugee rights

history of immigration 101

Immigration Time Line Variation 4

displacement of indigenous people around the world, displacing many people.
- Immigrants today, as well as in the past, have been subjected to xenophobia. Immigrants in the past and present have been blamed for problems such as unemployment, crime, overburdening public benefits, and other issues.
- Immigrants and other social movements have successfully fought for the expansion of rights and citizenship throughout U.S. history.

SOURCE   the authors

History Timeline exercise on Immigrant Worker Freedom Rides, 2003. Eunice Cho

history of immigration 101   module 1

History Under the Magnifying Glass

WHY DO IT?
- To more deeply explore issues of race and migration in U.S. history
- To familiarize participants (particularly if group is not that diverse) with historical cases of racism and xenophobia

TIME   60 minutes

MATERIALS NEEDED
- Easel paper, tape, markers
- Copies of small group discussion handouts for participants
- Copy of "Immigration timeline in pictures" if you are holding this activity on a different day than the timeline exercise

FACILITATOR PREP
- If you are holding this activity on a different day than the timeline exercise, post timeline dates on the wall.

DIRECTIONS:
1. Explain to the group that this activity will be an opportunity to more closely examine historical cases of racism and xenophobia.
2. Divide the large group into at least 6 small groups, if possible. Give a different scenario and set of discussion questions to each group. If you are starting this activity on a different day than Activity #1, re-post the Time Line on the walls around of the large group discussion room while the small groups are meeting.
3. Small groups should discuss their case study, and produce a drawing representing their group's discussion. (30 minutes)
4. Reconvene the large group, and have each small group present their drawing, then place their drawing under the date of their timeline.
5. Briefly process the activity with the large group. Ask:
   - Did anything surprise you about this activity? What did you notice?
   - How have people of color and immigrants been treated in the past? How has this treatment set up inequality for these groups?
   - Do you see any parallels to the present? If so, what?
   - If these cases happened today, what would you do?

SOURCE   the authors

history of immigration 101

Slavery & Race — 1705 Virginia Slave Codes Passed

group #1

Early U.S. colonial plantation owners of the U.S. depended on slaves captured from West Africa as their main workers. Historians estimate that Africa lost 50 million people to death and slavery at the hands of slave traders and plantation owners in Western Europe and the Americas. Only an estimated 1/3 of the Africans shipped across the Atlantic survived the rough journey. Each slave was chained into cramped spaces not bigger than a coffin. Survivors suffered hard labor under the whip, as well as rape and seeing family members sold off to other slavers.

Plantation owners tried but failed at enslaving Native Americans because they knew the land too well and escaped. White indentured servants got their freedom after working for several years. Increasingly, the rich began to justify slavery of Africans, not just through religion, but also through creating a whole system of white supremacy and black servitude. The white elite also worked hard to prevent white laborers from finding common cause with blacks, by getting them to identify more strongly as whites. Planters wrote laws that made sharp divisions between whites and blacks in opportunities and punishments.

According to historian John Horton, at one point Virginia state law defined a "black person" as "someone with one-sixteenth African ancestry." Florida's definition was someone with one-eighth African ancestry; and Alabama as anyone with any African ancestry at all. Horton said that meant "You give me the power, I can make you any race I want you to be, because it is a social, political construction. It is not a matter of biology. But regardless of how ridiculous it is, the defining of race is tremendously important…it defines your opportunities…your life chances."

WHAT DID YOU THINK OF THIS EXAMPLE?

1. Who benefited from defining anyone with any visible African heritage as Black?
2. What does the following statement mean to you: "race is a social, political construction…not a matter of biology" yet can define "your life chances?"
3. How does race operate today in the U.S.? How does it operate in other countries?
4. If you were born in another country, please share how race or ethnic divisions operate there. How is it similar and different to the U.S.?

WHAT WAS YOUR REACTION?

Draw a picture to place along the Time Line that reflects your small group discussion about "history under the magnifying glass" about African slavery and race.

BRIDGE: Building a Race and Immigration Dialogue in the Global Economy
www.nnirr.org

history of immigration 101 module 1

Native Americans — Forced Migration, Genocide & Resistance

group #2

The US government has carried out over two centuries of policies aimed at taking the land and resources of indigenous people. For example, the 1830 Indian Removal Act paved the way for the government to push whole nations from their homelands in the eastern U.S. all the way to Oklahoma. U.S. troops rounded up southeastern tribes like the Cherokee, Creek, Chickasaw, Choctaw, and Seminole nations and forced the people on death marches at gun-point, without adequate food, shelter, or medical attention. Many people died from the hunger and cold on the way to their newly designated "homelands." Some groups like the Sac and Fox nations of Illinois (Black Hawk War of 1832) and the Seminoles of Florida took up weapons to fight the forced migration. The Sac and Fox were then slaughtered by U.S. troops. After being pushed out of their lands the Seminoles moved to hard-to-enter territory in the Florida Everglades swampland. They refused to make peace with the U.S. until the 1960s.

The 1887 General Allotment Act is another example of U.S. attempts to annex Indian land. This time, the U.S. government imposed a racial classification system called "blood quantum." Those who could prove that they were at least of "one-half or more degree of Indian blood" and wanted to accept U.S. citizenship could obtain land. The rest of the tribe's communal land was then opened up to white settlers, big business, and the government. Indians lost another 100 million acres of their best land. This model was later used by the racist apartheid regime in South Africa which delegatd the best land to the white minority and moved the black majority to the worst land. Now some indigenous nations use blood quantum to define who can be legally registered as a member of the nation.

WHAT DID YOU THINK OF THIS EXAMPLE?

1. Talk about U.S. government policies of taking land from indigenous people. Do you know of any other groups of people who have gone through similar experiences?
2. Talk about the racial classification of "blood quantum." How did the creation of this system serve government interests at the time? Are there ways that it could serve indigenous people today?
3. If you were born in another country than the U.S., are there indigenous peoples there? If so, how are indigenous communities treated? What has been their response? Is there a sizeable section of the population that is of mixed ethnicity? If so, how are they treated and where do they stand within the ethnic stratification?

WHAT WAS YOUR REACTION?

Draw a picture to place along the Time Line that reflects your small group discussion about treatment of indigenous nations. You may also draw additional pictures related to the status of indigenous people in the home country/ies of members of the small group.

national network for immigrant and refugee rights
www.nnirr.org

history of immigration 101

"If You're White, You're All Right"—1790 Naturalization Act

group #3

The 1790 Naturalization Act declared citizenship available for whites only. Citizenship permitted the right to vote, own properties, file lawsuits, testify in court, and other essential rights. Foreign-born people of color were largely denied access to citizenship until the 1954 McCarran-Walter Act struck down racial barriers. U.S.-born blacks did not win the right to citizenship until 1868 when the 14th Amendment to the Constitution was passed. Yet many U.S.-born people of color were denied full citizenship rights until the Civil Rights movement of the 1950s and 60s pressured the government to grant reforms.

Before the 1954 Act removed racial restrictions on citizenship, many people tried to test the limits of the 1790 Naturalization Act. For example, in 1922 the U.S. Supreme Court ruled that Takao Ozawa, a Japanese immigrant who had attended the University of California at Berkeley, could not become a citizen because he was "clearly" "not Caucasian." Bhagat Singh Thind, a US army veteran, had argued that Asian Indians were part of the Aryan race and should thus be considered white and eligible for citizenship. In the 1923 U.S. vs. Bhagat Singh Thind decision, the Supreme Court argued that the definition of race had to be based on the "understanding of the common man"--white man, that is--not on science. The court said that although Asian Indians might technically be thought of as "Caucasian" by scientists, they were not white, and therefore not eligible for citizenship.

In 1914, a South Carolina judge ruled that while Syrians (which included many different Arab people) may be Caucasian, they were not "that particular free white person to whom the Act of Congress [1790] had denoted the privilege of citizenship"' – a privilege that was intended for persons of European descent.

WHAT DID YOU THINK OF THIS EXAMPLE?

1. Who was eligible for citizenship in 1790? Who was not?
2. Who was eligible for citizenship in 1954? Who was not?
3. Who is eligible for citizenship today? Who is not?
4. What rights and privileges do citizens have? Legal permanent residents? Undocumented workers? Refugees?
5. Do you think race still impacts who gets to be a US citizen today? How so? Or why not?

WHAT WAS YOUR REACTION?

Draw a picture to place along the Time Line that reflects your small group discussion about racism, immigration, and citizenship policies.

BRIDGE: Building a Race and Immigration Dialogue in the Global Economy
www.nnirr.org

history of immigration 101 module 1

Giant Labor Reserve –
1930s Deportations vs. WWII Bracero Program

group #4

Mexican workers have served as a giant reserve labor force for the US economy, cycling through boom and bust times.

From 1929-1939, the U.S. deported between 500,000 and 600,000 Mexicans, including many legal residents and U.S. citizens. U.S.-born children made up 60 to 75 percent of the total number of deportees. Although Mexicans workers had been recruited to work in agriculture, many restrictionists were against Mexican migration, especially after anti-Asian exclusion acts were passed. Employers, who benefitted from Mexican labor, favored an open border. The U.S. launched the Border Patrol in 1929. The Great Depression also began in 1929, and fueled anti-Mexican sentiments. The U.S. government set up urban-based programs to raid work and living areas and to deport Mexicans. By 1940, the Mexican population in the U.S. was cut down to about half of what it had been in 1930.

From 1942-1965, the U.S. began the Bracero ("Strong Arms") Program of Mexican workers, at first to fulfill wartime labor shortages in US agriculture. Nearly 5 million temporary labor contracts were issued to Mexican workers. Growers had wanted an open border and freedom to hire the workers at will, but the Mexican government insisted on a contract. Braceros worked on farms and U.S. railroads under brutal conditions. The work was backbreaking and often dangerous. Many workers got cheated out of their pay, and ended up with inadequate housing, food, water, sanitation facilities, and heating, compared to what they had been promised. Some workers found themselves getting set up to be used as strikebreakers.

WHAT DID YOU THINK OF THIS EXAMPLE?

1. What do you think pushed Mexicans to leave their country?
2. What pulled Mexicans to the U.S.?
3. What happened to Mexicans during times of economic prosperity?
4. What happened to Mexicans during times of economic hardship?
5. How did race, national origin status, and class impact deportation policy? Labor policy?
6. Can you think of other immigrant communities from other countries that shared similar experiences?

WHAT WAS YOUR REACTION?

Draw a picture to place along the Time Line that reflects your small group discussion about how race, nationality, and labor needs shape immigration policy.

national network for immigrant and refugee rights
www.nnirr.org

history of immigration 101

The Politics of Refugee Policy/1980 Refugee Act

group #5

The 1980 Refugee Act permitted immigration by a person who fears return to their country of origin because of "a well-founded fear of persecution on account of race, religion, nationality, membership in a particular social group or political opinion."

Unfortunately, the definition of "fear of persecution" depends on the relations the refugees' government has with the U.S. Take the cases of Haitian and Cuban refugees. While both sets of refugees are fleeing economic hardship, and often fear political violence, they are treated very differently. Haitians are locked up in the Krome detention center in Florida and await deportation hearings, while Cubans are often granted parolee status, the fast track route to green card and permanent residence status. This reflects the difference between the U.S. government's past support of Haitian dictatorships vs. its hard-line opposition to Cuba's Castro government.

This difference is reflected in the 1966 Cuban Adjustment Act. This law encourages Cubans to risk their lives to defect. The law says that if Cubans make it to the U.S., they can stay; if they are captured at sea by the Coast Guard, they are supposed to be deported. This is often called the "dry foot, wet foot" standard for refugee status. This discriminatory treatment adds up to a policy that favors Cubans, many of whom are racially white, and discriminates against Haitians, who are often black.

WHAT DID YOU THINK OF THIS EXAMPLE?

1. What was happening in world politics when the U.S. passed the 1980 Refugee Act?
2. Do you think the U.S. applies the standard of "well-founded fear of persecution" fairly equally to different countries' applicants for asylum? If not, please offer examples.
3. Do you think race influences asylum decisions? If so how? If not, why not?
4. After September 11, the number of refugees permitted to enter the U.S. was sharply curbed because of stated government fears about security. Do you think this is reasonable? Why? Why not?

WHAT WAS YOUR REACTION?

Draw a picture to place along the Time Line that reflects your small group discussion about how race, nationality, and politics shape refugee policy.

history of immigration 101   module 1

National Security, Race & Xenophobia – 1940s & Now

group #6

Xenophobia, national security, and racism have shaped the course of U.S. history. During World War II, President Franklin D. Roosevelt signed Executive Order 9066. The order gave the Army the power to arrest every Japanese American on the West Coast. Some 110,000 men, women and children of Japanese descent were sent to concentration camps in barren, isolated regions, and kept under armed guard. Three-quarters of those incarcerated were U.S. citizens. In 1944, the Supreme Court upheld the order, claiming it was a military necessity. Yet Americans of German and Italian descent (Germany and Italy were considered enemy nations), were not imprisoned in such wholesale way. The Japanese Americans spent over three years in the concentration camps. In 1988, after many years of campaigning by survivors of the camps, Congress passed a bill to pay reparations of $20,000 to each of the survivors, and President Reagan admitted that the US had committed "a grave wrong."

Racial profiling, xenophobia, and hate violence against Arab, South Asian, and Muslim communities have intensified since September 11, 2001. At the end of 2002, the U.S. Justice Department and INS launched the National Security Entry-Exit Registration System or "special registration" program. The government demanded that men from over 25 Arab, Asian, and African countries report to the INS to be fingerprinted, photographed, and questioned. Except for North Korea, all the countries listed were Arab and/or Muslim. Some men and boys whose immigration applications were pending because of INS' own delays were detained and sent from jail to jail. Many detainees also reported mistreatment, severe overcrowding, sleep deprivation, unnecessary restraints and racial slurs in detention. Many were unable to call family to inform them of what was happening.

WHAT DID YOU THINK OF THIS EXAMPLE?

1. Why were Japanese Americans, but not German or Italian Americans, sent to camps during World War II?
2. Do you think race, religious, and immigrant status profiling is justified during "periods of national emergency?" Why? Why not?
3. What messages is current government policy sending to the public about men and boys of Arab, South Asian, African, and Muslim descent?

WHAT WAS YOUR REACTION?

Draw a picture to place along the Time Line that reflects your small group discussion about how the US government treated race, religious, immigration and national security issues.

national network for immigrant and refugee rights
www.nnirr.org

history of immigration 101

Closing: Another Look at Our Names, Our Stories

WHY DO IT
- To reflect on the day's theme of immigration
- To provide a sense of closure for the day in a shared experience

TIME 15 minutes

MATERIALS NEEDED
- "Giant name tags" created by participants in opening exercise

DIRECTIONS
1. Collect the "giant name tags" created by participants in the opening exercise.
2. Ask participants to form a large circle, standing and facing inwards. Place the name tags in the middle of the circle so that each one is fully visible.
3. Remind participants that at the beginning of the workshop, they had thought of words related to immigration that corresponded with their name. Ask participants to look at all of the other name tags in the middle of the circle, and to find a word on someone else's name tag that is especially meaningful.
4. Go around the circle, and each participant should say the word that they found meaningful.
5. Thank the whole group for their participation.

SOURCE the authors

Eunice Cho

history of immigration 101 module **1**

- **U.S. Immigration History: a Handout**
- **Immigration History: Facilitator's Overview**
- **Immigration History Timeline in Pictures**

U.S. Immigration History: a handout

1492 COLUMBUS ARRIVES IN THE AMERICAS

LLEGADA DE COLON EN LAS AMERICAS

1600s –1865 SLAVERY OF AFRICANS: Millions of Africans forcibly removed from the continent, enslaved and transported to North America, primarily to work on plantations in the South.

ESCLAVITUD: Miliones de Africanos removidos por la fuerza de su continente, esclavizados y transportados a Norte América. Primeramente para trabajar en las plantaciones en el sur.

1790 NATURALIZATION ACT Only "free white persons" eligible to become U.S. citizens.

ACTA DE NATURALIZACION Solamente las "personas blancas libres" son elegibles para convertirse en ciudadanos estadounidenses.

1830 INDIAN REMOVAL ACT Forces 70,000 Native Americans to relocate in order to free land for settlement by European immigrants.

ACTA DE EXPULSION INDIGENA Forza 70,000 mil indígenas norteamericanos a ser removidos o trasladados para poder liberar tierra para la ocupación de los inmigrantes europeos.

1848 MEXICAN AMERICAN WAR: War between Mexico and the United States. The U.S. annexes all or parts of Texas, New Mexico, Arizona, California, Colorado, Nevada, and Utah. Mexicans in these areas lose their citizenship rights.

GUERRA MEXICANA AMERICANA: La Guerra entre México y EEUU. EEUU tomo áreas en los estados de Texas, Nuevo México, Arizona, California, Colorado, Nevada y Utah. Los Mexicanos que viven en esas áreas pierden sus derechos de ciudadanía.

1865-1870:
1865 13TH AMENDMENT outlaws slavery. Ku Klux Klan is founded.

ENMIENDA 13 prohibe la esclavitud. Se forma el Ku Klux Klan.

1866 CIVIL RIGHTS ACT grants citizenship to people born in the United States, except American Indians.

ACTA DE DERECHOS CIVILES le da la ciudadanía a todos los nacidos en los Estados Unidos excepto a los Indígenas norteamericanos.

1868 14th AMENDMENT grants equal protection of the law to African Americans.

ENMIENDA 14 le da protección igual de la ley a los afroamericanos.

BRIDGE: Building a Race and Immigration Dialogue in the Global Economy
www.nnirr.org

U.S. Immigration History: a handout

1870 — **15th AMENDMENT** establishes the right of African American males to vote. Specifically excludes all women.

1882-1943 — **CHINESE EXCLUSION ACT:** Denies citizenship for Chinese immigrants and suspends their entry to the U.S. During the late 1880s, Italians and the Irish also faced discrimination.

1890-1895 — **THE NEW SOUTH LAWS (JIM CROW LAWS)** Beginning with Mississippi, Confederate states enact amendments denying blacks the right to vote. Forms of disenfranchisement include poll taxes and ownership of property. In Texas, these laws are also used to deny Latinos the right to vote.

1919 — **PALMER RAIDS:** Deportations and round-ups of "aliens," anarchists, and communists, especially those from southern Europe and Latin America. 10,000 labor and immigrant activists are deported.

1920 — **20TH AMENDMENT:** Women win the right to vote

1921-1930 — **DEPORTATION OF MEXICAN WORKERS:** Thousands of Mexican workers, including many US citizens, are deported.

ENMIENDA 15 establece el derecho de los hombres afroamericanos a votar. Específicamente excluye a todas las mujeres.

ACTA DE EXCLUSION DE LOS CHINOS: Niega la ciudadanía a los inmigrantes chinos y suspende su entrada a los Estados Unidos. Durante el final de los 1800s, los italianos y los irlandeses también enfrentan mucha discriminación.

LAS LEYES DEL NUEVO SUR O LEYES DE "JIM CROW" Empezando con Mississippi, los estados confederados ponen enmiendas negando a los negros el derecho a votar, en forma de impuestos en las casillas y tenencia de tierras para poder votar. Texas adopta a las mismas leyes para excluir a los negros y también a los Latinos.

LAS REDADAS "PALMER" Deportaciones y redadas de extranjeros, anarquistas, y comunistas, especialmente los del sur de Europa y Latinoamerica que tenian un papel central en organizar los sindicatos en los Estados Unidos. 10,000 activistas de los movimientos laboral e inmigrante fueron deportados.

ENMIENDA 20: La mujer gana el derecho a votar.

DEPORTACIONES DE TRABAJADORES MEXICANOS: Miles de trabajadores mexicanos son deportados, incluyendo a muchos ciudadanos.

national network for immigrant and refugee rights
www.nnirr.org

U.S. Immigration History: a handout

1929	**U.S. BORDER PATROL CREATED**	**SE ESTABLECIO LA PATRULLA EN LA FRONTERA**
1942-1945	**JAPANESE INTERNMENT:** U.S. forcibly moves 120,000 Japanese-Americans from the western U.S. to detention camps for 3 years.	**CAMPOS DE DETENCION JAPONESES:** El gobierno EEUU remueve por la fuerza 120,000 americanos de descendencia japonesa del oeste de los Estados Unidos a campos de concentración por 3 años.
1943	**CHINESE EXCLUSION ACT REPEALED**	**EL ACTA DE EXCLUSION CHINO ES REPELADO**
1942-1964	**BRACERO PROGRAM:** Millions of contract workers from Mexico, Jamaica, British Honduras and Barbados brought to the U.S. to meet labor shortages created by WWII. Workers are still fighting for wages owed to them.	**PROGRAMA BRACERO:** Miliones de trabajadores contratados de México, Jamaica, Honduras Británicas, y Barbados son llevados a los Estados Unidos para responder a la falta de trabajadores debido a la Segunda Guerra Mindial. Hasta la fecha, los trabajadores siguen peleando por sueldos que nunca recibieron.
1954	**OPERATION WETBACK** Massive deportation campaign expelling more than 1.1 million Mexicans.	**ESPALDAS MOJADAS** Una campaña de deportaciones masivas, expulsando más de 1.1 milliones de mexicanos.
1961	**FREEDOM RIDES** challenge segregation on buses	**CARAVANAS DE LA LIBERTAD** enfrentan la segregación en los autobuses
1965	**VOTING RIGHTS ACT:** Literacy tests and other such requirements preventing citizens from voting become illegal.	**ACTA DE DERECHO A VOTAR:** Exámenes de alfabetismo y otros tales requísitos que impiden a ciudadanos votar son declarados ilegales.
1965	**IMMIGRATION ACT** Eliminates race, creed, and nationality quotas as basis for admission to the U.S.	**ACTA DE INMIGRACION Y NACIONALIDAD** Elimina raza, etnicidad y nacionalidad como base para el ingreso a los Estados Unidos

BRIDGE: Building a Race and Immigration Dialogue in the Global Economy
www.nnirr.org

U.S. Immigration History: a handout

1975 **INDOCHINA MIGRATION AND REFUGEE ASSISTANCE ACT/REFUGEE ACT:** Many refugees from Southeast Asia come in the aftermath of U.S. military and economic intervention in the region.

ACTA DE INMIGRACION Y ASISTENCIA PARA REFUGIADO/ACTA DE REFUGIADOS: Muchos refugiados del Este de Asia vienen después de la intervención militar y económica de los Estados Unidos en la región.

1986 **IRCA: IMMIGRATION REFORM & CONTROL ACT ESTABLISHED EMPLOYER SANCTIONS.** Makes it illegal for employers to knowingly hire any undocumented worker.

ACTA DE REFORMA Y CONTROL DE INMIGRACION Estableció las sanciones en contra de los empleadores. Se vuelve ilegal para los empleadores contratar trabajadores sabiendo que son indocumentados.

1990 **CONGRESS REPEALS BAN ON GAY & LESBIAN IMMIGRATION:** Congress removes homosexuality as a reason to disqualify foreigners from immigrating, or even visiting the U.S.

EL CONGRESO DEROGA LA PROHIBICION LA INMIGRACION DE GAYS Y LESBIANAS: El congreso remueve la homosexualidad como razón para descalifar a extranjeros de inmigrar, o aún vistar, a los Estados Unidos.

1996 **CHANGES IN IMMIGRATION POLICY** broaden grounds for deportation of immigrants

CAMBIOS EN POLITICAS MIGRATORIAS amplifican las condiciones para la deportación de los inmigrantes

2001 **U.S.A. PATRIOT ACT**

ACTA PATRIOTA DE LOS EE.UU.

Immigration History: Facilitator's Overview

This overview provides a brief background to key dates in U.S. immigration history for facilitators to familiarize themselves with larger trends and contextual events. Facilitators may want to refer to this overview when reviewing the timeline in large group discussions, to discuss other economic, social, and political forces taking place. This overview includes many dates, some of which are included in the "U.S. Immigration History Timeline In Pictures." Facilitators may want to use this overview as a way to supplement and customize the "timeline in pictures" when using it with different audiences.

*denotes inclusion in "Immigration History Timeline: In Pictures"

1492-1600s: Columbus arrives in the Americas.

*1492   Genocide of indigenous people begins with Christopher Columbus' voyage to the Americas. At the time of his arrival, the Northern Hemisphere is populated by 5,000,000+ Indigenous people.

1600s-1776: Colonial period, beginning of African slavery.

Demographics: During the 1600s, English, Dutch, Irish, Scots and French migrate to North America, the majority of whom are indentured servants, convicts, or prisoners. In 1619, the first shipload of African slaves arrives, and slavery strongly changes the racial makeup of the Colonies. By 1699, an estimated 33,200 African slaves were brought by force. About half of all people arriving in the 13 colonies from 1700 to 1775 were forcibly brought from Africa.

*1619   Slavery begins. First shipload of African slaves to American colonies arrives in Jamestown, Virginia.
1637   Pequot War—between Pequot Indians and European settlers
1675-1676   King Phillip's War—between Wampanoag, Narragansett Indians and English settlers
*1718   Large-scale Scottish and Irish immigration begins, with most settling New England, Maryland, and Pennsylvania. Immigrants from Scandinavia and Germany also arrive.

1776-1860s: Nation-building and Manifest Destiny

By 1800, the number of Native Americans/Indians had been reduced to about 600,000, due to policies of forced displacement and war. The white population of the U.S., however, increased to over 6 million in 1810, and the black population reached

Immigration History: Facilitator's Overview

approximately one and a half million. Although the importation of slaves was outlawed in 1807, Southern states largely ignored the law. The Mexican American War resulted in a huge loss of territory for the Mexican government,

Military/Expansion:

1776	American Independence from England
1803	Louisiana Purchase from France forms almost a third of current U.S. territory
1810-1819	Florida acquisitioned from Spain
1830	Indian Removal Act forces Native Americans from the Southeast U.S. to reservations in Oklahoma
1845	Republic of Texas joins Union after declaring independence from Mexico
1846	Oregon Territory--purchase gives the U.S. territory along the Pacific Ocean
1848	Treaty of Guadalupe Hidalgo—annexation from Mexico
*1790	Naturalization Act restricts citizenship to "free white persons."
*1798	Alien and Sedition Act: Allows the President to arrest, imprison or deport any non-citizen "dangerous to the peace and safety of the United States."
1803	Louisiana Purchase: the U.S. purchases the Louisiana Territory, colonized by France. The westward expansion that follows eventually leads to depletion of the buffalo, an animal central to some Native Americans' lifestyle.
*1807	Congress bans the importation of slaves. Southern states largely ignore the law. During the peak years of the slave trade, between 1740 and 1810, Africa supplied 60,000 captives a year --almost five times as many African slaves as European migrants.
*1830	Indian Removal Act mandates the removal of Native Americans from east of the Mississippi River to "Indian Territory" in Oklahoma. Over 30,000 people die during forced migration, which the Cherokee remember as "The Trail of Tears."
*1831-1861	Underground Railroad: Almost 100,000 slaves escape to the North on the Underground Railroad. Free African Americans and white sympathizers shelter and guide slaves. By 1850, Congress passes the Fugitive Slave Act, which penalizes anyone who helps a slave escape to freedom.
*1840s	Growing European Migration. Irish Potato Famine; crop failures in Germany; industrialization; and failed European revolutions begin a period of mass immigration.

Immigration History: Facilitator's Overview

*1845-1860 The "Know-Nothing" political party, a nativist political party, is founded in 1845 and reaches its peak of support ten years later.

*1846-1848 Mexican-American War. The U.S. invades Mexico seeking control of land and resources. The Treaty of Guadalupe Hidalgo is signed in 1848, transferring over 55% of Mexican land to the U.S. (present-day Arizona, California, New Mexico, Texas, and parts of Colorado, Nevada and Utah). Mexican citizens living in this territory have the choice assume U.S. citizenship within one year, although many forcibly lose their land.

*1849 California Gold Rush lures settlers from all over the world. California Indian population drops from about 120,000 in 1850 to fewer than 20,000 by 1880.

*1862: The Homestead Act encourages many new European immigrants to move to the western U.S. in territory once owned by Native Americans.

1860s-1910: Civil War, Reconstruction Era/Growing Nativism

From 1861-1880, the number of immigrants entering the U.S. reaches well over 5 million, more than the total number of immigrants that had arrived in the U.S. since independence. Germany, Great Britain, and Ireland send the most immigrants, although by the 1890s and 1900s, a growing number of immigrants hail from China, Southern and Eastern regions of Europe, the Caribbean, and the Middle East. Growing nativist and white supremacist movements in the Reconstruction era tried to maintain power after the end of slavery.

1861-1865 The U.S. Civil War is fought over the issue of slavery.

1863 Emancipation Proclamation legally frees slaves, although many slaves do not learn this for years.

*1865-1870 Beginning of Reconstruction

1865 Congress passes the Thirteenth Amendment, outlawing slavery.

1865 The Ku Klux Klan is founded to maintain white supremacy through intimidation and violence.

1868 Congress passes the 14th Amendment, which grants equal protection of the laws to African Americans.

1870 Congress passes the 15th Amendment, which gives African American males the right to vote.

1875 Page Law ends the arrival of Chinese women immigrants based on the fear that Asian immigrants would begin to form families in the U.S.

*1882 Chinese Exclusion Act is passed, barring most Chinese immigrants from entering the U.S. The act also bans "lunatics" and people likely to become public charges.

Immigration History: Facilitator's Overview

1885   Alien Contract Labor Law bars anyone from bringing in foreigners under work contracts, except for domestic workers or skilled workmen.

1890s   Indian Boarding Schools. U.S. government begins an aggressive campaign to "civilize" Indian people by rounding up Indian children, separating them from their families, and sending them away to boarding schools. Many Indian children die as a result.

1890s   Lynchings of African Americans and Mexicans and the burning of Chinatowns increase during this period.

*1898   Spanish-American War. U.S. invades and occupies Cuba, the Philippines, Puerto Rico, and other Spanish colonies in the Pacific Islands. Hawaii is also annexed by force this year.

1904-1999   U.S. establishes permanent military bases in the Panama Canal zone

1901   Anarchist Exclusion Act allows immigrants to be excluded on the basis of their political opinions.

1907   "Gentlemen's Agreement" forbids the emigration of Japanese and Korean laborers to the U.S.

1909   Halladjian Ruling: federal government re-classifies Armenians from "Asiatics" to Caucasians. "…They [Armenians] learned a little bit more English than the Japanese did and they look more American…"

1909   National Association for the Advancement of Colored People (NAACP) formed to fight for civil rights through legal action and education.

1910-1940: World War I, Great Depression

The decade from 1910-1920 marks one of the largest influxes of immigrants to the United States. New immigration from southern and eastern Europe easily outnumbers northern European migration, and brought new militancy to socialist and anarchist movements. This era marks the passage of numerous anti-immigrant policies, such as the 1917 Literacy requirement and the 1921 and 1924 National Origin Quotas. The Great Depression of the 1930s also fuels intolerance, evidenced by the mass deportations of Mexican Americans during this time.

*1910   Mexican Revolution sends thousands of peasants to the U.S. border seeking safety and employment.

*1910-1940s   Great Migration. Over 1 million African Americans migrate from the South to the North to escape lynchings, Jim Crow laws, and economic hardship.

1912   Lawrence Textile Mill Strike is largely led by southern and eastern European immigrant organizers.

Immigration History: Facilitator's Overview

*1915-1925   Ku Klux Klan grows in strength; Klan membership peaks in 1925, with over 5 million members.

*1917   Literacy requirement for immigrants. Mexicans exempted from anti-immigration laws so that they could provide labor. All Asian immigration is banned.

1918   Passport Act prevents arrival and departure to and from the U.S. without documentation.

*1919   Palmer Raids. Deportations and round ups of "aliens," anarchists, and communists, especially those from southern Europe and Latin America influential in labor organizing.

1920   "Ladies Agreement" ends the arrival of Japanese and Korean picture brides. European women are also affected—they are banned from entry if they cannot show that either a man or a job is available to support them.

1920   20th Amendment gives women the right to vote.

*1921   In response to growing anti-immigrant sentiment and the growing power of white supremacists, the Quota Act establishes a "national origins quota system" that favors immigration from Europe.

1922   Ozawa Ruling. Japanese immigrant, Takao Ozawa, challenges the Supreme Court saying he qualifies for citizenship. His case is denied because he is not "Caucasian."

1923   Bhagat Singh Thind Ruling. Supreme Court rules that while Asian Indians might be "Caucasian," they are not white, and therefore not eligible for citizenship.

*1924   Immigration Act of 1924 establishes quotas that even more heavily favor Northern and Western European immigrants. Immigration from Asia is banned, including wives and children of Chinese Americans.

1929   U.S. Border Patrol is created, introducing the distinction between "legal" and "illegal" immigrants for the first time.

*1930s   United States government deports thousands of Mexicans, including many U.S. citizens to Mexico during the Great Depression.

*1934   Tydings-McDuffie Act grants independence to the Philippines, and limits Filipino immigration to a quota of fifty persons per year, and all Filipinos in the United States were reclassified as 'aliens.'

1940-1950: World War II era

World War II changed the Depression-era landscape for immigrant communities. Wartime alliances required that the U.S. reverse aspects of its immigration policy, such

Immigration History: Facilitator's Overview

as Chinese exclusion, and labor shortages created a need that Mexican workers readily filled. Wartime hysteria led to the tragedy of Japanese internment, while African American, Asian, and Mexican American soldiers faced discrimination when they returned.

*1940: Alien Registration Act requires registration & finger-printing of "aliens" over 14 years old.

1941-1945 U.S. becomes involved in World War II, and fights against Germany, Italy, and Japan. Soldiers away at war leave a labor shortage at home.

*1942 Japanese Internment. Over 112,000 Japanese Americans, most of them U.S. citizens, are placed in military internment camps during World War II.

Filipinos are reclassified as U.S. citizens, making it possible for them to register for the military.

1943 The Chinese Exclusion Act is repealed. By the end of the 1940s, all restrictions on Asians acquiring U.S. citizenship are abolished.

*1943-1964 The Bracero Program brings in over 5 million temporary workers from Mexico, mostly to fill an agricultural labor shortage during World War II.

1945 The War Brides Act allows foreign-born wives of U.S. citizens who had served in the U.S. armed forces to enter the United States. African American, Mexican, and Asian veterans of World War II return to face racism and segregation.

1950-1960: Cold War era

1950-1953 Korean War: The U.S. fights Communist forces in Korea, leading to the division of Korea into two countries. The Korean War ends in an armistice; the war is not officially ended.

*1951 1951 United Nations Refugee Convention is signed, defining rights of refugees, including protections for employment and welfare, on the issue of identity papers and travel documents. This Convention is amended in 1967 to apply to all people who become refugees after 1951.

*1952 McCarren Walter Act eliminates racial barriers to citizenship, but also tightens quotas for immigrants and allows deportation of immigrants for "subversive activities."

*1954 Operation Wetback targets Mexican American communities in search for "illegal immigrant." Nearly 4 million people are deported to Mexico.

Immigration History: Facilitator's Overview

  1954 Brown v. Board of Education of Topeka bans racial segregation of public schools.

*1955 Rosa Parks begins the Montgomery Bus Boycott to protest segregation of African Americans in the South.

1960-1980: Civil Rights Gains, Vietnam War

1960-1975 U.S. military involvement in Vietnam, Laos, Cambodia.

1961 U.S. invades Cuba in Bay of Pigs and the Dominican Republic

*1961-1968 Height of Civil Rights Movement

1961 Integrated groups of protesters join Freedom Rides on buses across the South to protest segregation.

1963 Hundreds of thousands of Americans take part in the March on Washington to call for racial equality.

1964 24th Amendment outlaws poll taxes for national elections; Civil Rights Act outlaws discrimination in public accommodations.

1965 Voting Rights Act nullifies local laws and practices that prevent minorities from voting; Malcolm X is assassinated.

1968 Martin Luther King is assassinated.

*1962 Cesar Chavez and Dolores Huerta organize the National Farm Workers Association, which becomes the United Farm Workers in 1966.

*1965 Immigration and Nationality Act repeals the national origins quota system that favors European migration, leading to increased immigration from Latin America, Asia, and other regions. Immigration policy now gives priority to family reunification, labor skills, and political refugees.

1965 Cuban Refugee Airlift begins. Cubans admitted under special quotas.

1969 Stonewall Riots spark a new era for the LGBT rights movement, taking place in New York City. Gays fight off police during a raid on the Stonewall Inn. One of the customers at Stonewall Inn on the night of the raid is an immigrant man who committed suicide in fear that he would be deported for being gay.

*1975 Indochina Migration and Refugee Assistance Act allows refugees from Southeast Asia to the U.S. 1980 Refugee Act brings U.S. refugee law in accordance with international standards.

1980-1989 US military intervention in El Salvador, Guatemala, Nicaragua, Grenada, Lebanon, Libya, Iran, and Panama.

Immigration History: Facilitator's Overview

1980   INS announces new policy on homosexuality: If an immigrant admits that s/he is homosexual to an INS inspector, s/he is excluded from entering the U.S. If a homosexual person denies that s/he was homosexual, but is later found out, s/he could be deported for perjury (lying under oath).

*1982   More than 250 churches provide "sanctuary" to Salvadoran and Guatemalan refugees.

*1986   The Immigration Reform and Control Act gives amnesty to approximately three million undocumented residents, and makes it illegal for employers to hire undocumented workers.

1989-present: New World Order: Globalization and Human Rights

1990s   U.S. military intervention in Iraq, Somalia, Bosnia, Macedonia, Yugoslavia, Kosovo, Sudan, and East Timor.

1990   The Immigration Act of 1990 increases the number of immigrants allowed into the United States each year to 700,000. Congress removes homosexuality as a reason to disqualify foreigners from immigrating, or even visiting, the United States.

*1993   The U.S. government implements a blockade strategy along the U.S. Mexico border, forcing migrants to cross through the desert: Operation Gatekeeper (CA), Operation Safeguard (AZ), and Operation Blockade/Hold The Line (TX). By 2003, over 3,000 people have died while trying to cross the border.

1993   Congress places ban on immigrants who are HIV+.

*1995   California voters pass Proposition 187, which prohibits public educational, welfare, and health services to undocumented immigrants. The proposition is later found to be unconstitutional.

*1996:   Three major bills affecting immigrants are passed, including:
The Illegal Immigration Reform and Immigrant Responsibility Act (IIRIRA) and Anti-Terrorism and Effective Death Penalty Act. Increases jailing of non-violent, non-criminal immigrants and allows deportation of immigrants for minor crimes. Results in the deportation of over 200,000 people. Welfare reform ends monetary and medical assistance for most immigrants.

1997   Nicaraguan Adjustment and Central American Relief Act (NACARA) allows Nicaraguans and Cubans who have been in the U.S. since December 1, 1995 to apply for permanent residence. Salvadorans and Guatemalans can legalize if they have been in the U.S, since 1990 and could prove extreme hardship if deported.

Immigration History: Facilitator's Overview

2000 Legal Immigration and Family Equity (LIFE) Act restores ability of some immigrants to secure legal status, mainly spouses and children of permanent residents whose cases were mishandled during the 1986 amnesty.

*2001 U.S. military intervention in Afghanistan and Iraq

*2001 Events of September 11 attacks set the stage for "national security" based immigration policy. Congress passes the PATRIOT Act, which gives the federal government broad powers to detain suspected "terrorists" for unlimited periods of time without access to legal representation. Over 1,200 Arab, Muslim, and South Asian men are detained in secret.

*2002 U.S. government demands "special registration" for men from 25 Arab, Muslim, and South Asian countries, or face deportation. Border Security and Visa Reform Act increases number of border patrol agents, and creates a centralized database for immigration and law enforcement.

*2003 Department of Homeland Security takes over responsibility for all immigration enforcement and security.

Immigration History Timeline in Pictures — module 1

1492

Artistic rendering of European man in metal helmet attacking Indians.

Genocide of indigenous people begins with Christopher Columbus' voyage to the Americas.

El genocidio contra los pueblos indígenas se inicia con el viaje de Cristobal Colón a las Américas.

Immigration History Timeline in Pictures

1619

"Remarks on the slave-trade ..." Printed and sold by Samuel Wood, No. 362 Pearl-Street [1807].

SLAVERY BEGINS. First shipload of African slaves to American colonies arrives in Jamestown, Virginia.

EMPIEZA LA ESCLAVITUD. El primer cargamento de viente esclavos llega en barco a la colonia de Jamestown, Virginia.

Immigration History Timeline in Pictures

module 1

1790/1798

Signing of the Declaration of Independence, painting by John Trumbull.

1790: Naturalization Act restricts citizenship to "free white persons."

Acta de Naturalización restringe la ciudadanía a "personas blancas libres."

1798: Alien and Sedition Act: Allows the President to arrest, imprison or deport any non-citizen "dangerous to the peace and safety of the United States."

Acta de Extranjeros y Sedición: Autoriza al Presidente arrestar, encarcelar o deportar a cualquier no-ciudadano "peligroso para la paz y seguridad de los Estados Unidos."

Immigration History Timeline in Pictures

1807

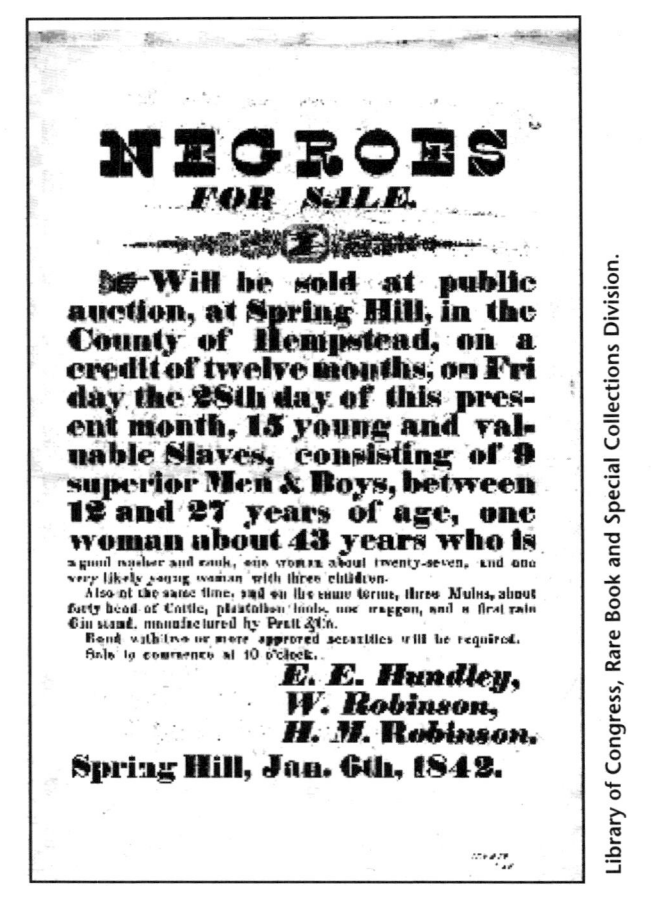

"Negroes for sale. Will be sold at public auction, at Spring Hill, in the County of Hempstead, on a credit of twelve months, on Friday the 28th day this present month ... Spring Hill, [Ark.] Jan. 6th, 1842"

Congress bans the importation of slaves into the U.S. Southern states largely ignore the law.

El Congreso prohíbe la importación de esclavos africanos a los Estados Unidos. Los estados del sur ignoran la ley.

Immigration History Timeline in Pictures — module 1

1830

Painting by Robert Lindneux

Removal Act mandates the removal of Native Americans from east of the Mississippi River to "Indian Territory" in Oklahoma. Over 30,000 people die during forced migration, which the Cherokee remember as "The Trail of Tears."

El Acta de Remover Indios autoriza el desplazamiento de los pueblos originales Nativos Americanos del éste del Río Misisipi al "Territorio Indio" en Oklahoma. Más de 30,000 mueren durante el destierro forzado, que es recordada por los Cherokee como "El Sendero de Lágrimas."

Immigration History Timeline in Pictures

1831-1860

Harriet Tubman, a former slave, led more than 300 slaves to freedom on the Underground Railroad.

Underground Railroad: Almost 100,000 slaves escape to the North on the Underground Railroad, with the help of free African Americans and white sympathizers shelter and guide slaves. By 1850, Congress passes the Fugitive Slave Act, which penalizes anyone who helps a slave escape to freedom.

El ferrocarril clandestino: Casi 100,000 esclavos se escapan al Norte por el Ferrocarril Clandestino, con la ayuda de Africanos Americanos libres y simpatizadores blancos que amparan y guían a los esclavos. En 1850, El Congreso aprueba el Acta de Esclavos Fugitivos, que castiga a cualquiera que ayude a un esclavo escaparse a la libertad.

Immigration History Timeline in Pictures

module 1

1840s

Irish Immigrants on Ship, 'Queenstown,'" from Harper's Weekly, May 1874.

Large wave of immigration begins, due to Irish Potato Famine; crop failures in Germany; industrialization; and failed European revolutions.

Hambruna de la Papa Irlandesa; fracasan cosechas en Alemania; la industrialización; y fracasan revoluciones europeas creando un périodo de emigración masiva.

Immigration History Timeline in Pictures

1846-1848

Mexican American War: American forces in formation at the Battle of Palo Alto, 1846 / Lith. by Klauprech & Menzel. Library of Congress Prints and Photographs Division

Mexican-American War: The U.S. invades Mexico for control of land and resources. The Treaty of Guadalupe Hidalgo is signed in 1848, transferring over 55% of Mexican land to the U.S. (present-day Arizona, California, New Mexico, Texas, and parts of Colorado, Nevada and Utah). Mexican citizens living in this territory have the choice to gain U.S. citizenship within one year, although many forcibly lose their land.

EEUU desata una guerra contra México: Los EEUU invade a México para anexar tierras y recursos. El Tratado de Guadalupe Hidalgo es ratificado en 1848, cediendo más de 55% del territorio mexicano a los EEUU (actualmente a Arizona, California, Nuevo México, Tejas, y partes de Colorado, Nevada, y Utah). Ciudadanos mexicanos que viven en este territorio tienen la opción de conseguir la ciudadanía estadounidense dentro de un año, aunque muchos pierden forzosamente sus tierras.

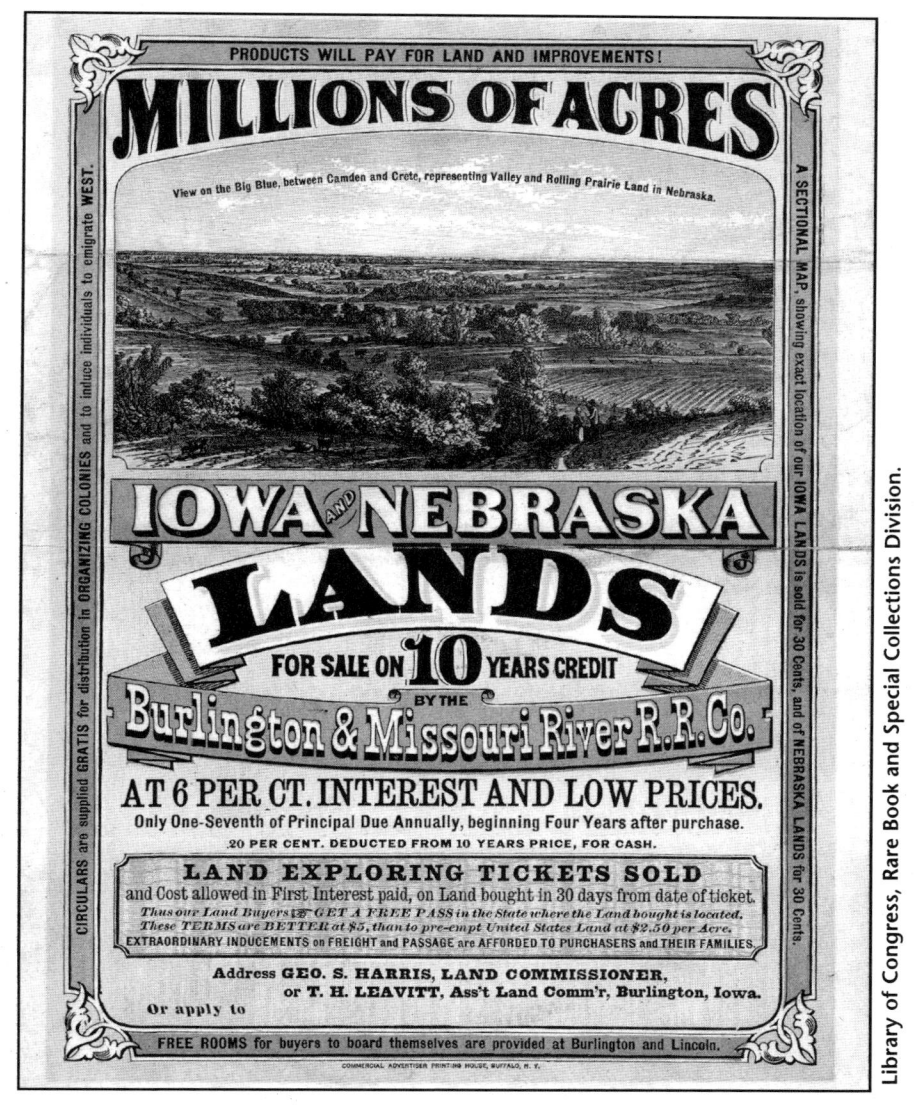

Immigration History Timeline in Pictures — module 1

1862

Advertising circular: "Millions of acres. Iowa and Nebraska. Land for sale on 10 years credit by the Burlington & Missouri River R. R. Co. at 6 per ct interest and low prices," printed 1873

The Homestead Act encourages many new European immigrants to move to the western U.S. in territory once owned by Native Americans.

El Acta de Haciendas estimula la emigración europea con la promesa de tierra en el oeste de los EEUU antes de los Indios.

Immigration History Timeline in Pictures

1865-1870

"Significant Election Scene at Washington, 1867." Harper's Weekly, June 22, 1867.

1865: 13th Amendment outlaws slavery. The Ku Klux Klan is founded to maintain white supremacy through intimidation and violence.

1868: 14th Amendment grants equal protection rights.

1870: 15th Amendment grants African American men right to vote.

1865: la Décima Tercera Enmienda, declarando que la esclavitud es ilegal. El Ku Klux Klan es fundado para mantener la supremacía blanca a través de la intimidación y la violencia.

1868: la Décima Cuarta Enmienda, que otorga la igualdad de protección frente las leyes.

1870: la Décima Quinta Enmienda, que otorga el derecho al voto a los varones Africanos Americanos.

Immigration History Timeline in Pictures

module 1

1882

"The Nigger Must Go, and the Chinese Must Go: The Poor Barbarians Can't Understand our Civilized Republican Form of Government," Harper's Weekly, September 13, 1879.

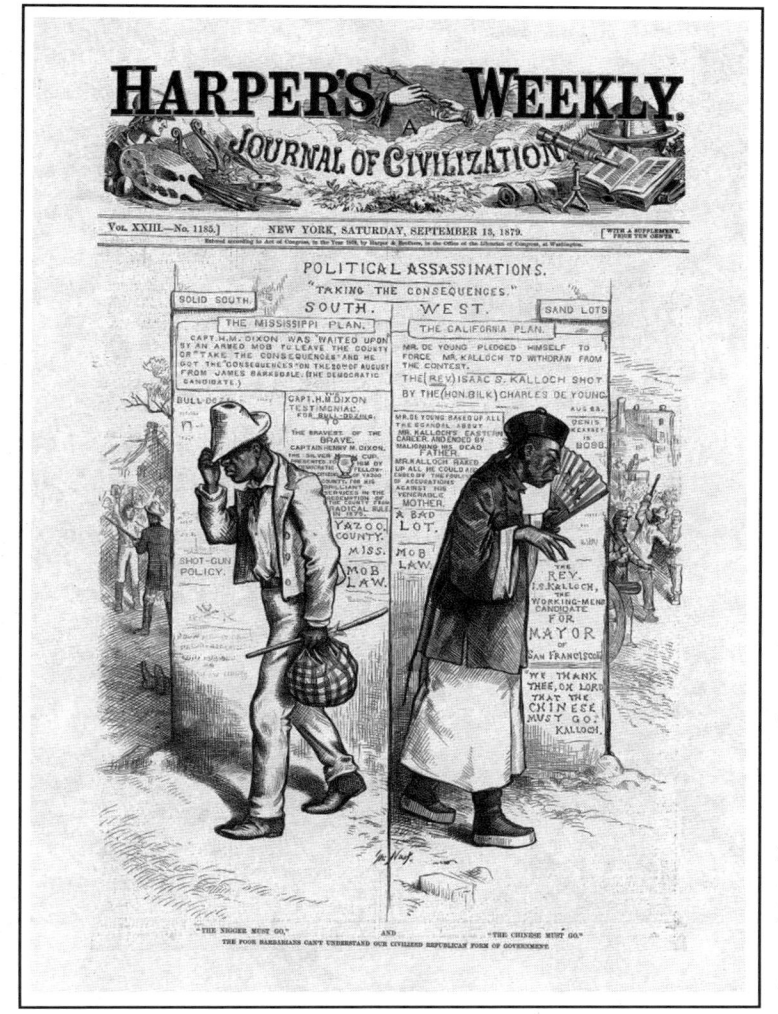

Harper's Weekly, courtesy Library of Congress Prints and Photographs Division, and National Archives: Still Pictures Division

Chinese Exclusion Act is passed, barring most Chinese immigrants from entering the U.S.

El Acta de Exclusión de Chinos es aprobada, prohibiendo a la mayoría de inmigrantes chinos de entrar a los EEUU.

national network for immigrant and refugee rights | 85
www.nnirr.org

Immigration History Timeline in Pictures

1898

Spanish-American War: US invades and occupies Cuba, the Philippines, Puerto Rico, and other Spanish colonies in the Pacific Islands. Hawaii is also annexed by force this year.

La Guerra entre España y EEUU: EEUU invade y ocupa a Cuba, las Filipinas, Puerto Rico, y otras colonias españolas en las Islas Pacíficas. Hawaii también es anexada por fuerza este año.

Immigration History Timeline in Pictures — module 1

1910-1940

"Having fun at roller skating rink of Savoy Ballroom," and "House and children in Negro section of Chicago, Illinois 1941."

Photos by Russell Lee, 1941. Farm Security Administration - Office of War Information Photograph Collection, Library of Congress Prints and Photographs Division

Great Migration: Over 1 million African Americans migrate from the South to the North to escape lynchings, Jim Crow laws, and economic hardship. They seek out better jobs and an overall better life in the North.

La Gran Migración: Más de un millón de americanos de descendencia africana migraron del sur al norte para escapar los linchamientos, las leyes de Jim Crow, y la dura condición económica. Buscan tener mejores trabajos y una mejor calidad de vida en el norte.

Immigration History Timeline in Pictures

1910

Mexican refugees fleeing Revolution in 1914.

Mexican Revolution sends thousands of peasants to the U.S. border seeking safety and employment.

La Revolución Mexicana causa que miles de campesinos lleguen a la frontera estadounidense buscando seguridad y empleo.

Immigration History Timeline in Pictures — module 1

1915

"Parade of the Ku Klux Klan in Virginia, bordering on the District of Columbia," 1922.

Ku Klux Klan grows in strength; Klan membership peaks in 1925, with over 5 million members.

El Ku Klux Klan crece en fuerza; la membresía del Klan alcanza una cumbre en 1925, con más de 5 millones de miembros.

Immigration History Timeline in Pictures

1917

THE AMERICANESE WALL, AS CONGRESSMAN BURNETT WOULD BUILD IT.
UNCLE SAM: You're welcome in — if you can climb it!

From Clash of Cultures in the 1910s and 1920s, http://www.history.ohio-state.edu/projects/clash/Imm_KKK/Immigration%20Pages/Immigration-page1.htm

"The Literacy Test: You're welcome in, if you can climb it!"

Congress also enacts a literacy requirement for immigrants. Mexicans exempted from anti-immigration laws so that they could provide labor.

El Congreso promulga el requisito de alfabetismo para inmigrantes. Se exceptúa a los mexicanos de las leyes anti-inmigración para que puedan proveer mano de obra.

Immigration History Timeline in Pictures — module 1

1919

"Police searching Max Dolinger after bomb throwing in Anarchist riot, Union Sq., New York"

Palmer Raids: Deportations and round ups of "aliens," anarchists, and communists, especially those from southern Europe and Latin America influential in labor organizing.

Las Redadas Palmer: Se detienen y deportan a "extranjeros," anarquistas, y comunistas, especialmente a esos provenientes del sur de Europa y América Latina que son influyentes en la organización de trabajadores.

Immigration History Timeline in Pictures

1921-1924

"Uncle Sam is a Man of Strong Features," Judge Magazine, 1898

In response to growing anti-immigrant sentiment and the growing power of white supremacists, the Quota Acts of 1921 and 1924 establish a "national origins quota system" that favors immigration from Europe.

Respondiendo al creciente sentimiento anti-inmigrante y el creciente poder de racistas blancos, el Acta de Cuotas 1921 y 1924 establece un "sistema de cuotas de origen nacional" que favorece a la emigración de Europa.

Immigration History Timeline in Pictures — module 1

1929

"Martial law on Colorado border stops migratory laborers," 1936

Farm Security Administration - Office of War Information Photograph Collection, Library of Congress Prints and Photographs Division

United States government deports thousands of Mexicans, including many U.S. citizens to Mexico during the Great Depression.

El gobierno estadounidense deporta a miles de mexicanos, incluyendo a ciudadanos estadounideses durante la Gran Depresión.

Immigration History Timeline in Pictures

1934

Filipino farm workers cut lettuce in the fields of Salinas, CA, in 1935. Photo by Dorothea Lange.

Farm Security Administration - Office of War Information Photograph Collection, Library of Congress Prints and Photographs Division

Tydings-McDuffie Act grants independence to the Philippines, and limits Filipino immigration to a quota of fifty persons per year, and all Filipinos in the United States were reclassified as 'aliens.'

El Acta Tydings-McDuffie otorga la independencia a las Filipinas y limita la emigración filipina a una cuota de cincuenta personas por año, y todos los filipinos en los EE.UU. son re-clasificados como "extranjeros."

Immigration History Timeline in Pictures

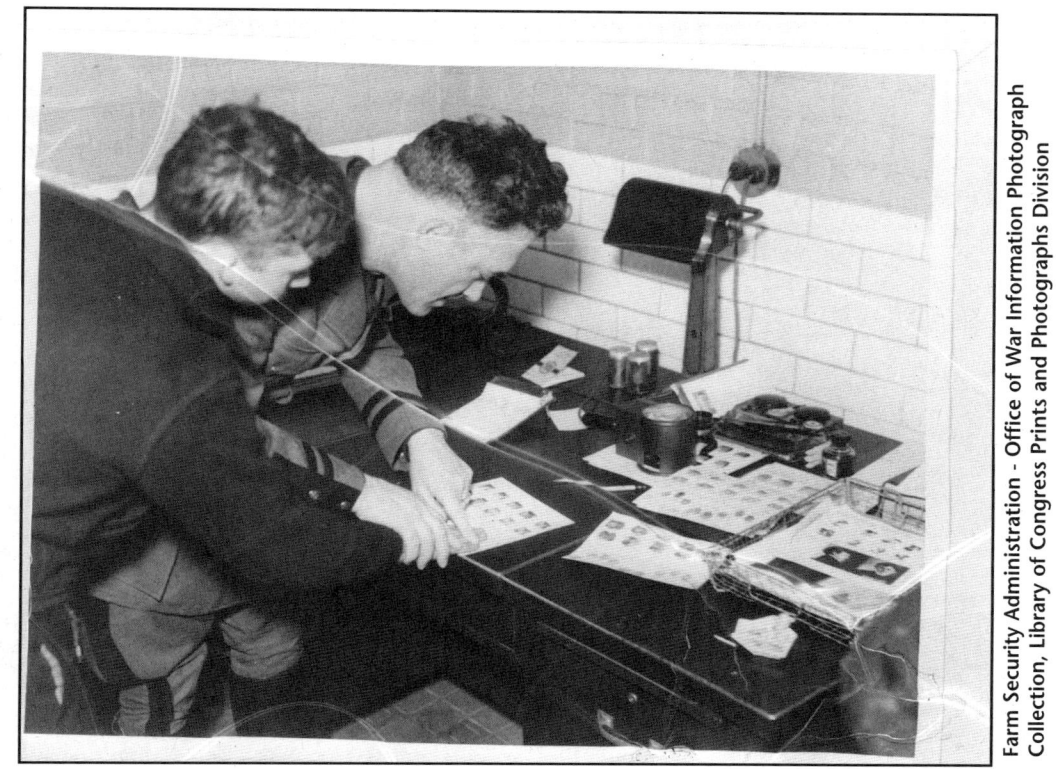

module 1

1940

"Fingerprinting," 1935.

Alien Registration Act requires registration & finger-printing of "aliens" over 14 years old.

Ley de Registración de Extranjeros requiere que todo "extranejro" mayor de 14 años de edad se registren y se les tome las huellas digitales.

Immigration History Timeline in Pictures

1942

Japanese American internment center at Manzanar, CA. Families in Turlock, CA await evacuation. Sign announcing interment policy. Photos by Dorothea Lange

National Archives Still Pictures Division.

Japanese Internment. Over 112,000 Japanese Americans, most of them U.S. citizens, are placed in military internment camps during World War II.

Más de 112,000 Japonéses Americanos, la mayoría de ellos ciudadanos estadounidenses, son encarcelados en campos de concentración militares en la Segunda Guerra Mundial.

Immigration History Timeline in Pictures

module 1

1943

Mexican agricultural laborers arrive by train to help in the harvesting of beets, 1943.

The Bracero Program brings in over 5 million temporary workers from Mexico, mostly to fill agricultural labor shortage during World War II.

El Programa Braceros importa a más de cinco millones de trabajadores temporarios de México, la mayoría para cubrir la escaséz de mano de obra agrícola durante la Segunda Guerra Mundial.

Immigration History Timeline in Pictures

1951

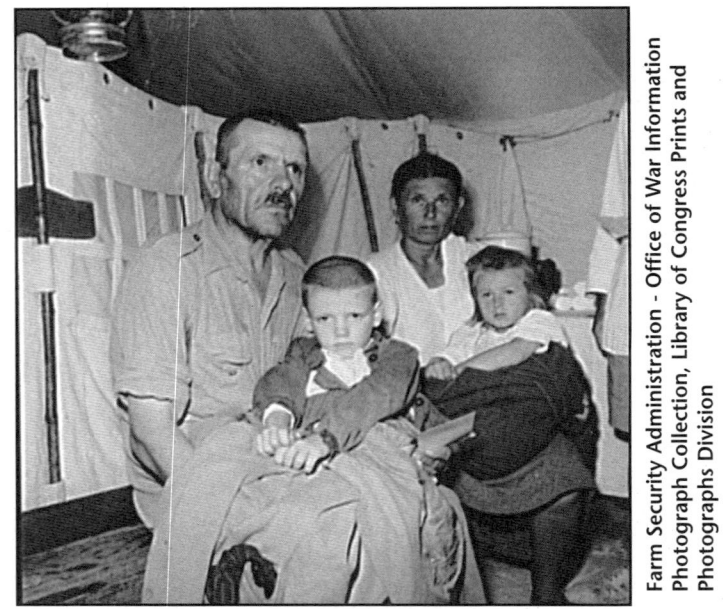

Refugees at El Shatt, the United Nations Relief and Rehabilitation Administration's refugee camp for Yugoslavs, 1944

1951 United Nations Refugee Convention is signed, defining rights of refugees, including protections for employment and welfare, on the issue of identity papers and travel documents. This Convention is amended in 1967 to apply to all people who become refugees after 1951.

La Convención de 1951 sobre Refugiados de las Naciones Unidas es suscrita, definiendo los derechos de los refugiados, incluyendo a protecciones de empleo y bienestar, la emisión de papeles de identificación y documentos para viajar. Esta Convención es enmendada en 1967 para aplicarse a toda persona que haya sido refugiado después de 1951.

Immigration History Timeline in Pictures module 1

1952

Immigrants—of all races—participate in a naturalization ceremony in California. Courtesy David Bacon.

McCarren Walter Act eliminated racial barriers to citizenship, but also tightens quotas for immigrants and allows deportation of immigrants for "subversive activities."

El Acta McCarren Walter elimina las barreras raciales a la ciudadanía, pero también reforza las cuotas para inmigrantes y permite la deportación de inmigrantes por "actividades subversivas."

Immigration History Timeline in Pictures

1954

"Deported workers back in Mexico."

500 Years of Chicano History in Pictures by Elizabeth Martinez

Operation Wetback targets Mexican American communities in search for "illegal immigrants," and deports over 3.8 million people to Mexico.

Operación Espaldas Mojadas desata redadas contra comunidades México Americanas buscando a "inmigrantes ilegales" y deporta a más 3.8 millones de personas a México

Immigration History Timeline in Pictures — module 1

1955

Parks photo, 1956. Library of Congress Prints and Photographs Division

Rosa Parks begins the Montgomery Bus Boycott to protest segregation.

Rosa Parks empieza el Boicoteo del Transporte de Montgomery para protestar la segregación racial.

Immigration History Timeline in Pictures

1961-1968

Martin Luther King and Malcolm X waiting for press conference, 1964. Photo by M. Triosko

U.S. News & World Report Magazine Photograph Collection, Library of Congress Prints and Photographs Division.

1961: Freedom Rides

1963: March on Washington

1964: Height of Civil Rights Movement; Civil Rights Act outlaws discrimination in public accommodations and by employers.

1965: Voting Rights Act; Malcolm X is assassinated.

1968: Martin Luther King is assassinated.

1961: las Caravanas de Libertad

1963: la Marcha sobre Washington

1964: Auge del Movimiento de Derechos Civiles; el Acta de Derechos Civiles proscribe la discriminación en alojamientos públicos y por empleadores.

1965: El Acta de Derechos al Voto. Malcom X es asesinado.

1968: Martin Luther King es asesinado.

Immigration History Timeline in Pictures

module 1

1965

Immigration and Nationality Act repeals the national origins quota system that favors European migration.

El Acta de Inmigración y Nacionalidad deroga el sistema de cuotas de origen nacional que favorecía a la emigración europea.

Immigration History Timeline in Pictures

1975

Vietnamese refugee family, 1975.

Indochina Migration and Refugee Assistance Act allows refugees from Southeast Asia to the U.S.

El Acta de Asistencia de Migración y Refugiados de Indochina permite que refugiados del Sudeste de Asia entren a EEUU.

Immigration History Timeline in Pictures

module 1

1982

Protest against U.S. military intervention in Central America.

Sanctuary Movement. More than 250 churches provide "sanctuary" to Salvadoran and Guatemalan refugees.

Más de 250 iglesias ofrecen "santuario" a refugiados salvadoreños y guatemaltecos.

Immigration History Timeline in Pictures

1986

Immigrant rights activists protest against Simpson-Rondino, a legislative forerunner to IRCA. 1985.credit

The Immigration Reform and Control Act gives amnesty to approximately three million undocumented residents, and makes it illegal for employers to hire undocumented workers.

El Acta de Reforma y Control Migratorio otorga la amnistía a aproximadamente tres millones de residentes indocumentados, y prohíbe a empleadores que ocupen a trabajadores indocumentados.

Immigration History Timeline in Pictures

module 1

1990

Congress removes homosexuality as a reason to disqualify foreigners from immigrating, or even visiting, the United States.

El Congreso elimina la homosexualidad como razón para descalificar a extranjeros de emigrar, o aún visitar, a los Estados Unidos.

Immigration History Timeline in Pictures

1993

A worker looks over the fence between Mexico and the U.S., trying to find a moment when the Border Patrol may not be looking so that he can cross.

By David Bacon

The U.S. government implements a blockade strategy on the U.S. Mexico border, forcing migrants to cross through the desert. By 2003, over 3,000 people have died while trying to cross the border.

El gobierno de EEUU implementa una estrategia de bloqueo en la frontera EEUU-México, forzando a migrantes de cruzar a través del desierto. Para el 2003, más de 3,000 migrantes han muerto intentando cruzar la frontera.

Immigration History Timeline in Pictures   module 1

1995

Two Hmong children listen to their parents urge a California legislator to maintain bilingual education for them.

By David Bacon

California voters pass Proposition 187, which prohibits providing of public educational, welfare, and health services to undocumented immigrants. This is later found unconstitutional.

Los votantes de California aprueban la Proposición 187, que prohíbe la educación pública, la asistencia social, y servicios de salud a inmigrantes indocumentados. Después un fallo determina que es inconstitucional.

Immigration History Timeline in Pictures

1996

Three major bills affecting immigrants are passed, including: The Illegal Immigration Reform and Immigrant Responsibility Act (IIRIRA) and Anti-Terrorism and Effective Death Penalty Act: which increases jailing of non-violent, non-criminal immigrants and allows deportation of immigrants for minor crimes, and results in the deportation of over 200,000 people. Welfare reform ends monetary and medical assistance for most immigrants.

Tres leyes notables que afectan a inmigrantes son aprobadas, incluyendo: El Acta de Reforma de Inmigración Ilegal y Responsabilidad del Inmigrante (IIRIRA) y el Acta Contra el Terrorismo y Pena de Muerte Efectiva: que incrementan el encarcelamiento de inmigrantes no-violentos, no-criminales y permite la deportación de inmigrantes por ofensas menores, resultando en la deportación de más de 200,000 personas. La reforma de la asistencia pública termina la ayuda económica y médica para la mayoría de inmigrantes.

Immigration History Timeline in Pictures

module 1

2001-3

A march and rally in protest against the beginning of bombing in Afghanistan.

Events of September 11 attacks set the stage for "national security" based immigration policy. Congress passes the PATRIOT Act, which gives the federal government broad powers to detain suspected "terrorists" for unlimited periods of time without access to legal representation. Over 1,200 Arab, Muslim, and South Asian men are detained in secret.

Los eventos tras los ataques del 11 de Septiembre instauran las condiciones para políticas migratorias de seguridad nacional. El Congreso aprueba el Acta Patriota, que otorga al gobierno federal poderes amplios para detener a presuntos "terroristas" por tiempo indefinido sin acceso a representación legal. Más de 1,200 árabes, musulmanes, y sudasiáticos son detenidos en secreto

history of immigration 101

Sources and Suggested Reading:

Carla Blank, *Rediscovering America: The Making of Multicultural America*, 1900-2000 (New York: Three Rivers Press, 2003.)

Louise Cainkar, "No Longer Invisible: Arab and Muslim Exclusion After September 11," *Middle East Report*, Fall 2002, 22-29.

Kitty Calavita, *Inside the State: The Bracero Program, Immigration, and the INS* (New York: Routledge Press, 1992.)

Ellis Cose, *A Nation of Strangers: Prejudice, Politics, and the Populating of America* (New York: Morrow Press, 1992.)

David Eltis, "Free and Coerced Transatlantic Migrations: Some Comparisons," *The American Historical Review*, Volume 88, No. 2 (Apr., 1982), 251-280.

John Higham, *Strangers In the Land: Patterns in American Nativism*, 1860-1925, (New Brunswick, Rutgers University Press, 1988.)

Bill Ong Hing, *Defining America Through Immigration Policy*, (Philadelphia: Temple University Press, 2004.)

Matthew Jacobson, *Whiteness of A Different Color: European Immigrants and the Alchemy of Race*, (Cambridge: Harvard University Press, 1999.)

Elizabeth Martinez, *500 Years of Chicano History in Pictures*, (Albuquerque: South West Organizing Project, 1991.)

Ronald Takaki, *Strangers from a Different Shore: A History of Asian Americans*, (New York: Penguin Books, 1989.)

William Tamayo, "The Evolution of United States Immigration Policy," in *Domestic Violence in Immigrant and Refugee Communities: Asserting the Rights of Battered Women*, ed. Deeana Jang et al. eds., 1991.

Russell Thornton, *American Indian Holocaust and Survival: A Population History Since 1492*, (Norman: University of Oklahoma Press, 1987.)

Richard Wright, *12 Million Black Voices*, with a preface by David Bradley and photo direction by Edwin Rosscam, (New York: Viking Press, 1941, reprint New York: Thunders Mouth Press, 1988.)

Howard Zinn and George Kirschner, *A People's History of the United States: The Wall Charts*, (New York: The New Press, 1995.)

References:

1. Russell Thornton, *American Indian Holocaust and Survival: A Population History Since 1492*, Norman: University of Oklahoma Press, 1987.
2. Matthew Jacobson, *Whiteness of a Different Color: European Immigrants and the Alchemy of Race*, Cambridge: Harvard University Press, 1999.
3. California Newsreel. "Race Timeline." *Race: the Power of An Illusion*, 2003. Available at www.pbs.org.
4. Howard Zinn, *A People's History of the United States: 1492—Present*. New York: Harper Perennial, 1995, p. 23-38.
5. California Newsreel. "Interview with James O. Horton," *Race: the Power of An Illusion*. Background Readings, 2003. Available at www.pbs.org
6. Ward Churchill, *From a Native Son: Selected Essays on Indigenism, 1985-1995*. Boston: South End Press, 1996, p. 197.
7. Churchill, p. 26.
8. Ronald Takaki. *Strangers from a Different Shore: A History of Asian Americans*. Boston, Toronto & London: Little, Brown & Co. 1989. pp. 208 & 298.
9. Takaki, p. 298 & 299. California Newsreel. "Episode 3: The House We Live In." 11 Rodolfo Acuña, *Occupied America: A History of Chicanos*. New York: Harper & Row. 1988. p. 198-206.
10. González, 1983, cited in Pierette Hondagneu-Sotelo, Domestica, University of California Press, 2001. p.22.
11. Acuña, pp. 261-266.
12. Saul Landau, "*Haitian and Cuban Refuges: Wet foot/dry foot; black foot/white foot*," October 30, 2000, Znet Daily Commentaries, http://www.zmag.org/sustainers/content/2000-10/30landau.htm
13. Howard Zinn, p. 407.
14. Ronald Takaki, p 485-486.
15. National Immigration Law Center, "Urgent Alert, February 04, 2003," Washington DC.
16. Working Group on Enforcement & Justice Issues, c/o NNIRR, "Immigrant Rights Groups Fear Domestic War Will Escalate Against Immigrants and Refugees as Homeland Security Department takes over Immigration Controls," February 27, 2003.

globalization, migration and workers rights!

globalization, migration, and workers rights — module 2

OVERVIEW

The goals of this workshop are to:

- Connect our personal stories to larger forces that compel people to migrate
- Discuss globalization's impact on migration
- Analyze and discuss the connections between globalization and migration
- Identify policies and institutions that affect corporate globalization and immigration flows
- Examine how globalization affects our communities and how our communities are responding

WHAT WILL WE BE TALKING ABOUT?

In this workshop, we will think about the following questions:

- What are some of the reasons that we have moved and/or immigrated?
- How has globalization forced people to migrate?
- How do corporations benefit from globalization? How have communities been affected by globalization?
- What are some ways that our communities are responding to globalization?

globalization, migration, and workers rights

Backgrounder: Migration, Globalization, and Workers' Rights

Corporations and business interests praise globalization as the increased flow of technology, communication, and trade as elements that strengthen the world market and build human progress. But globalization, which enhances the capacity of wealthy countries and corporations to maintain control of resources and wealth, has devastated workers and the poor, and has widened the disparity between rich and poor in the world. For example, the richest 1/5 of the world's population now consumes over 86% of the world's goods and services, while 2.8 billion people, almost half the world's population survives on less than $2 a day.

Global economic restructuring builds on patterns of domination that have existed between rich and poor countries for centuries. In order to attract foreign investment and create jobs, governments of many developing countries have favored foreign-owned firms that pay starvation wages while exposing workers to a variety of health and safety hazards. Blatant violations of labor rights are tolerated. Globalization also hurts workers in richer countries, as corporations have sent jobs overseas, and have discouraged organizing by threatening to move their operations abroad.

International migration has jumped in the past few decades, greatly accelerated by the process of globalization. The United Nations estimates that there are currently over 175 million people in migration today, compared to 80 million only three decades ago. Globalization also increased migration both inside and outside the U.S. Unemployment, hunger, poverty, landlessness, displacement, war, political violence, and other causes spur migration. U.S. foreign and economic policies—including corporate welfare—have played a strong role in creating these conditions in sending countries, by supporting military conflict, "structural adjustment" programs, and other interventions that disrupt the social, economic, and political fabric of other nations.

Despite increased immigration enforcement and difficult work conditions, migrants worldwide send over $111 billion to their home countries. Worldwide, remittances to developing countries total about $60 billion a year, roughly equivalent to the total aid that rich countries give to poor countries each year. U.S. policy attempts to address immigration from a law enforcement perspective are both harmful and misguided. As long as global economic and political factors that compel migration continue to exist, immigration policies designed to stop migration by militarizing borders, detention, deportation, and intimidation will not halt the flow of migration. Instead, they will result in increased abuse, discrimination, and human rights violations. Recognizing this, migrants' rights activists around the world are taking bold steps to address the international dimensions of migration.

globalization, migration, and workers rights — module 2

SUMMARY POINTS

- Immigration to the United States is a small part of total world migration.
- Individual reasons for migration are often shaped by larger economic, social, and political factors.
- Globalization has forced developing countries to adopt policies that increase poverty, labor abuses, social instability, and political conflict, while corporations benefit from these policies. These conditions often displace communities and force people to migrate. Local elites are often complicit and benefit from these policies as well.
- Corporate and governmental policies allow corporations "freedom of movement" across borders, while restricting the movement of immigrants.
- Groups and individuals are raising awareness and forming international alliances, resisting the harmful effects of corporate globalization, and fighting for their rights.

WORKSHOP MENU

Exercise:	Time:
Welcome, introduction to the workshop, review of goals	10 minutes
Icebreaker Activity: Let's Move! A Miming Introduction or The Most Unusual Job	20 minutes
Immigration and Globalization Quiz	15-45 minutes
Screening and discussion of video: Uprooted: Refugees of the Global Economy*	1 hour, 20 minutes
Closing: Another World is Possible	25 minutes
Evaluation	10 minutes

*core exercise

Total Time: 2 - 3 hours

globalization, migration, and workers rights

Let's Move! A miming introduction

WHY DO IT?
- To use as an introduction and a fun, physical icebreaker
- To connect personal experiences of moving (both immigrating to and moving within the U.S.) to the issue of global migration

TIME: 20 minutes

MATERIALS NEEDED: none

DIRECTIONS:
1. Form a large circle, with all participants standing and facing inwards.
2. Explain to participants that this is an exercise for everyone to introduce themselves. Ask each person to:
   - Say their name
   - Say a place where they used to live
   - Make a motion that illustrates the reason that they moved

After someone introduces her/himself, everyone in the circle repeats their name and motion.

You may want to demonstrate this with an example before you begin. Encourage participants not to repeat an action that someone else has already done to get the creative juices flowing!

Here are two examples:

Example 1: First, a participant states her name: Consuelo
Then she states one place where she used to live: Mexico City
Then she makes an action: Holding her arms in front of her like she is hugging someone.
(Her reason: wanting to join her family)

Example 2: First, a participant states his name: John
Then he states one place where he used to live: Springfield, Illinois
His action could be: pulling his pockets out and showing that they are empty
(His reason for moving from Illinois: needed a new job)

3. When all participants have introduced themselves, ask the participants to find a partner. Each participant should explain what their action represented to their partner.

globalization, migration, and workers rights — module 2

4. After the partners are finished sharing, ask the large group how they felt about the exercise. What did they notice? What were some of the reasons why people moved? What were some of the similarities?

5. At this point, revisit the teaching points of this exercise.

TEACHING POINTS:
- Personal reasons for migration are often affected by economic, social, and political factors/ structures and policies.
- These reasons also lead other people in similar situations around the world to migrate.

VARIATIONS:
- For sessions with less time or with many participants, have them say their name, a place they have moved from, and make a motion while they state out loud why they moved. Done this way, it is one of the quickest introductions/icebreakers we have seen!

CHALLENGES:
- The amount of information that a participant has to remember to present (name, place they moved from, motion) can become confusing or overwhelming. A clear demonstration before the exercise starts can help.

SOURCE: authors, adapted from Kristina Bennett of Navigating Transitions

national network for immigrant and refugee rights
www.nnirr.org

globalization, migration, and workers rights

The Most Unusual Job I Ever Had...

WHY DO IT?
- To use as a humorous introduction
- To introduce the concept of labor and work into the discussion

TIME: 20 minutes

MATERIALS NEEDED: slips of paper, pens, and a basket

DIRECTIONS:
1. Ask all participants to gather in a circle. Ask everyone to introduce themselves by name and by organization or place where they live.
2. Pass a slip of paper to each participant. Ask each participant to write down the "most unusual" job that they have ever had. Then collect the slips of paper in the basket.
3. Mix up the slips of paper, and pass the basket around the circle. Ask each participant to take out a slip of paper, and read the job listed on the piece of paper. After the "unusual job" is read, the person who held that job should identify herself/himself.

CHALLENGES:
- This activity works best in groups that share a common class background
- Facilitator needs to set a respectful tone for everyone's labor: for example, warn the group that a job that someone may consider "most unusual" may be a job that someone currently holds.

globalization, migration, and workers rights — module 2

The Immigration and Globalization Quiz

WHY DO IT?
- To present information and focus discussion on immigration and globalization
- To assess the group's knowledge on issues of immigration and globalization
- Can be used to energize a group, especially with the "tic-tac-toe" version

TIME 15-45 minutes

MATERIALS NEEDED
- Copies of quiz for participants to read
- Small prizes for participants, such as candy or a small toy (optional)
- Masking tape or easel paper and markers (optional: for tic-tac-toe)

FACILITATOR PREP
- Review quiz questions before exercise

DIRECTIONS

Variation 1: The Quick Version (15 minutes):
1. Pass out copies of the quiz to all participants.
2. Read off the questions, one at a time, and ask participants to choose their answer by raising their hands. Read the correct answer, and ask participants to think about their own response and that of the group. You can make the quiz more entertaining by acting like a game show host, even giving out small prizes to participants.

Variation 2: Small Group Discussions (30-45 minutes):
1. Pass copies of the quiz to all participants.
2. Divide participants into small groups, and ask each small group to complete the quiz together. (15-20 minutes)
3. After the small groups have completed the quiz, read through the answers. Then lead the group in a discussion about the quiz. Here are some questions to ask:
   - What answers were the most surprising? Why?
   - What purpose does misinformation serve?
   - What can we do about it?

Variation 3: Large Group "Tic-tac-toe" (30-45 minutes):
1. Explain that the group will play a game of "Immigration and Globalization Tic-Tac-Toe." Ask for two volunteers: one who will act as the human "tic-tac-toe" board, and one who will be the game "host or hostess." Make sure that the person who will be the "tic-tac-toe" board feels comfortable with the host or hostess putting masking tape on their chest.
2. Divide the room into two teams, the "x" team and the "o" team. Have team members sit together.

globalization, migration, and workers rights

The Immigration and Globalization Quiz

3. Take the masking tape and draw a tic-tac-toe board on the volunteer's belly. The other volunteer will put "x's" or "o's" on the tic-tac-toe board when a team answers a question correctly. The team can decide where to put their "x" or "o."
Flip a coin to decide which team goes first. The teams will take turns answering a question.

The rules of the game are simple:
- The facilitator will ask the first team to answer a question. If the team answers the question correctly, they get to play "tic-tac-toe," and put either their "x" or an "o" on the board.
- If the team does not answer the question correctly, then they lose a chance to place their "x" or "o" on the board. The other team gets a chance to answer the same question.
- The facilitator will keep asking the teams questions until someone wins "tic-tac-toe!"

4. Have the group discuss the game. Here are some questions to ask:
  - What answers were the most surprising? Why?
  - What purpose does misinformation serve?
  - What can we do about it?

CHALLENGES
- If playing in teams becomes too competitive, then participants may lose focus of the activity's goals, so be sure to help participants refocus on the issues. Also, this is a good opportunity to create teams at random; break up any cliques to ensure diversity among teams.
- Quizzes can provide information, but can disempower participants and remind them of unpleasant school experiences. Emphasize the general amount of misinformation in our society, instead of what people don't know.
- Consider the literacy of the group as you plan the exercise. You may want to plan that all information is read aloud by choosing people who are comfortable reading questions aloud ahead of time, or by asking for volunteers during the session. This variation will lend a different rhythm to the exercise.

SOURCE authors and Project South, "How to Use the Myth-Buster Quiz," Popular Education for Movement Building: Resource Guide Volume 2, 2001. www.projectsouth.org. Quiz by NNIRR.

handout

Immigration and Globalization Quiz

1. How many migrants are there in the world?
   a. 9 million people
   b. 50 million people
   c. 175 million people
   d. 1 billion people

2. What percent of the U.S. population was born in another country?
   a. 5%
   b. 11.5%
   c. 27.3%
   d. 50%

3. True or false? The percentage of immigrants (vs. non-immigrants) living in the U.S. is the highest in the whole world.

4. What have been the effects of NAFTA (North American Free Trade Agreement, passed in 1994) and the creation of the WTO (World Trade Organization) on workers?
   a. U.S. workers have lost over 766,000 jobs
   b. Corporations have used the threat of moving jobs overseas to bust unions in the U.S.
   c. Over 4 million Mexican people have been pushed into severe poverty
   d. all of the above

5. What percent of all immigrants coming to the U.S. are women?
   a. 75%
   b. 55%
   c. 30%
   d. 10%

6. In 1970, corporate executives in the U.S. were paid more than 30 times the wages of an average worker. How much do corporate executives make in comparison to average workers in the U.S. today?
   a. 30 times the income of an average worker
   b. 100 times the income of an average worker
   c. 250 times the income of an average worker
   d. 450 times the income of an average worker

7. What three countries send the most immigrants to the U.S.?
   a. Haiti, China, Mexico
   b. Mexico, India, Philippines
   c. Mexico, China, Philippines
   d. Mexico, El Salvador, China

8. What international human rights treaty has the U.S. government ratified?
   a. UN Convention on the Elimination of Racial Discrimination
   b. UN Convention on the Rights of the Child
   c. UN Convention for Migrant Workers and Their Families
   d. UN Convention Against Torture

9. What rights does the UN International Convention for Migrant Workers and Their Families protect?
   a. the right to participate in a union
   b. respect for your cultural identity
   c. right to family reunification
   d. all of the above

10. Worldwide, how much money do immigrants send back to their home countries?
    a. 10 million dollars
    b. 1 billion dollars
    c. 50 billion dollars
    d. 111 billion dollars

national network for immigrant and refugee rights
www.nnirr.org

globalization, migration, and workers rights

Answers to Immigration and Globalization Quiz:

1. **c.** The United Nations estimated in 2002 that there were over 175 million people in migration in the world, more than 2/3 of the total population of the United States. The number of migrants in the world has more than doubled since 1970, with the majority of migrants living in developed countries. Source: United Nations, International Migration Report, 2002.

2. **b.** 11.5% of the U.S population was born outside the United States. Today's proportion of foreign-born residents to U.S.-born residents is less than at the turn of the century, when foreign-born immigrants comprised 15% of the population. Source: U.S. Census Bureau, The Foreign Born Population in the United States, March 2002, issued 2003.

3. **False.** Many countries have higher percentages of foreign-born populations than the U.S. For example, over 17% of Canada's population are immigrants, and over 21% of Australia's population is foreign born, as compared to 11.5% in the United States. Source: Organisation for Economic Co-Operation and Development, Trends in International Migration: Annual Report 2000, 2001.

4. **d.** All of the above. Many U.S. companies moved production to Mexico to take advantage of lower wages and weaker environmental protections. Growing trade deficits and job flight has resulted in the loss of 3 million U.S. jobs. Companies have also used the threat of moving overseas to discourage union organizing. One study found that five years after NAFTA, 90% of 400 plant closings or threatened plant closings occurred during organizing drives. Mexican workers have also seen little benefit, due to economic crises caused by agreements within NAFTA, which resulted in over 4 million Mexican people pushed into severe poverty. Sources: Economic Policy Institute, "Fast Track to Lost Jobs: Trade Deficits and Manufacturing Decline Are the Legacies of NAFTA and the WTO," 2000, and "NAFTA at Seven: Its Impact on Workers in All Three Nations," 2001; Commission for Labor Cooperation, "Plant Closings and Labor Rights," 1997, and Sarah Anderson, Institute for Policy Studies, "Seven Years Under NAFTA," 2001.

5. **b.** Over one half of all immigrants to the U.S. are women, which is a new trend in migration to the U.S., reflecting global trends of the growing number of female migrants. Source: U.S. Census Bureau, The Foreign Born Population in the United States, March 2002, issued 2003.

globalization, migration, and workers rights — module 2

6. d. Since 1970, the average earnings of an American chief executive have gone from 30 times to 450 times that of the average worker. Source: Bruce R. Scott, "The Great Divide in the Global Village," Foreign Affairs, January/February 2001.

7. c. The three countries that sent the most immigrants to the U.S. in 2000 were Mexico, with 173, 914 immigrants; China, with 45,652 immigrants; and the Philippines, with 42,474 immigrants. India is a close fourth, with 42, 046 immigrants. Other countries that sent over 20,000 immigrants to the U.S. in 2000 include Vietnam, Nicaragua, El Salvador, and Haiti. Source: INS 2002 Statistical Yearbook.

8. a. The U.S. ratified the UN Convention to Eliminate Racial Discrimination in 1994. The U.S. has yet to ratify the other listed human rights treaties, unlike most of the world. For example, the U.S. and Somalia are the only remaining countries in the world that have not yet ratified the UN Convention on the Rights of the Child. Source: Office of the United Nations High Commissioner for Human Rights, Status of Ratification of the Principal International Human Rights Treaties, November 2003.

9. d. All of the above. The International Convention for the Protection of Migrant Workers and Their Families protects all of these rights, and many more. The Convention entered into force in 2003. For full text of the Convention, visit: http://www.unhchr.ch/html/menu3/b/m_mwctoc.htm.

10. d. According to the World Bank in 2001, immigrants worldwide sent over $111 billion to their home countries. Internationally, remittances to developing countries total about $60 billion a year, roughly equivalent to the total aid that rich countries give to poor countries each year. Sources: Migration Policy Institute, "Remittances from the U.S. in Context," 2003, and Bruce Stokes, "Foreign Aid: Making Migration Work Better," National Journal, 2003.

globalization, migration, and workers rights

Uprooted: Refugees of the Global Economy

WHY DO IT?
- To explore how the global economic forces hve displaced communities
- To discuss the impact of corporate and governmental policies on workers and their communities worldwide and locally

TIME 1 hour, 20 minutes

MATERIALS NEEDED
- Easel paper, markers, and tape
- Copies of small group discussion questions
- Copy of Uprooted: Refugees of the Global Economy video, produced by the National Network for Immigrant and Refugee Rights (visit www.nnirr.org to purchase a copy)
- Television and VCR player

FACILITATOR PREP

DIRECTIONS

1. Review goals of this activity, and introduce the video.
Some useful points about the video:
- Uprooted: Refugees of the Global Economy follows the lives of three immigrant organizers now living in the U.S.
- The characters in Uprooted discuss how globalization caused them to migrate, and the conditions that they faced when they moved to the U.S.

2. Before watching the video, divide the large group into three small groups, each group paying closer attention to one of the stories in the video: Maricel, Jessy and Jaime, and Luckner.
If you have a large amount of people, you may want to divide up into more than 3 groups, with some groups watching the same character—we have found that 4-6 people per group is ideal.
Ask participants to think about the following questions while watching the video:
- What are some of the corporate policies that forced people to migrate?
- What are some of the governmental policies that forced people to migrate?

3. Watch *Uprooted: Refugees of the Global Economy* (30 minutes)
4. After watching the video, have groups divide into their small groups to discuss the video. Give each of the groups a handout of "Small Group Discussion Questions for Uprooted: Refugees of the Global Economy." (20 minutes)

globalization, migration, and workers rights — module 2

5. Bring the small groups back together. Each small group should discuss these questions, and report back to the large group by representing their character's story in a symbolic way (i.e. a skit, a drawing, human sculpture, poem, song, etc.)
6. Discuss with the large group:
    - Did you identify with any of the stories in the video in particular? Why?
    - What were some of the government and corporate policies that forced the characters in the video to migrate?
    - How are the conditions faced by the characters in the video similar or different from those in your community?
    - What can be done to build solidarity between workers and communities affected by globalization?

After the group has discussed these questions, review the teaching points.

TEACHING POINTS

- Globalization has forced developing countries to adopt policies that increase poverty, labor abuses, social instability, and political conflict, while corporations benefit from these policies. These conditions often displace communities and force people to migrate.
- Corporate and governmental policies allow corporations "freedom of movement" across borders, while restricting the movement of immigrants.
- Groups and individuals are raising awareness and forming international alliances, resisting the harmful effects of corporate globalization, and fighting for their rights.

VARIATIONS

- Facilitators can expand the large group discussion into a comparison of results of such economic policies in the U.S. For example, facilitators can ask, "What are some of the similarities you see between the countries in the video and the U.S?" Some examples would include unemployment, deterioration of social services, increasing poverty, etc.
- Facilitators can ask each small group to identify three corporate/government policies in the "sending" country that forced the characters to migrate, and three immigration policies in the U.S. that made it difficult for the characters to migrate. They should include this information as part of their report-back. The resulting discussion can focus on how and who decides these policies, and some possible ways to impact these decision-makers.

SOURCE the authors

handout

Small Group Discussion Questions for *Uprooted: Refugees of the Global Economy*

- Why did your character(s) decide to move from their home country to the U.S.?
- What were the government policies that forced them to migrate? What were the corporate policies that forced them to migrate? How are they related?
- What were the immigration policies that shaped their experience in the U.S.? How do these policies compare to policies for corporations?
- Why do you think your character became a community activist?

Now plan how your small group can briefly report back your discussion to the large group by representing your character's story in a symbolic way (such as a short skit, a drawing, human sculpture, poem, song, etc.)

globalization, migration, and workers rights module 2

Closing—Another World Is Possible

WHY DO IT?
- To focus on solutions and activism around the issues raised in the module
- To use as a closing activity, and to reflect upon the day's activity

TIME 25 minutes

MATERIALS NEEDED
- Sticky notes and pens
- Large world map
- Easel paper and marker

DIRECTIONS

1. Distribute a sticky note and pen to each participant. Ask each participant to think about the day's activities. Instruct participants to complete the following phrase and to write it on their sticky note:

    Another world is possible when we: _____

2. Gather the group into a large circle. In the middle of the circle, place the large world map. (If the map is hung on the wall, create a circle facing the map.)

3. Go around the circle, and ask each participant to read their statement aloud, and then place their sticky note on a place on the map that is special to them.

SOURCE the authors

E. Cho

national network for immigrant and refugee rights | 129
www.nnirr.org

globalization, migration, and workers rights

Resources

Organizations:

Coalition of Immokalee Workers. http://www.ciw-online.org. P. O. Box 603, Immokalee, FL, 34143. Tel: 239-657-8311.

Global Trade Watch, www.tradewatch.org. 1600 20th Street, NW, Washington, DC 20009. Tel: (202) 588-1000.

Grassroots Global Justice (GGJ), http://www.uevermont.org/ggj/.

Highlander Research & Education Center, www.highlandercenter.org. 1959 Highlander Way, New Market, TN 37820. Tel: (865) 933-3443

Institute for Food and Development Policy/Food First. www.foodfirst.org. 398 60th St., Oakland, CA 94618. Tel: 510-654-4400.

International Forum on Globalization, www.ifg.org. 1009 General Kennedy Avenue #2, San Francisco, CA 94129. Tel: 415-561-7650.

Jobs With Justice. www.jwj.org. 501 3rd St. NW, Washington, DC 20001. Tel: 202-434-1106.

JustAct - Youth Action for Global Justice. www.justact.org. 333 Valencia, Suite 325, San Francisco, CA 94103. Tel: 415-431-4204.

Miami Workers Center. http://miamiworkerscenter.org. 6127 NW 7th Avenue, Miami, Florida 33127. Tel: 305-759-8717.

Tennessee Economic Renewal Network (TERN). www.tirn.org. 1515 E. Magnolia, Suite 403, Knoxville, TN 37917. Tel: 865-637-1576.

Southwest Organizing Project (SWOP). www.swop.net. 211 10th St. SW, Albuquerque, NM 87102. Tel: 505-247-8832.

Southwest Workers Union (SWU). www.swunion.org. P.O. Box 830706, San Antonio TX 78283-0706. Tel: 210-299-2666.

globalization, migration, and workers rights — module 2

Educational Materials and Resources:

Field Guide to the Global Economy. By Sarah Anderson with John Cavanagh with Thea Lee and the Institute for Policy Studies. This guide describes how the global flow of goods and services, money, and people affects communities, workers, the poor, and the environment. Available at http://www.ips-dc.org/pubs/pb_fieldguide.htm.

Globalization for Beginners. By United for a Fair Economy. What is globalization? How does it affect us? Who's winning, who's losing, and who's making the rules? What are the IMF, World Bank, and WTO? How can people around the world assert democratic control over the global economy? A guide to presenting a 3-hour workshop. Available at www.faireconomy.org.

Today's Globalization: A Popular Education Toolkit. Published by Project South: Institute for the Elimination of Poverty and Genocide. Using interactive exercises and games this curriculum introduces the basic terms, concepts and history of globalization. Available at www.projectsouth.org.

Trade Secrets: The Hidden Costs of the FTAA. By Jeremy Blasi and Casey Peek. This 16-minute documentary examines in clear, concise language how NAFTA and FTAA impact workers' rights, the environment, and our democracy. Includes "Understanding the FTAA," including a set of fact sheets, background materials, and fun interactive role plays. Available at http://laborcenter.berkeley.edu.

Uprooted: Refugees of the Global Economy. By the National Network for Immigrant and Refugee Rights. This award-winning documentary explores how the global economy has forced people to leave their home countries. UPROOTED presents three stories of immigrants who left their homes in Bolivia, Haiti, and the Philippines after global economic powers devastated their countries, only to face new challenges in the United States. 28 minutes, bilingual in English/Spanish (with subtitles.) $20, available at www.nnirr.org.

WEdGE: Women's Education in the Global Economy. Published by the Women of Color Resource Center. A popular education workbook increases understanding of how women around the globe are affected by the global economy and how they are organizing to defend their rights. Available at www.coloredgirls.org.

introduction to race, migration, and multiple oppressions

race, migration, and multiple oppressions — module 3

Introduction to Race, Migration, and Multiple Oppressions

OVERVIEW

The goals of this workshop are to:
- Examine negative stereotypes and their relationship to unjust policies, practices, and structures of oppression and privilege
- Explore all parts of our identities—including race, immigration status, gender, sexual orientation, class, religion, and others
- Discuss policies and structures that create oppression, and explore our individual experiences with these structures, especially race and nationality oppression
- Discuss potential strategies to support one another in fighting different forms of oppression

WHAT WILL WE BE TALKING ABOUT?

In this workshop, we will think about the following questions:
- What are stereotypes? How are we affected by negative stereotypes?
- What privileges do I have in society? What oppressions do I face in society?
- What are some policies or institutions that create oppression in our communities?
- What are some ways that we can support each other to fight different forms of oppression?

NOTE TO FACILITATORS

This module can serve as a starting point for facilitators who plan to use the BRIDGE curriculum in a long-term process, as it builds a framework for other exercises in the curriculum. This module uses the metaphor of a shared circle and the image of the heart to anchor most of the activities, providing a centering theme for participants. Music, percussion, and dance, when adapted to the style of the group, can also play an important role and be helpful to enter deeper dialogues about complex issues that involve strong opinions, emotions and feelings.

race, migration, and multiple oppressions

Backgrounder: Introduction to Race, Migration, and Multiple Oppressions

We all have multiple ways in which we see ourselves and how others view us. No one is simply a woman or man, rich or poor, black or white; our experiences as human beings are shaped by many factors. These factors include race, nationality, ethnicity, immigration status, gender, religion, sexual orientation, gender identity, disability, age, and others.

In addition, our experiences of oppression and privilege, injustice and power are often shaped by one or more of these factors at a time. The combined aspects of one's identity can either intensify (through multiple oppression) or buffer (via privilege) the full force of oppression that individuals and groups of people experience. For example, a woman of color born in the U.S. will often face both sexism and racism in a discriminatory situation, but experience the protection of U.S. citizenship, while a white gay man will face homophobia, but still has privilege when it comes to race and sex. People tend to be more aware of inequities when they are on the oppressed side of a particular power relation, but less conscious when they are on the privileged side. We can experience oppression and privilege in different ways at the same time.

Discussing and examining stereotypes can be useful in discussing the ways that oppression and privilege operate in society. Stereotypes, which are negative messages about specific groups of people, can foster mistreatment of people, and grant a whole system of privileges to one sector of the population at the expense of the other. Related, but distinct sets of stereotypes have developed throughout history, tailored to different groups depending on economic and political needs of those in power.

While each of us has been shaped by how we relate to different people based on our race, nationality, gender, sexual orientation, etc. status, we have a bit of "wiggle room" to move beyond the labels forced upon us, both individually and as a group, especially when we link up with others to organize for our human rights and in solidarity with other disenfranchised groups. Because stereotypes, policies and practices stemming from race, nationality, and other distinctions are not neutral, we do well to raise critical questions like "For whose benefit?" and "At whose expense?" Through promoting open and honest dialogue and active listening we can start to break through the wedges that divide us and build more healthy and sustainable communities.

race, migration, and multiple oppressions — module 3

SUMMARY POINTS

- Race and nationality, as well as class, ethnicity, gender, religion, sexual preference, disability, and other factors, shape our own experiences.
- Different groups of people face related, but distinct sets of stereotypes.
- Stereotypes are negative messages about specific groups of people. These negative messages can foster mistreatment of people, and grant a whole system of privileges to one sector of the population at the expense of the other.
- Oppression is the systematic and institutionalized mistreatment, exploitation, and exclusion of people who are members of a certain group.
- Forms of oppression and privilege are related to one another—we can experience oppression and privilege in different ways at the same time.
- The combined aspects of one's identity can either intensify or buffer the full force of oppression that one experiences.
- People tend to be more aware of inequities when they are on the oppressed side of a particular power relation, but less conscious when they are on the privileged side.
- Institutional policies are not neutral, so we should raise critical questions like "For whose benefit?" and "At whose expense?"
- Through open and honest dialogue and active listening, we can start to break through the wedges that divide us and nurture more healthy and sustainable people and communities.

national network for immigrant and refugee rights

race, migration, and multiple oppressions

WORKSHOP MENU

Activity:	Time:
Welcome, introduction to the workshop, review of goals	10 minutes
Opening/Introductions: Circle of Strength	15 minutes
Review Objectives/Ground Rules	10 minutes
*How Strong Beats My Heart?	
Looking at Our Individual Oppressions and Privileges	40 minutes
*Exploring Stereotypes We Face	30 minutes
*What's Behind These Stereotypes?	60 minutes
The Multiple Jeopardy Conga Line: Our Intersecting Identities	15 minutes
Closing: Spider's web exercise	15 minutes
Evaluation	10 minutes

*core exercise

Total Time: 3 hours, 25 minutes

Michelle Yamashita

race, migration, and multiple oppressions — module 3

Opening/Introductions: Circle of Strength

WHY DO IT?
- To use as an introduction and a fun, physical icebreaker
- To establish the group circle as a space of sharing and processing—which will be a central theme in the module.

TIME Approximately 15 minutes

MATERIALS NEEDED none

DIRECTIONS

1. Form a large circle, with all participants standing and facing inwards.
2. Explain to participants that this is an exercise for everyone to introduce themselves. Ask each person to:
   - Say their name
   - Name a positive quality that they bring to their work
   - Make a physical motion or gesture that illustrates the positive quality

After someone introduces her/himself, everyone in the circle should repeat their name and motion.

You may want to demonstrate this before you begin. For example:

First, a participant states her name: Victoria
Then she states a good quality she brings to her work: energy
Then she makes an action: jumps up and down

Encourage participants not to repeat a word or action that someone else has already done to get the creative juices flowing! Note that the group will wade deeper into playing with these patterns in this and other modules.

If this is a multi-organizational group, you may want to ask people to also share their organization's name.

SOURCE Kristina Bennett of *Navigating Transitions*

race, migration, and multiple oppressions

How Strong Beats My Heart?
Looking at Our Individual Oppressions and Privileges

WHY DO IT?
- To reflect on race, nationality, gender, class, sexual orientation and other aspects of our identity
- To connect individual experiences to systems of privilege and oppression, and impacts on different groups of people
- To introduce the intersections of racism, nationality and other forms of oppression that will be explored in greater depth in other BRIDGE modules

TIME 40 minutes

MATERIALS NEEDED
- Copies of "How Strong Beats My Heart?" handout for each participant
- Pens for each participant

DIRECTIONS

1. Distribute the "How Strong Beats My Heart?" materials to each participant.
2. Ask participants to spend the next 10 minutes filling out their responses to the handout.
3. After about 10 minutes, ask participants to pair with someone near them, (preferably someone they don't already know well) to share what they've written or drawn about each of the different aspects of their identity. (*Be sure to signal for partners to switch off speaking after 5 minutes*)
4. Reconvene the whole group back into the circle and process the exercise. Ask for reactions to the exercise. How did people feel about the exercise? Was there anything surprising that they heard from their partner? From themselves? (*10 minutes*)

SOURCE the authors

handout

How Strong Beats My Heart?

Many cultures see the heart as the center where our feelings, spirits, emotions and compassion live. We are going to use the imagery of our hearts to reflect on different parts of who we are and how that links us to broader communities of people.

Take time to think about the different aspects of your identity in terms of: immigration status, race and/or ethnicity, gender, class, sexual orientation, religious affiliation/spiritual beliefs, age, any other piece of who you are that is important to you. Then answer the following questions:

DIRECTIONS

1. How do I identify under these categories? Are there any other parts of my identity that I also want to name? Write them in the veins and arteries leading to your heart.
2. What positive experience can I remember having because of this identity?
3. What negative experience can I remember having because of this identity?

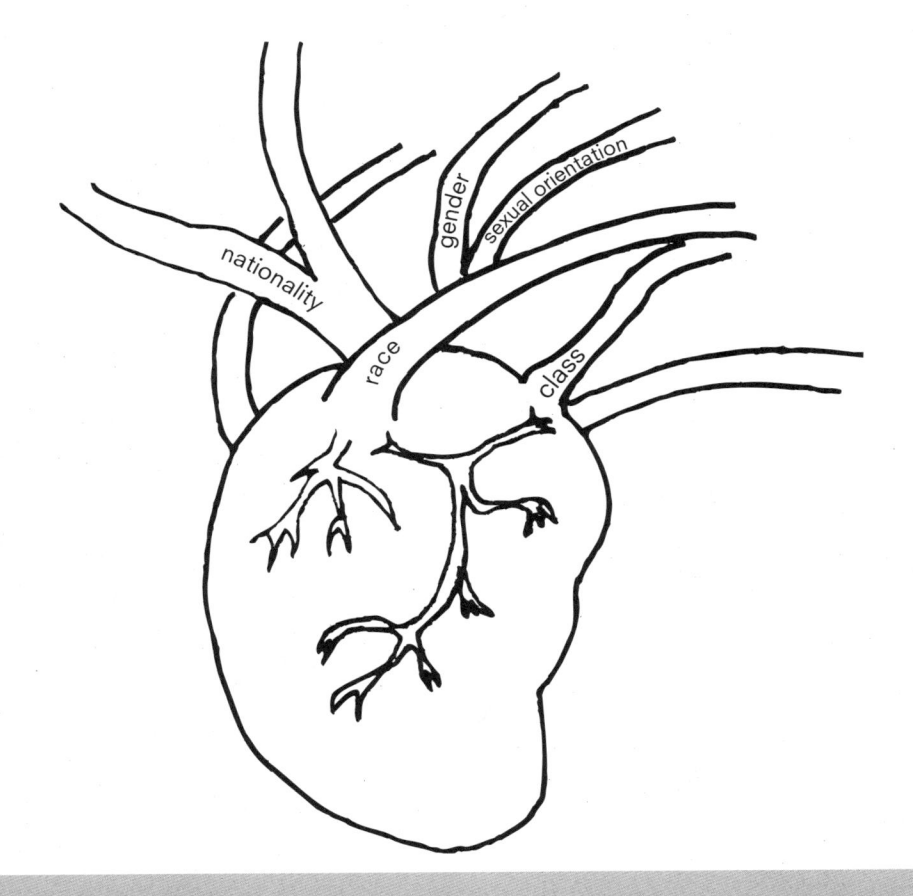

national network for immigrant and refugee rights
www.nnirr.org

race, migration, and multiple oppressions

Exploring Stereotypes We Face
(This exercise builds on the previous one)

WHY DO IT?
- To build on the discussions of identity from the previous exercise
- To explore the idea of stereotypes, their effects, and their social function
- To identify and challenge ways in which we reproduce stereotypes

TIME 30 minutes

MATERIALS NEEDED
- Small slips of paper or sticky notes
- Basket
- Pens for participants
- Easel paper, markers, tape
- Drums or other percussion instruments (optional)

FACILITATOR PREP
- You may want to schedule a break after this activity to prepare for the next one, as some of the materials generated in this activity will be used in the next activity, "What's Behind These Stereotypes?"

DIRECTIONS

1. Explain that the group will now look more closely at the statements developed in the last exercise. Ask participants to think about all the statements that they wrote on their "heart" handout.

2. Write the following sentence on the board:

   I am _____ (an identity that you wrote),
   but I am not _____ (a stereotype about that identity.)

After you have written the sentence on the board, pass out a slip of paper to each participant. Ask participants to think about their own experiences, and write the sentence on their piece of paper, filling in the blanks. Ask participants to write as clearly as possible, since other people will be reading it. After participants have finished writing their statements, collect the slips of paper in a basket. (10 minutes)

Some examples we have seen:
I am Arab, but I am not a terrorist.
I am Latino, but I don't speak Spanish.
I am lesbian, but I don't hate all men.

race, migration, and multiple oppressions module 3

Exploring Stereotypes We Face

3. Convene the large group to share the statements they wrote. This step has two options:

> **Option A:** This option is useful for groups that have not worked together before or for a group where participants face a greater challenge sharing information that makes them feel vulnerable.

Place a basket into the middle of the circle. Mix up the papers and pass the basket around the circle, asking each participant to take one slip of paper, and to read the statement on the slip of paper. After all participants have finished, collect the slips of paper for the next exercise.

> **Option B:** This option is useful for groups that have worked together before, plan to work together for a longer term, or in a setting where participants want to take a risk towards building deeper trust.

Ask participants to beat on their upper chest with one open palm to make a heartbeat sound, ba-boom, ba-boom, while gently swaying from side to side. Begin by modeling the beat.

Once the group has a good rhythm going, ask participants to take turns calling out their sentences. Let people know that they can briefly "stop their heartbeat" when they share their sentence if it's too hard to "make the motion and talk at the same time. But they can rejoin the community heartbeat once they're done. The group will find that some of that people's sharing will be a mix of humorous, painful, ironic, and angry statements.

After everyone (who wanted to) has shared, ask people to give a round of applause in accelerating tempo for all the great work and creativity and risk participants demonstrated.

4. Briefly discuss the exercise with the participants.
- What does it feel like to be put in a group with a negative stereotype?
- What does it feel like to be in a group with a positive stereotype?
- How did it feel when you discovered that you had stereotyped another group?

race, migration, and multiple oppressions

TEACHING POINTS
- Our race and nationality, as well as class, ethnicity, gender, religion, sexual preference, disability, and other factors shape our own experiences, good and bad.
- Stereotypes are negative messages about specific groups of people. These negative messages and misinformation allows mistreatment and oppression of these groups.
- Different groups of people face related, but distinct sets of stereotypes.
- No person is born with these stereotypes—but we are all exposed to misinformation from messages in society that perpetuate stereotypes.

SOURCE the authors; "I am__ but not___" exercise adapted from Paul Gorski, "Circles of My Multicultural Self"

Michelle Yamashita

142 | BRIDGE: Building a Race and Immigration Dialogue in the Global Economy
www.nnirr.org

race, migration, and multiple oppressions — module 3

What's Behind These Stereotypes?

WHY DO IT?
- To examine the impact stereotypes have on different groups of people
- To identify and challenge some ways in which we replicate stereotypes
- To connect stereotypes about our identity to systems and structures of privilege and oppression
- To think and strategize about ways to challenge these ideas, systems, and structures, and how allies can better support one another
- To reflect on the connection between personal healing and social resistance

TIME: Approximately 60 minutes

MATERIALS NEEDED
- "Stereotype statements" from previous activity
- Basket
- Copies of "What's Behind the Stereotypes?" handout for each participant
- Sticky notes, or small pieces of paper and tape
- Butcher paper and markers enough for small groups of participants to use
- Paper clips

FACILITATOR PREP
- Depending on the number of participants in the group, determine how many small groups to form. (4-6 participants per group seems to work best.)
- Take the "stereotype statements" from the former activity and sort them out according to identity category. (For example, put all the stereotypes that deal with race/ethnicity into one pile; all the stereotypes that have to do with gender in another; for religion, sexual orientation, etc.) These "stereotype statements" will be the basis for the discussion. Choose 2-3 statements per group. If you don't have enough statements for a specific category, you may want to write a few on new slips of paper. Clip each stack of statements together, and place in the basket.

Here are some examples of stereotypes that we've heard:
- "I am a Black man, but not interested in snatching your purse."
- "I am Asian, but I'm not good at math."
- "I am Native American, but I don't live in a Teepee."
- "I am white and from the South, but I'm not a Republican."
- "I am an immigrant, but I'm not trying to steal your job."
- "I am gay, but I'm not out to get your children."
- "I am a woman, but I don't always get emotional."
- "I am on welfare, but I'm not lazy."

race, migration, and multiple oppressions

What's Behind These Stereotypes?

DIRECTIONS

1. Explain to the group that this exercise will further examine the use of stereotypes in our society. Pass out "What's Behind the Stereotype?" handouts to each participant. Quickly explain the directions for the small group activity.

2. Divide the participants into groups of 4-6 people. Ask each group to pick one group of "stereotype statements" from the basket. Give each group butcher paper and markers for their discussion.

3. Ask each small group to examine each of their "stereotype statements," according to the instructions on the handout (about 30 minutes).

4. Each small group should quickly report back their discussion, by choosing one of their statements, and describing their answers to each of the questions on the handouts.

5. Build on each of the small group discussions. Ask the large group:
   - What did you notice about this exercise? Was anything surprising? If so, what?
   - Focus on the small group report-backs. Are there any other examples of laws, policies, or institutions that help to perpetuate inequality?
   - What can people who are not directly affected by a stereotype do to be a good ally?

TEACHING POINTS

- Stereotypes help to rationalize unjust and inhumane actions and policies against a group of people.
- Unjust policies, laws, and institutions perpetuate inequality, exploitation, and oppression.
- Institutional policies are not neutral so we should raise critical questions like "For whose benefit?" and "At whose expense?"
- Through open and honest dialogue and active listening we can start to break through the wedges that divide us and nurture more healthy and sustainable people and communities.

SOURCE The authors. Special thanks to Stacy Kono of AIWA for her helpful suggestions on the handout.

handout

Before you start, pick someone in your group to chair the discussion, and someone to record your group's discussion on a large sheet of paper.

Answer the following questions for each "stereotype" that your group receives, and record your answers on the easel paper.

1. What is the stereotype/negative idea? Who is this stereotype/negative idea attacking?

2. How does this stereotype impact the people it is attacking? How does this stereotype impact other groups of people?

3. Who benefits from these negative ideas? What are some policies and institutions that help these people/groups benefit?

4. What can we do to address this oppression? What can other people do to address this oppression and support one another?

After you have finished looking at each stereotype your group has been given, decide one stereotype that your group will present to the rest of the participants.

race, migration, and multiple oppressions

Multiple Jeopardy Conga Line: Our Intersecting Identities

WHY DO IT?
- To connect our personal identities and examine how different combinations of oppression and privilege operate within ourselves
- To talk about how different combinations of identity serve to intensify or buffer oppression and privilege

TIME Approximately 15 minutes

MATERIALS NEEDED
- Drums, percussion instruments, or music to play to mark the beat

DIRECTIONS

1. Ask the group to form a large circle.
2. Ask participants to stretch out for this exercise by first squatting as low as they comfortably go, then standing up and stretching and standing and reaching as far up as they can go. Ask them to think back to how they filled out their hearts in the earlier execise and what they learned from all the exercises today.
3. Begin to beat out a beat on your drums/instruments, or turn on the music. Ask people to start dancing around in a circle with a hand on the shoulder or back of the person in front of them. Get a good rhythm of the conga line going.
4. Ask participants to dance their "height" for privilege/oppression when it comes to race, with the highest for most privileged, to the lowest for least privileged. For example, those who have a lot of racial privilege should stand tall and those without should squat down for a few low beats. Explain that when we have privilege in certain areas, it allows us to stand taller and reach heights more easily. Let people look around for a few beats.
5. Repeat this for other categories, such as nationality, immigration status, gender, sexual orientation, etc.
6. Ask participants to think of all the categories that they identified with today. Ask them to dance at their "average height," representing the combination of identity aspects.

TEACHING POINTS
- Forms of oppression and privilege are related to one another—we can experience oppression and privilege in different ways at the same time. The combined aspects of one's identity can either intensify or buffer the full force of oppression that one experiences.
- People tend to be more aware of inequities when they are on the oppressed side of a particular power relation, but less conscious when they are on the privileged side.

race, migration, and multiple oppressions module 3

Multiple Jeopardy Conga Line: Our Intersecting Identities

VARIATIONS
- For groups that may not be as comfortable with the "conga line," participants can do this exercise standing in a circle.

CHALLENGES
- Self-identifying for some of the categories, such as sexual orientation, may be risky for some participants. Remind participants that they only need to share that aspect if they are comfortable and safe enough to publicly identify with a particular group.

SOURCE the authors

Michelle Yamashita

race, migration, and multiple oppressions

Closing: Spider's Web

WHY DO IT?
- To evaluate the day's activities
- To acknowledge and appreciate participants
- To provide a sense of closure for the day

TIME Approximately 15 minutes

MATERIALS NEEDED
- Ball of yarn or string

DIRECTIONS
1. Ask the large group to form a big circle. The group can stand or sit, depending on the participants' energy.
2. Ask participants to take a look around the circle, at all the other participants. Explain that the group will be building a "web of solidarity," to appreciate what each person brings to the group.
3. Start off by holding on to the end of the string, and throwing the ball of string to another person. Say one thing that you appreciate about her/him. S/he should then hold her piece of string, and throw the ball of string to another person in the group, repeating the process. Repeat until everyone in the group has received the ball of string; people should not receive it more than once.
4. At the end explain that this exercise shows all of the connections that make us strong; the web is weakened if someone lets go.

SOURCE unknown—we have seen many educators use this one!

Michelle Yamashita

race, migration, and multiple oppressions — module 3

Resources

Organizational Resources:

Challenging White Supremacy Workshops. www.cwsworkshop.org. 2440 16th St. PMB 275. San Francisco, CA 94103. Tel: 415-647-0921.

Colours of Resistance. http://colours.mahost.org. c/o Student-Worker Solidarity QPIRG at McGill, 3647 University Street, 3rd Floor, Montréal, Quebec H3A 2B3, Canada

Committee on Women, Population, and the Environment. www.cwpe.org. P.O. Box 16178, Baltimore, MD 21218.

Incite! Women of Color Against Violence. www.incite-national.org. (National group.) P.O. Box 6861, Minneapolis, MN 55406. Tel: (415) 553-3837.

National Center for Human Rights Education. www.nchre.org. PO Box 311020, Atlanta, GA 31131. Tel: 404-344-9629.

Poverty & Race Research Action Council (PRRAC), www.prrac.org. 3000 Connecticut Ave., N.W., Suite 200, Washington, DC 20008. Tel: 202-387-9887.

TODOS: Sherover Simms Alliance Building Institute. 1203 Preservation Park Way, Suite 200. Oakland, CA 94612. Tel: 510-967-2888.

Women of Color Resource Center. www.coloredgirls.org. 1611 Telegraph Ave. #303, Oakland, CA 94612. Tel: 510-444-2700.

Educational Resources and Publications:

Ed. Gloria Anzaldúa. Making Face, Making Soul: Haciendo Caras, Creative and Critical Perspectives by Feminists of Color. San Francisco: Aunt Lute Books, 1990.

Ed. Cherrie Moraga and Gloria Anzaldua, This Bridge Called My Back: Writings By Radical Women of Color. Berkeley: Third Woman Press, 2002 (reissue).

Lee, E. & Okazawa-Rey, Margo. Handout: Tolerance vs. transformation. In Beyond heroes and holidays: A practical guide to K-12 anti-racist, multicultural education and staff. Washington, D.C.: Network of Educators on the Americas, 1998.

bell hooks. Ain't I A Woman? Black Women and Feminism. Boston: South End Press, 1981.

Ronald Takaki. A Different Mirror: A History of Multicultural America. Boston: Back Bay Books, 1993.

Hugh Vasquez and Isoke Femi. No Boundaries: A Manual for Unlearning Oppression and Building Multicultural Alliances. Todos Institute, 1993. To order, call 510-444-6448.

Women of Color Resource Center. Time To Rise: U.S. Women of Color: Issues and Strategies. WCRC, 2001. To order, visit www.coloredgirls.org.

migrant rights are human rights!

migrant rights are human rights! module 4

OVERVIEW

The goals of this workshop are to:

- Explore the connection between the rights of immigrants and refugees and human rights
- Reflect on the role of human rights in our lives and in our communities' experiences
- Explore how broader community needs and issues impact our own lives and our families
- Discuss how the denial of human dignity and human needs are violations of human rights
- Learn about human rights mechanisms relevant to immigrant and refugee communities
- Examine ways that communities have organized against human rights abuses and promoted human rights

WHAT WILL WE BE TALKING ABOUT?

In this workshop, we will think about the following questions:
- What are human rights, and who has human rights?
- What role do human rights play in our lives?
- What are some ways in which human rights are violated in our community?
- What happens to our communities, families, and our lives when human rights are violated?
- How have communities organized against human rights abuses and promoted human rights?

NOTE TO FACILITATORS

The process of building strong community awareness and organizing around human rights is a lengthy one, hardly able to be completed in just one session. This module is intended as a tool to provide a basic introduction of human rights to immigrant and refugee communities. For other community-based human rights resources, please see the list at the end of this module.

migrant rights are human rights!

Backgrounder: Migrant Rights are Human Rights!

Immigrant and refugee communities living in the U.S. experience human rights abuses every day. These abuses take place in cities, in rural areas, and at borders, in schools, workplaces, on the road—in many walks of life. Immigrant communities organizing for fair wages, the right to work, legalization, access to education and social services, and against immigration enforcement abuse, discrimination, detention, and deportation are all fighting for one common goal: human rights.

The human rights framework is a powerful tool for organizing in many ways. The U.S. legal system does not guarantee the same basic civil rights enjoyed by U.S. citizens to immigrants. For example, non-citizen immigrants and refugees frequently do not have access to due process and legal representation. Recent legislation, such as the U.S. PATRIOT Act, also makes it possible for naturalized citizens to lose their status. A human rights framework, however, supports the rights of all people, regardless of their immigration status or citizenship, and provides a more comprehensive and supportive vision of immigrant and refugee rights. International agreements, such as the UN Convention for the Protection of Migrant Workers and Their Families, and the United Nations Convention relating to the Status of Refugees transcend national borders. The human rights framework also provides immigrant communities with an additional tool to build solidarity with other movements. Sharing a human rights perspective allows communities to recognize that all struggles and issues are interconnected, and provides a common language to build understanding and support between seemingly divergent issues.

Immigrant and refugee communities in the U.S. carry on a long tradition of organizing for human rights at the local, national, and international level. Local community groups support the human rights of immigrants and refugees through service provision, organizing, and advocacy work. Community groups have conducted "know your human rights" trainings, documented human rights abuses, and have used human rights language in framing campaigns and media work. At the national and international level, groups have worked together to form international alliances, to raise the visibility of migrant and refugee issues in international forums, and have celebrated December 18, International Migrants Day.

migrant rights are human rights! module 4

SUMMARY POINTS

- Everyone, as a human being, has human dignity, and therefore has human rights. Human rights can never be taken away from a human being.
- Human rights support the needs of human beings, and are universal, interconnected, and indivisible.
- The United Nations Universal Declaration of Human Rights is an international agreement that supports the civil, political, economic, social, and cultural rights of every human, as well as their environmental, development, and sexual rights.
- International human rights agreements such as the International Convention of Migrant Workers and Their Families and the 1951 UN Refugee Convention and 1967 Protocol promote the human rights of migrants and refugees.
- Communities around the world have used human rights principles to fight for justice, equality and democracy. Many immigrant and refugee communities bring deep knowledge and experience about the importance of human rights learned in their own countries to the U.S.
- Immigrant communities continue to successfully organize to uphold their human rights.

WORKSHOP MENU

Activity:	Time:
Welcome, introduction to the workshop, review of summary points	10 minutes
Suggested Introduction/Icebreaker:	
"Our Names, Our Stories" (page 154)	20 minutes
*Opening: Three Questions—Talking about Human Rights in Our Lives	40 minutes
*The Human Rights Circle: Human Rights in Our Communities	90 minutes
Organizing for Human Rights: Discussing Case Studies	40 minutes
Closing: Poetic Justice	30 minutes
Evaluation	10 minutes
*core exercise	

Total Time: 3 hours

NOTE The exercises in this module do not go into specifics of international human rights institutions, law, or history, although reviewing the "human rights fact sheet" collectively, or as part of a brief facilitator presentation after the "Human Rights Circle" exercise may be useful.

migrant rights are human rights!

Three Questions—Talking about Human Rights in Our Lives

WHY DO IT?
- To open the workshop and to have participants introduce themselves and connect with each other
- To build increased trust within the group
- To connect personal experiences to the idea of human dignity and human rights

TIME 40 minutes or more

MATERIALS NEEDED
- Easel paper and marker

FACILITATOR PREP
- Write the "three questions" for reference on easel paper

DIRECTIONS

1. Assemble the group. Have participants find a partner, preferably someone they don't know. If there is an odd number of participants, form one group of three.

2. Ask participants to introduce themselves to their partner and to answer the following three questions and share with their partners (10 minutes):
   - Name one time when your human dignity was violated
   - Name one time when you denied someone else their human dignity
   - Name one time when your human dignity was upheld, or you upheld someone else's human dignity

3. After everyone has had a chance to share with their partners, bring the large group back together in a circle. Ask each person to introduce her/himself, and then share the answer to one of the questions with the large group. Give the option for participants to pass. (For groups with more time, you may want to go around the circle three times, focusing on a different question each time.)

4. When people have finished, process the activity with the large group. Ask:
   - How did this make you feel? What did you notice?
   - Did anything surprise you?
   - What does human dignity mean to you?
   - What is the connection between human dignity and privilege?

After the group has discussed these questions, review the teaching points.

migrant rights are human rights! module 4

TEACHING POINTS
- Our human dignity can be upheld and violated in our daily lives.
- We also have the capacity to violate or uphold other people's human dignity.
- The denial or affirmation of our human dignity is often based on our relative power or privileges of race, class, gender, sexual orientation, immigration status, age, educational level, disability and others.
- Every human being has equal dignity, and therefore, has equal human rights, which can never be taken away.
- Human rights are ethically and morally based in upholding everyone's human dignity.

CHALLENGES
- Talking about human rights violations may be challenging for participants, especially in a climate without trust. In some instances, this exercise can also trigger difficult memories or experiences for participants.
- It is important set a tone of mutual trust and respect before this activity by conducting an icebreaker activity, emphasizing ground rules before the exercise, and giving participants the option to pass. Emphasizing the group's collective responsibility to one another also reinforces an atmosphere of trust and shared experience.
- It is important to stress confidentiality; what is shared in the group remains in the group and should not be discussed outside the group, even with the person who self-disclosed.

SOURCE Loretta Ross, National Center for Human Rights Education, adapted by the authors

Michelle Yamashita

migrant rights are human rights!

The Human Rights Circle: Human Rights in Our Communities

WHY DO IT?
- To identify key issues facing our communities
- To examine how community needs and crises impact the lives of families and individuals
- To connect the idea of human needs to human rights
- To apply the Universal Declaration of Human Rights to participants' realities

TIME 90 minutes

MATERIALS NEEDED
- Copies of "Human Rights Circle" handout for all participants
- One copy of "Human Rights cards," cut along dotted lines, tape
- Basket or jar
- Easel paper, markers, tape

DIRECTIONS

1. Divide the large group into smaller groups of 4-6 participants.

2. Distribute the "Human Rights Circle" handout to all participants, and review the instructions. Give each small group a large piece of easel paper, markers, and pens.

3. Small groups will complete the community survey on human rights, and produce a piece of easel paper with a diagram of their group's discussion. (20-25 minutes)

4. Bring the small groups back together. Ask each group to quickly present the results of their discussion. To shorten the report-backs, suggest that each group report back on only one community issue. Applaud the efforts of each group, and place all of the diagrams on the wall. Discuss with the large group:
   - What were some of the common needs and problems identified in the small group discussions?
   - How did all of the needs connect with each other?
   - Did your discussions surprise you in any way? Why?

5. After the small group presentation and discussion, pass out a "Human Rights Card" to each participant. Explain that each card is a human right listed in the Universal Declaration of Human Rights, an international agreement signed by nearly every country in the United Nations in 1948.

migrant rights are human rights! module 4

6. Ask participants to look at their cards, and to look at the circles on the wall. Then ask participants to find a need in the circles that is related to their card, and to place their card on it.

(Some rights may be applicable in more places than one; ask participants to put their "human rights card" on only one need, but to keep in mind places where it could fit. Other "human rights cards" may not correspond with the needs listed; ask participants to put them outside the circle.)

For example: Need: children need better schools
Right: Article 26: Right to Education

Need: Family can't pay bills
Right: Article 25: Right to Adequate Living Standard

7. Ask each participant to read their "human rights card" aloud, and to quickly read the need they've selected. If a "human rights card" does not correspond with the need listed, ask the group to think of a situation where this right would apply.

8. To summarize, ask:
- Did anything surprise you? Why?
- After having done this exercise, what do you think is a human right? Who do you think has human rights?
- What happens to us when our human rights are violated?
- What happens to a society that produces and allows human rights violations?
- What are some ways that we—ourselves, our families, and our communities—can make sure that our human rights are respected?

9. After the group has discussed these questions, you may want to review the Teaching Points.

national network for immigrant and refugee rights
www.nnirr.org

migrant rights are human rights!

TEACHING POINTS
- Human needs are human rights.
- Humans have many needs, and these needs and rights are interconnected with one another, at the individual, family, and community level.
- The realities of families and communities are multi-issue: many needs, corresponding with many rights.
- While all humans have the same human rights, we each need something different to protect them. (For example, all children have the right to education, but blind children will need books in Braille in order to secure this human right met.)

VARIATIONS
- Consider reviewing and presenting the "human rights fact sheet" included at the end of the module for groups that have more interest in learning about international human rights institutions, law, or history.

SOURCE authors, with Alma Maquitico

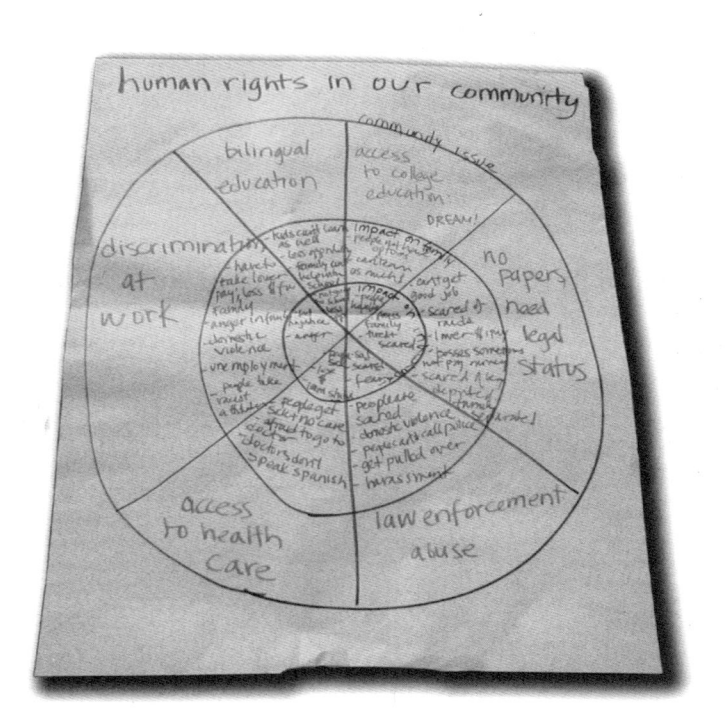

credit: E. Cho

handout

The Human Rights Circle

Before you start, pick someone in your group to keep the discussion going, and someone to record your group's discussion on a large sheet of paper.

Copy the circle drawing on the worksheet onto a large sheet of paper, and answer the questions together as a group. Remember to choose someone to write your discussion on the paper, and 1-2 people to quickly share your group's discussion with the rest of the large group.

1. What are some problems or needs faced by your community?
Write each need in a section of the outer-most circle.
2. What happens to families in your community when this need is not met?
Write what happens to families in the second circle.
3. What happens to you (or people you work with) when this need is not met?
Write what happens in the inner-most circle.

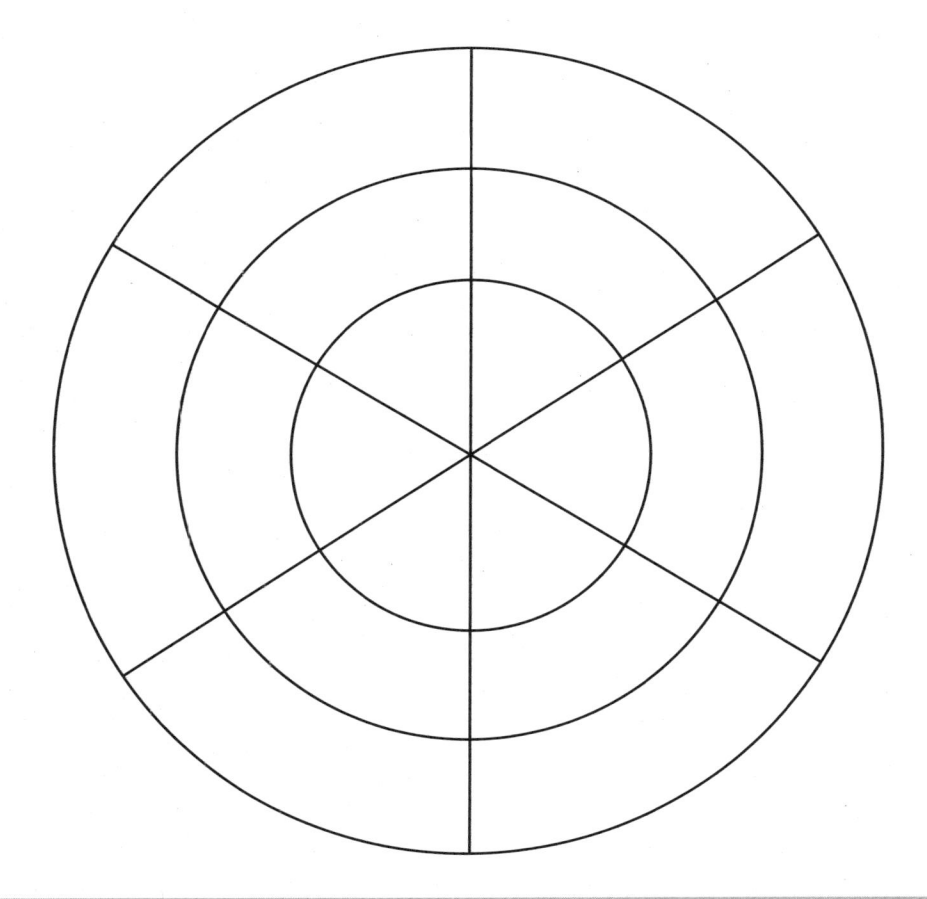

national network for immigrant and refugee rights
www.nnirr.org

Article 1	Article 2	Article 3	Article 4	Article 5
Right to Equality	**Freedom From Discrimination**	Right to Life, Liberty, and Personal Security	Freedom From Slavery	Freedom From Torture and Degrading Treatment
Article 6	Article 7	Article 8	Article 9	Article 10
Right to Recognition as a Person Before the Law	Right to Equality Before the Law	Right to Remedy by Competent Tribunal	Freedom from Arbitrary Arrest and Exile	Right to Fair Public Hearing
Article 11	Article 12	Article 13	Article 14	Article 15
Right to be Considered Innocent until Proven Guilty	Freedom from Interference with Privacy, Family, Home and Correspondence	Right to Free Movement in and out of the Country	Right to Asylum in other Countries from Persecution	Right to a Nationality and the Freedom to Change Nationality

Article 16	Article 17	Article 18	Article 19	Article 20
Right to Marriage and a Family	Right to Own Property	Freedom of Belief and Religion	Freedom of Opinion and Information	Right of Peaceful Assembly and Association
Article 21	**Article 22**	**Article 23**	**Article 24**	**Article 25**
Right to Participate in Government and in Free Elections	Right to Social Security	Right to Desirable Work and to Join Trade Unions	Right to Rest and Leisure	Right to Adequate Living Standard
Article 26	**Article 27**	**Article 28**	**Article 29**	**Article 30**
Right to Education	Right to Participate in the Cultural Life of a Community	Right to a Social Order that Articulates this Document	Community Duties Essential to Free and Full Development	Freedom from State or Personal Interference in the Above Rights

migrant rights are human rights!

Organizing for Human Rights: Discussing Case Studies

WHY DO IT?
- To examine some specific examples of immigrant communities' successful human rights organizing
- To discuss strategies for community organizing for human rights

TIME 40 minutes or more

MATERIALS NEEDED
- Copies of small group handouts for participants (note: there are three case studies)
- Easel paper and marker

DIRECTIONS
1. Divide the participants into three small groups. Give each small group a testimony to read and discuss.
2. Small groups will read and discuss a case study of community human rights organizing. (20 minutes)
3. Reconvene the small groups, and ask each group to briefly give a summary of their group's story, and to name three strategies they discussed for using human rights in their organizing. (15-20 minutes)

TEACHING POINTS
- Immigrant rights organizations have successfully used human rights to organize their communities.
- Documenting and reporting abuses and educating communities about human rights can help to stop human rights abuses by authorities.

SOURCE the authors

E. Cho

BRIDGE: Building a Race and Immigration Dialogue in the Global Economy
www.nnirr.org

Migrant Rights are Human Rights!

Community Organizing Case Studies

Case Study #1:
DRUM: Desis Rising Up and Moving
Human Rights for South Asian Immigrants in New York City After September 11, 2001

After September 11, 2001, immigrants living in the U.S.—particularly those of South Asian, Arab, and Muslim origin—became the target of hate violence and discriminatory policies. In the months following September 11, the U.S. government secretly rounded up and detained over 1200 South Asian, Muslim, and Arab men at their jobs, schools, or homes. Family members often had no idea where their loved ones had disappeared. The U.S. government refused to release names of the detainees, and held the men in detention without access to lawyers. At least one man died while in government custody.

Community members became even more afraid when the INS announced the start of its "special registration" program, requiring men and boys from over 25 mainly Arab or Muslim countries to report to the INS for fingerprints, photographs, and questioning. Over 150,000 men and boys registered, and over 13,000 of them now face deportation. Many of them had applications pending with the INS for legal status. The men held in detention have reported mistreatment, severe overcrowding, sleep deprivation, unnecessary restraints and racial slurs. Many were unable to contact family members, and the INS charged high bonds from those it did release. Meanwhile, none of these detentions have led to any charges related to acts of violence or terrorism.

DRUM (Desis Rise Up and Moving) is a community organization of working class South Asian immigrants in New York City. After September 11, family members, neighbors, and friends of detainees began to organize through DRUM. Together, they visited local detention centers and connected with over 100 detainees, with the goal of ensuring that their human rights and due process rights. The group established a toll-free number for immigrants in detention to call for assistance, and distributed the phone number during visits to the detention centers. They also began monthly protests and meetings with local prison and detention center officials to fight for better conditions. In addition, DRUM organized "action teams" of 5-10 people for each person they reached in detention, to write letters, organize protests, help provide legal support, and advocate for better conditions in jails and detention centers.

DRUM has led trainings on human rights with family members of detainees, as well as some former detainees. Through their work, they have won the release of approximately 60 people from detention, and have continued to fight for better

Case Study #1:

conditions in detention. DRUM has collected stories and testimonies of immigrants in detention, some which have been published in human rights reports, including a government report criticizing the Attorney General's policies of secret detention after September 11.

Discussion questions:
1. What human rights were being violated in this community?
2. What were the causes of these human rights violations? Who was responsible?
3. How has DRUM promoted the human rights of community members in their organizing work? What do you think would happen without their organizing work?
4. What are some ways that your community can work to uphold human rights in your community?

DRUM: Desis Rising Up and Moving, 72-26 Broadway, 4th Fl. Jackson Heights, NY 11372. Tel: (718) 205-3036, www.drumnation.org.

Case Study #2:
The Border Network for Human Rights
Community Human Rights Promoters Challenge Abuses at the U.S. Mexico Border

Over the last fifteen years, the U.S. government has developed a "seal the border" policy along the U.S.-Mexico border. This policy has increased the number of border patrol officers, military personnel, and the use of military equipment and technology along the border. The result: communities have increasingly faced harassment, intimidation, and even death.

From 2001 to 2003, Border Patrol agents shot at least five people in Arizona alone. In 2003, three people were killed by Border Patrol agents in separate incidents. Anti-immigrant vigilante groups along the border, some with white supremacist ties, have rounded up undocumented immigrants at gunpoint, and turned them into the Border Patrol. As the U.S. government has constructed concrete and steel walls along the border, migrants have been forced to cross through dangerous areas in the desert. From 1998-2003, over 2,038 migrants have died trying to cross the border.

This policy has heightened tension and fear for immigrant communities living near the border. The Border Patrol targets anyone they perceive to be an undocumented immigrant—even those with papers or U.S. citizens of Mexican origin. Documented cases of abuse by the Border Patrol take place in all walks of life: at traffic stops, in homes, at work, even in school buses. Agents have torn up or taken away identity documents and birth certificates, and searched people, cars, and homes without any warrant, even at gunpoint.

The Border Network for Human Rights is composed of organized groups of immigrant community members, who work together to challenge human rights abuses on the U.S.-Mexico border. Based mostly in Texas and New Mexico, the Border Network has trained community members to become human rights promoters and to form human rights committees. Human rights promoters go through a training process where they learn about their own human rights, how to document abuses and file human rights abuse reports, and how to train and organize other community members about their human rights.

The Border Network has organized documentation campaigns on abuses in the community and published them in a report, which in turn has strengthened the visibility of the human rights committees. As the power of the community has grown, the attitude of local Border Patrol and other immigration enforcement officials has changed. Border Network members have met with Border Patrol officials to discuss the findings of their reports. "We've not only learned our rights," said one community member, "but we've developed a commitment to fight for them."

Case Study #2:

Discussion questions:
1. What human rights were being violated in this community?
2. What were the causes of these human rights violations? Who was responsible?
3. How has the Border Network for Human Rights promoted the human rights of community members in their organizing work? What do you think would happen without their organizing work?
4. What are some ways that your community can work to uphold human rights in your community?

Border Network for Human Rights, 611 Kansas, El Paso, TX 79901. Telephone: 915-577-0724.

*this case study was based in part on "Building Community Capacity: The Border Network for Human Rights," in Close To Home, Ford Foundation, 2004.

Case Study #3:
The Interfaith Coalition for Immigrant Rights
Faith Communities Celebrate December 18, International Migrant Rights Day for the Human Rights of Migrants

For the past few years, the Interfaith Coalition for Immigrant Rights (ICIR) has held events every December 18 in celebration of International Migrants Day. ICIR is a coalition of faith-based organizations in California that works to educate congregations and public officials about immigrant rights. It also trains immigrant leaders about improving community access to health and welfare benefits. Many immigrant community members are afraid of using public resources for fear of jeopardizing their ability to adjust their legal status or gain citizenship.

"December 18 is important because it helps us to remember that migration is important in all of our societies as a global phenomenon, and not only in our local communities," said Betty Cantón, the Director of ICIR. "It also shows that human rights are not different from immigrant rights: no matter what, we are advocating for the human dignity of all immigrants." December 18 is the date that the International Convention for the Protection for All Migrant Workers and Their Families—the only international agreement that exists to protect the rights of migrants—was approved by the United Nations General Assembly in 1990.

For the past few years, ICIR has spread the word about International Migrants Day to congregations around the state, and has encouraged them to dedicate a sermon, or a celebration to talk about the meaning of migration and immigrant rights. December 18 is an important opportunity to raise awareness, especially because it falls around important celebrations for many faith traditions, including Ramadan, Hanukah, Kwanzaa, and Christmas. ICIR has also organized posadas, which are traditionally celebrated in Latin America, Spain, the Philippines and many other parts of the world, reenacting Joseph and Mary's journey to Bethlehem. The Posadas Without Borders raises awareness about the hundreds of immigrants who die each year crossing the border. ICIR also holds press conferences and public interfaith services to highlight important immigrant rights issues on December 18.

Case Study #3:

Discussion questions:
1. What human rights violations does the work of ICIR address?
2. What were the causes of these human rights violations? Who was responsible?
3. How does ICIR promote the human rights of community members in their organizing work? What is significant about December 18?
4. What are some ways that your community can work to uphold human rights in your community?
5. How can culture be used to help teach about human rights?

Interfaith Coalition for Immigrant Rights: 965 Mission St. #514, San Francisco CA 94107. Tel: (415) 227-0388. www.icironline.org.

For more information about International Migrants Day, visit www.nnirr.org and www.december18.net.

migrant rights are human rights! module 4

Closing: Poetic Vision of Human Rights

WHY DO IT?
- To reflect on the day's theme of human rights
- To build a vision for human rights in our lives
- To provide a sense of closure for the day in a creative, shared experience

TIME 30 minutes

MATERIALS NEEDED
- Copies of the "Poetic Vision of Human Rights" handout for all participants
- Pens and pencils for all participants

DIRECTIONS

1. Explain to the group that to close the day's activities, we will be reflecting on what our world would look like if all of our human rights were upheld by writing poetry.

2. Divide the large group into groups of 2-3 people.

3. Distribute copies of the "Poetic Vision of Human Rights" to all participants, and review the instructions on the handout. Give each group 10-15 minutes to work on their poem.

4. After groups are finished writing their poems, hold a "poetry slam" where participants present their poems. Applaud each group's performance.

5. (Optional) Ask the group if you can collect the poems, make copies, and send them to everyone.

SOURCE National Organizers Alliance and Applied Research Center, Social Justice Dialogues: When Wedge Issues Collide, adapted by authors

handout

A Poetic Vision of Human Rights

instructions

- Complete each sentence in the poem using a mixture of seriousness and humor. (Be sure to add the humor.) You have total creative license—don't worry about rhyming, rhythm, or reason!
- When we reconvene, we will hold a poetry slam. Decide who in your group will present a spoken word performance of the poem.
- After writing the poem, be sure to have all the authors sign it.

A World of Human Rights...

By:

We want human rights because

We want a world where our families...

We want a world where our communities...

We want a world where our leaders...

We want a world where justice means...

We want a world where no borders means...

We want a movement where human rights...

We want a world of human rights.

BRIDGE: Building a Race and Immigration Dialogue in the Global Economy
www.nnirr.org

BRIDGE Fact Sheet

Migrant Rights are Human Rights!

What are human rights?
Human rights are those rights that are considered vital for all people.
>Human rights are **universal**: *every human being has the same human rights*
>Human rights are **inalienable**: *human rights can never be taken away from you*
>Human rights are **indivisible**: *no person's human rights are more important than another's*
>Human rights are **interconnected**: *all human rights are equally important*

The primary types of human rights include:
- **Political rights**: Political rights include the rights to take part in the government of one's country, such as the rights enshrined in the U.S. Bill of Rights, which include voting rights, freedom of speech, etc.
- **Civil rights**: the right to be equal to anyone else in society.
- **Economic rights**: the right to have an economy that meets people's economic needs, such as the right to a living wage, and the right to organize labor unions
- **Social rights**: includes the right to food, shelter, education, health care, and social services.
- **Cultural rights**: includes the right to freedom of religion, to speak your own language, and maintain a distinct cultural identity.

Other sets of rights are beginning to emerge. These include:
- **Environmental rights**: includes the right to clean drinking water and air, the right not to live in toxic communities, the right not to be poisoned by pesticides or other dangerous chemicals at work.
- **Developmental rights**: includes the right of countries to control their own natural resources without interference or domination by richer countries.
- **Sexual rights**: includes the right of women and men to determine their own sexual behavior, including the right to determine when and who to marry, and the right to determine with whom and the conditions under which they will engage in sexual activity.

What is the Universal Declaration of Human Rights?
The Universal Declaration of Human Rights (UDHR) was adopted by the United Nations in 1948 to create a basic international standard for human rights. It was the first comprehensive agreement among nations about the specific rights and freedoms of all human beings. The UDHR has 30 articles that specify the fundamental rights to which all human beings should be entitled.

BRIDGE Fact Sheet

Who developed the UDHR and how?

The Universal Declaration of Human Rights is a relatively recent document. The development of the UDHR coincides with the founding of the United Nations after the end of World War II. During World War II, the United States, Britain, China and Russia—nations that emerged from the war with the most power—developed plans for an international forum that would help to maintain peace and security, and to foster prosperity. These plans eventually led to the formation of the United Nations (UN) in 1945.

The UN Charter gave human rights a new international legal status, and identified human rights as one of the four founding purposes of the United Nations. The inclusion of human rights language in the UN Charter, however, was less a result of governmental discussions, but was instead born from pressure from social justice movements, Latin American governments and other non-governmental organizations. The UN Charter mandated the formation of a Human Rights Commission, which drafted the United Declaration of Human Rights. On December 10, 1948, after three years of drafting, the UN General Assembly adopted the UDHR.

What is the UN Migrant Rights Convention?

The UN Migrant Rights Convention (officially known as the International Convention for the Protection of the Rights of All Migrant Workers and Members of Their Families), is the first international treaty to specifically address the rights of migrants. The Convention extends the protection of fundamental human rights to all migrant workers and their families, including both documented and undocumented migrants.

The United Nations General Assembly approved the convention on December 18, 1990, and was brought 'into force' in 2003. The United Nations has established an office to monitor the Convention's implementation among those countries that have ratified the treaty, as well as an international treaty body to review countries' adherence to the treaty.

Why do we need the UN Migrant Rights Convention?

The UN Migrant Rights Convention provides a set of international standards to address the treatment, welfare and human rights of both documented and undocumented migrants and the obligations and responsibilities on the part of the sending and receiving countries. It extends the concept of "equality of treatment" between nationals and non-nationals, between women and men migrant workers and between documented and undocumented workers. Overall, the Convention seeks to play a role in preventing and eliminating the exploitation of all migrant workers and members of their families throughout the entire migration process. In particular, it seeks to put an end to the illegal or clandestine recruitment and trafficking of migrant workers and to discourage the exploitation of migrant workers in an irregular or undocumented situation. Finally, the Convention establishes mechanisms for its implementation that provide new opportunities for increased participation from the global community to protect the rights of migrants. To see the full text of the convention, visit: http://www.unhchr.ch/html/menu3/b/m_mwctoc.htm

What are some human rights tools specific to refugees?
The 1951 United Nations Convention relating to the Status of Refugees, and its 1967 Protocol relating to the Status of Refugees form the basis for the human rights of refugees. The 1951 Convention defines a refugee as any person who has a "well-founded fear of being persecuted for reasons of race, religion, nationality, membership of a particular social group or political opinion, is outside the country of his nationality and is unable…or unwilling to return to it." The Convention protects the rights of refugees, including protections for employment and welfare, especially in regards to identity papers and travel documents. To see the full text of the conventions, visit: www.unhcr.ch.

The United Nations High Commissioner for Refugees is an international agency responsible for providing international protection for refugees, facilitating voluntary return of refugees to their home countries, or helping them integrate into their new countries.

What are some critiques and limitations of the human rights framework?
The human rights framework has become a powerful tool to point to injustices that take place in our world. However, there have been many critiques about the limitations of using human rights. First, using UN human rights treaties to act on specific violations can prove challenging. While the UN and the international community can condemn a human rights violation, it often has little enforcement power. The power of public opinion, shame, and international pressure from social justice movements is the force behind most UN human rights enforcement. Critics of human rights have also pointed to situations where international arguments for human rights have conflicted with practices of local communities. Other critiques of the human rights framework have pointed to the fact that powerful countries—often decry human rights violations in poorer, weaker countries. Meanwhile, these powerful countries' own economic and military policies create conditions that encourage massive violations of human rights. It is important to consider these critiques and limitations when using human rights to strengthen and build the power of our communities.

migrant rights are human rights!

Resources

Organizational Resources:

Global Campaign for the Ratification of the Convention on the Rights of Migrants. www.migrantsrights.org.

Migrant Rights International. www.migrantwatch.org. c.p. 135, route des Morillons 1211 Geneva, Switzerland. Tel: +41.22.9177817. MRI is an international network of migrant rights organizations from around the world.

Human Rights Education Associates. www.hrea.org. An international non-governmental organization that supports human rights learning.

National Center for Human Rights Education. www.nchre.org. PO Box 311020, Atlanta, GA 31131. Tel: 404-344-9629. NCHRE provides a variety of resource material for human rights educators, including trainings tailored to specific social justice issues, fact sheets, and more.

National Network for Immigrant and Refugee Rights. www.nnirr.org. 310 8th St. Suite 303, Oakland, CA 94607. Tel: 510-465-1984.

People's Movement for Human Rights Education. www.pdhre.org. 526 West 111th Street, New York, NY 10025. Tel: 212-749-3156

www.december18.net. This site is an international web portal that promotes and provides resources for International Migrants Day, December 18.

Educational Resources:

The Human Rights Education Handbook: Effective Practices for Learning, Action, and Change. This handbook provides activities, exercises, and helpful tools for human rights educators. To order, visit www.hrusa.org or call 1-888-473-3828 for more information.

Learning, Reflecting, and Acting: 149 Activities Used in Learning Human Rights. Available from the People's Decade for Human Rights Education, www.pdhre.org.

Manual Para Promotores de Derechos: A Training Manual (in Spanish) for Community Based Human Rights Organizing. Available from the Border Network for Human Rights, 611 Kansas, El Paso, TX 79901. Telephone: 915-577-0724.

Publications:

Achieving Dignity: Campaigner's Handbook for the Migrant Rights Convention.
Published by Migrant Rights International. This guide provides analysis, background and ideas for potential activities around the Migrant Rights Convention. To order, visit the campaign website at www.migrantsrights.org.

A World on the Move: A Resource Guide on International Migrant Rights. Published by the National Network for Immigrant and Refugee Rights. A comprehensive look at the results of the 2001 UN World Conference Against Racism, background articles on human rights mechanisms for

migrant rights are human rights! module 4

immigrants. Also tips on preparing for international conferences, and connecting local issues with international human rights campaigns and systems. To order, visit www.nnirr.org.

Fact Sheet No. 20: Human Rights and Refugees. Published by the Office of the High Commissioner for Human Rights. Gives a brief overview of international refugee organizations, international refugee law, and the human rights of refugees. Visit www.unhchr.ch/html/menu6/2/fs20.htm.

Fact Sheet No. 24: The Rights of Migrant Workers. Published by the Office of the High Commissioner for Human Rights. Provides a brief overview of the Migrant Rights Convention, and examines various global forums addressing migrant rights has been discussed. Visit www.unhchr.ch/html/menu6/2/fs24.htm.

Forefront Handbook Series, including: Making the Most of the Media: Tools for Human Rights Groups Worldwide; A Handbook of Practical Strategies for Local Human Rights Groups; Human Rights Institution-Building; A Quick Guide to Funding Sources for Human Rights Organizations. To order, visit www.forefrontleaders.org.

The Human Rights Abuse Documentation Reference Manual. A publication of Casa de Proyecto Libertad, Immigration Law Enforcement Monitoring Project, and the Border Network for Human Rights. This manual provides information on documenting human rights abuses in the U.S. immigration law enforcement context. Contact Nathan Selzer, Casa de Proyecto Libertad, 113 N. 1st St., Harlingen, TX 78550. Tel: 956-425-9552, or email: selzernj@hushmail.com.

Making the Mountain Move: An Activist's Guide to How International Human Rights Mechanisms Can Work For You. By Scott Long, formerly of the International Gay and Lesbian Human Rights Commission. This well-written and accessible guide explains the structures of the UN and regional human rights mechanisms, NGO accessibility. Available at www.iglhrc.org/news/factsheets/unguide.html.

Promoting and Protecting the Rights of Migrant Workers: A UN Road Map—A Guide for Asian NGOs to the International Human Rights System and Other Mechanisms. Published by the Asian Migrant Center. This comprehensive guide provides specific information for migrant rights NGOs to access and utilize current international structures, including the UN, ILO, and IOM. Available free to download at: www.chrf.ca/english/publications_eng/files/un-roadmap.htm.

Something Inside So Strong: A Resource Guide on Human Rights in the United States. Published by the U.S. Human Rights Network. Available at www.ushrn.org.

U.S. Campaign for the Ratification of the UN Convention on the Protection of the Rights of All Migrant Workers and Members of Their Families: Endorsement Packet, 1998. Published by NNIRR. This packet outlines the global campaign for the ratification of the convention, and a guide to the text of the convention. To obtain a copy, visit www.nnirr.org, and visit the news/publications section.

Universal Declaration of Human Rights

On December 10, 1948, the General Assembly of the United Nations adopted and proclaimed the Universal Declaration of Human Rights (UDHR). The UDHR is an international agreement that outlines a moral standard for the rights of all humans. This Declaration guarantees the rights of all people and upholds a broad spectrum of economic, social, cultural, political, and civil rights.

Preamble

Whereas recognition of the inherent dignity and of the equal and inalienable rights of all members of the human family is the foundation of freedom, justice and peace in the world,

Whereas disregard and contempt for human rights have resulted in barbarous acts which have outraged the conscience of mankind, and the advent of a world in which human beings shall enjoy freedom of speech and belief and freedom from fear and want has been proclaimed as the highest aspiration of the common people,

Whereas it is essential, if man is not to be compelled to have recourse, as a last resort, to rebellion against tyranny and oppression, that human rights should be protected by the rule of law,

Whereas it is essential to promote the development of friendly relations between nations,

Whereas the peoples of the United Nations have in the Charter reaffirmed their faith in fundamental human rights, in the dignity and worth of the human person and in the equal rights of men and women and have determined to promote social progress and better standards of life in larger freedom,

Whereas Member States have pledged themselves to achieve, in cooperation with the United Nations, the promotion of universal respect for and observance of human rights and fundamental freedoms,

Whereas a common understanding of these rights and freedoms is of the greatest importance for the full realization of this pledge,

Now, therefore, The General Assembly, proclaims this Universal Declaration of Human Rights as a common standard of achievement for all peoples and all nations, to the end that every individual and every organ of society, keeping this Declaration constantly in mind, shall strive by teaching and education to promote respect for these rights and freedoms and by progressive measures, national and international, to secure their universal and effective recognition and observance, both among the peoples of Member States themselves and among the peoples of territories under their jurisdiction.

migrant rights are human rights!

Article 1

All human beings are born free and equal in dignity and rights. They are endowed with reason and conscience and should act towards one another in a spirit of brotherhood.

Article 2

Everyone is entitled to all the rights and freedoms set forth in this Declaration, without distinction of any kind, such as race, colour, sex, language, religion, political or other opinion, national or social origin, property, birth or other status.

Furthermore, no distinction shall be made on the basis of the political, jurisdictional or international status of the country or territory to which a person belongs, whether it be independent, trust, non-self-governing or under any other limitation of sovereignty.

Article 3

Everyone has the right to life, liberty and security of person.

Article 4

No one shall be held in slavery or servitude; slavery and the slave trade shall be prohibited in all their forms.

Article 5

No one shall be subjected to torture or to cruel, inhuman or degrading treatment or punishment.

Article 6

Everyone has the right to recognition everywhere as a person before the law.

Article 7

All are equal before the law and are entitled without any discrimination to equal protection of the law. All are entitled to equal protection against any discrimination in violation of this Declaration and against any incitement to such discrimination.

Article 8

Everyone has the right to an effective remedy by the competent national tribunals for acts violating the fundamental rights granted him by the constitution or by law.

Article 9

No one shall be subjected to arbitrary arrest, detention or exile.

Article 10

Everyone is entitled in full equality to a fair and public hearing by an independent and impartial tribunal, in the determination of his rights and obligations and of any criminal charge against him.

Article 11

Everyone charged with a penal offence has the right to be presumed innocent until proved guilty according to law in a public trial at which he has had all the guarantees necessary for his defence.

No one shall be held guilty of any penal offence on account of any act or omission which did not constitute a penal offence, under national or international law, at the time when it was committed. Nor shall a heavier penalty be imposed than the one that was applicable at the time the penal offence was committed.

Article 12

No one shall be subjected to arbitrary interference with his privacy, family, home or correspondence, nor to attacks upon his honour and reputation. Everyone has the right to the protection of the law against such interference or attacks.

Article 13

Everyone has the right to freedom of movement and residence within the borders of each State.

Everyone has the right to leave any country, including his own, and to return to his country.

national network for immigrant and refugee rights
www.nnirr.org

migrant rights are human rights!

Article 14

Everyone has the right to seek and to enjoy in other countries asylum from persecution.

This right may not be invoked in the case of prosecutions genuinely arising from non-political crimes or from acts contrary to the purposes and principles of the United Nations.

Article 15

Everyone has the right to a nationality. No one shall be arbitrarily deprived of his nationality nor denied the right to change his nationality.

Article 16

Men and women of full age, without any limitation due to race, nationality or religion, have the right to marry and to found a family. They are entitled to equal rights as to
marriage, during marriage and at its dissolution.

Marriage shall be entered into only with the free and full consent of the intending spouses.

The family is the natural and fundamental group unit of society and is entitled to protection by society and the State.

Article 17

Everyone has the right to own property alone as well as in association with others.

No one shall be arbitrarily deprived of his property.

Article 18

Everyone has the right to freedom of thought, conscience and religion; this right includes freedom to change his religion or belief, and freedom, either alone or in community with others and in public or private, to manifest his religion or belief in teaching, practice, worship and observance.

Article 19

Everyone has the right to freedom of opinion and expression; this right includes freedom to hold opinions without interference and to seek, receive and impart information and ideas through any media and regardless of frontiers.

Article 20

Everyone has the right to freedom of peaceful assembly and association.

No one may be compelled to belong to an association.

Article 21

Everyone has the right to take part in the government of his country, directly or through freely chosen representatives.

Everyone has the right to equal access to public service in his country.

The will of the people shall be the basis of the authority of government; this will shall be expressed in periodic and genuine elections which shall be by universal and equal suffrage and shall be held by secret vote or by equivalent free voting procedures.

Article 22

Everyone, as a member of society, has the right to social security and is entitled to realization, through national effort and international co-operation and in accordance with the organization and resources of each State, of the economic, social and cultural rights indispensable for his dignity and the free development of his personality.

Article 23

Everyone has the right to work, to free choice of employment, to just and favourable conditions of work and to protection against unemployment.

Everyone, without any discrimination, has the right to equal pay for equal work.

Everyone who works has the right to just and favourable remuneration ensuring
for himself and his family an existence worthy of human dignity, and supplemented, if necessary, by other means of social protection.

Everyone has the right to form and to join trade unions for the protection of his interests.

Article 24

Everyone has the right to rest and leisure, including reasonable limitation of working hours and periodic holidays with pay.

migrant rights are human rights!

Article 25

Everyone has the right to a standard of living adequate for the health and well-being of himself and of his family, including food, clothing, housing and medical care and necessary social services, and the right to security in the event of unemployment, sickness, disability, widowhood, old age or other lack of livelihood in circumstances beyond his control.

Motherhood and childhood are entitled to special care and assistance. All children, whether born in or out of wedlock, shall enjoy the same social protection.

Article 26

Everyone has the right to education. Education shall be free, at least in the elementary and fundamental stages. Elementary education shall be compulsory. Technical and professional education shall be made generally available and higher education shall be equally accessible to all on the basis of merit.

Education shall be directed to the full development of the human personality and to the strengthening of respect for human rights and fundamental freedoms. It shall promote understanding, tolerance and friendship among all nations, racial or religious groups, and shall further the activities of the United Nations for the maintenance of peace.

Parents have a prior right to choose the kind of education that shall be given to their children.

Article 27

Everyone has the right freely to participate in the cultural life of the community, to enjoy the arts and to share in scientific advancement and its benefits.

Everyone has the right to the protection of the moral and material interests resulting from any scientific, literary or artistic production of which he is the author.

Article 28

Everyone is entitled to a social and international order in which the rights and freedoms set forth in this Declaration can be fully realized.

Article 29

Everyone has duties to the community in which alone the free and full development of his personality is possible.

In the exercise of his rights and freedoms, everyone shall be subject only to such limitations as are determined by law solely for the purpose of securing due recognition and respect for the rights and freedoms of others and of meeting the just requirements of morality, public order and the general welfare in a democratic society.

These rights and freedoms may in no case be exercised contrary to the purposes and principles of the United Nations.

Article 30

Nothing in this Declaration may be interpreted as implying for any State, group or person any right to engage in any activity or to perform any act aimed at the destruction of any of the rights and freedoms set forth herein.

national network for immigrant and refugee rights
www.nnirr.org

migrant rights are human rights!

UN Convention on the Protection of Rights For All Migrant Workers and Members of Their Families

The following summary highlights some of the most important aspects of the convention on migrant workers, and can act as a general guide to the concepts and content of the document. However, the full text of the Convention provides a comprehensive definition of the rights of migrant workers and their families and should be consulted for a full understanding of its provisions. The text can be obtained in any of the six working languages of the United Nations by writing to the U.N. Center for Human Rights, 8-14 avenue de la Paix, 1211 Geneva 10, Switzerland.

Preamble

The Preamble declares among its 16 points, that the States Parties—the nations signing and ratifying the Convention:

- Take into account the principles embodied in the basic instruments of the United Nations concerning human rights, such as the Universal Declaration of Human Rights, and conventions on women's and children's rights;
- Take into account the principles and standards of the international Labor Organization;
- Realize the importance and extent of the migration phenomenon, which involves millions of people and affects a large number of States in the international community;
- Consider the situation of vulnerability of migrant workers and their families, and that their rights have not been sufficiently recognized everywhere;
- Consider that recourse to the employment of migrant workers who are in an irregular situation will also be discouraged if the fundamental human rights of all migrant workers are more widely recognized;
- Are convinced of the need for international protection of the rights of all migrant workers and their families, reaffirming and establishing basic norms in a comprehensive convention which could be applied universally.

migrant rights are human rights! module 4

Part I: Scope and Definitions

Article 1 states that the present Convention is applicable, except as otherwise provided, to all migrant workers and members of their families without distinction of any kind such as sex, race, color, language, religion or convictions, political opinion.

Article 2 defines the term migrant worker" as a person who is to be engaged in a remunerated activity in a State of which he or she is not a national. Other terms are also identified such as "frontier worker", "seasonal worker", and "specified-employment worker" for persons required to depart from the State of employment at the expiration of their authorized period of stay.

Articles 4 and 5 differentiate migrant workers and "members of the family" as documented, in a regular situation, or as non-documented, in an irregular situation.

Part II: Non-discrimination

Article 7 provides that non-discrimination with respect to rights shall exist without distinction of any kind on the basis of sex, race, color, language, religion or convictions, political or other opinion, national ethnic or social origin, nationality, age, economic position, property, marital status, birth or other status.

Part III: Human Rights of All Migrant Workers and Members of Their Families

This section defines rights of migrant workers and members of their families such as:

Article 8 freedom to leave any State, including their state of origin and the right at any time to re-enter their State of origin.

Article 9: the right to life.

Article 10: no subjugation to torture or to cruel, inhuman or degrading treatment or punishment.

Article 11: prohibition against being held in slavery or servitude, or being required to perform forced or compulsory labor (excepting what is normally required of a person who is under detention in consequence of a lawful order, or in cases of emergency or calamity, or normal civil obligations).

Article 12 and 13: the right to freedom of thought, expression, conscience, and religion: and the right to hold opinions without interference.

Article 16: the rights to liberty and security of person and effective protection by the State against violence. Verification of identity must be carried out in

migrant rights are human rights!

accordance with the law. No individual or collective arbitrary arrest or detention. Information on the reasons for arrest shall be given in a language the detained understands.

Article 17: if deprived of liberty, treatment with humanity and with respect for the inherent dignity of the human person and cultural identity. Detained migrants are entitled to the same rights as nationals in the same situation.

Article 18: the right to equality with nationals of the State before the courts and tribunals.

Article 21: it is unlawful other than by a public official duly authorized by law, to confiscate, destroy or attempt to destroy identity documents. No authorized confiscation of such documents shall take place without delivery of a detailed receipt.

Article 22: prohibits measures of collective expulsion. Expulsion may only be in pursuance of a decision taken by the competent authority in accordance with law and the decision shall be communicated to migrant workers in a language they understand. In case of expulsion, the person concerned shall have a reasonable opportunity before or after departure to settle any claims for wages.

Article 23: the right to have recourse to the protection and assistance of their State of origin.

Article 24: the right to recognition everywhere as a person before the law.

Article 25 requires treatment no less favorable than that which applies to nationals of the receiving State regarding remuneration.

Article 26: the right to take part in meetings and activities of trade unions; with no restrictions other than those prescribed by law.

Article 27 stipulates the same treatment for social security granted to nationals insofar as applicable requirements are fulfilled.

Article 28: the right to receive any medical care that is urgently required for the preservation of their life regardless of any irregularity in their situation or that of their parents.

Article 29 provides children the right of access to education on the basis of equivalence with nationals.

Article 30 provides children the right to a name, to registration of birth, and to a nationality.

Part IV: Other Rights of Migrant Workers and Members of Their Families in a Regular Situation

Article 39 provides for the right to liberty of movement in the territory of the State of employment without any restrictions except those provided by law and are necessary to protect national security and public order.

Article 40 upholds the right to form associations and trade unions.

Article 41 provides for the right to participate in public affairs, to vote and to be elected at elections in their State of origin.

Article 43 stipulates equality of treatment with nationals such as access to educational institutions, vocational guidance and training, housing, social and health services, cooperatives and self-managed enterprises, and participation in cultural life.

Article 44 recognizes that the family is the natural and fundamental group unit of society and is entitled to protection by society, and requires appropriate measures to ensure the protection of the unity of the family of the migrant worker.

Article 45 mandates that members of the family of migrant workers shall enjoy equality of treatment with nationals in the State of employment, in relation to access to educational institutions, vocational guidance, social and health services, and participation in cultural life. States of employment are to facilitate the integration of children of migrant workers in the local school system and to facilitate for the children of migrant workers the teaching of their mother tongue and culture.

Article 52 upholds the right to freely choose remunerated activity.

Article 53 provides that family members who have an authorization of residence or admission that is without limit of time or is automatically renewable shall be permitted freely to choose their remunerated activity.

Article 54 provides that without prejudice to the terms of their authorization, migrant workers shall receive equal treatment with nationals in respect of protection against dismissal, unemployment benefits, access to public work schemes intended to combat unemployment, and access to alternative employment.

Article 56 limits expulsion from a State of employment, to reasons defined in the national legislation of that State and subject to the safeguards established in Part III.

migrant rights are human rights!

Part V: Provisions Applicable to Particular Categories

Articles 58 to 63 define particular categories of frontier workers, seasonal workers, itinerant workers, project-tied workers, specified-employment workers and self-employed workers, and allow for certain limited exceptions to the rights set forth in part IV.

Part VI: Promotion of Sound, Equitable, Humane and Lawful Conditions

Article 64 mandates States Parties concerned to cooperate with a view to promoting sound, equitable and humane conditions.

Article 65 stipulates that States Parties shall maintain appropriate services to deal with international migration of workers, such as the formulation and implementation of policies, an exchange of information, consultation and cooperation with the other States Parties, provision of appropriate information particularly to employers, and provision of information and appropriate assistance to migrant workers.

Article 68 requires States Parties to collaborate to prevent and eliminate illegal or clandestine movements and employment of migrant workers in an irregular situation. Included are appropriate measures against the dissemination of misleading information; measures to detect and eradicate illegal or clandestine movements of migrant workers and to impose effective sanctions on persons or entitles who organize such movements, and persons in an irregular situation.

Article 70 obligates the States Parties to take measures equal to those applied to nationals to ensure that working and living conditions of migrant workers are in keeping with the standards of fitness, safety, health and principles of human dignity.

Part VII: Application of the Convention

Article 72 establishes a Committee on the Protection of the Rights of All Migrant Workers and Their Families. Initially, it is to consist of ten and, after entry of the forty-first State Party, of fourteen experts of high moral standing, impartiality and recognized competence in the field covered by the Convention. Members of the Committee shall be elected by secret ballot by the State Parties from a list of persons nominated by the State Parties.

Article 73 requires States Parties to report on the legislative, judicial, administrative and other measures they have taken to give effects to the provisions of the Convention as follows: within one year after the entry into force of the Convention: and thereafter every five years.

Article 77 provides for States Parties to permit the Committee to receive and consider claims by individuals regarding violations of any provisions.

Part VIII: General Provisions

Article 79: States retain the right to establish criteria for admission of migrant workers and their families but stipulate that legal and other treatment remain in accord with the Convention.

Article 82 prohibits renunciation of any rights and any pressure on individuals to relinquish any rights.

Article 83 requires States to ensure effective remedies to any violation, including review of claims by competent authorities, and enforcement of remedies when granted.

Part IX: Final Provisions

Article 85 through 87 provide for depositing at the UN, signing, ratification and entry into force of the Convention.

Article 88 disallows exclusion of application of any part of the Convention by States Parties.

Article 92 provides for arbitration in the case of disputes between States arising from the Convention not settled by negotiation.

Source: Proclaiming Migrant Rights, World Council of Churches and Churches' Committee for Migrants in Europe, Briefing Papers No. 3

immigrant rights & LGBT rights!

immigrant rights and LGBT rights

module 5

OVERVIEW The goals of this workshop are to:
- Explore the connections between immigrant rights and the rights of lesbian, gay, bisexual, and transgender (LGBT) people
- Discuss how the struggle for human dignity and human rights includes a struggle for the rights of sexual minorities
- Explore how homophobic messages about gender and sexual orientation are shaped very early on from our cultures, families, and communities
- Discuss some of the ways immigration policies affect sexual minorities, in the past and present

WHAT WE WILL BE TALKING ABOUT? In this workshop, we will think about the following questions:
- How do immigrant rights and LGBT (lesbian, gay, bisexual, and transgender) rights relate to each other?
- Why is it important to support the rights of LGBT people?
- What is homophobia, and how is it used to take power away from people? How does it relate to other forms of oppression?
- What are some of the issues that LGBT immigrants face?

NOTE TO FACILITATORS This module works best with groups that are largely unfamiliar with L/G/B/T issues, but who may have more familiarity with immigrant rights issues. However, portions of this module, such as "Xenophobia, Homophobia, and More," and "Looking At Our Stories: Testimonies of LGBT Immigrants" could be useful for L/G/B/T audiences not as familiar with immigrant rights issues. This module can be used with the other sections of the BRIDGE curricula or as a stand-alone module.

immigrant rights and LGBT rights

Backgrounder: Challenges Faced by LGBT Immigrants

Lesbian, gay, bisexual, and transgendered immigrants living in the U.S. face many levels of discrimination, including xenophobia, racism, homophobia, and sexism. Many obstacles exist even before an immigrant arrives in the United States. Although laws that banned lesbian and gay immigrants were officially repealed in 1990, LGBT immigrants still face substantial difficulties in obtaining legal immigration status. For example, current immigration policy only recognizes "direct family ties" as heterosexual. Same-sex partners are therefore denied such immigration privileges. Transsexual immigrants may not be able to have gender changed on official documents from his/her country, resulting in enormous, sometimes insurmountable, difficulties with the INS.

Lesbians and gay men have also historically experienced great difficulties in gaining political asylum. In 1994, lesbians and gay men were finally recognized as a social group for purposes of applying for political asylum. Poor LGBTs are particularly likely to be dismissed simply as "economic migrants," while those from countries with whom the US has a friendly relation are often denied asylum for foreign-policy reasons. Few transgender people have ever been awarded asylum, because gender and sexual orientation persecution often operates in ways that are difficult to document.

The continued ban on the immigration of HIV positive individuals also affects LGBT immigrants. Though HIV is not strictly a LGBT issue, it remains of great concern, because the current ban on HIV positive immigrants reinforces multiple forms of inequality that affect LGBT communities. Individuals are excludable if they are HIV+, and "ironically" HIV testing is required for all applicants for permanent residency. Individuals can still apply for political persecution based on HIV-related discrimination in their home countries.

LGBT people who succeed in migrating face constraints within the US because of their immigration status. They may remain vulnerable to deportation until becoming naturalized citizens. Although being lesbian or gay is no longer officially a ground for denial of citizenship or for deportation, immigration officials may search for other permissible reasons - such as "lack of good moral character" - to exclude, deport, or deny citizenship to immigrants who are not heterosexual or do not conform to gender norms. Legal immigrants certainly face constraints, but undocumented LGBT immigrants confront even more draining and multiple forms of disenfranchisement. Lacking secure access to such basics as work, housing, and health care, as well as increased discrimination and social isolation, they are also constantly vulnerable to exploitation, violence, and deportation.

immigrant rights and LGBT rights

module 5

SUMMARY POINTS

- Like all immigrants, gay and lesbians, including LGBT immigrants, have faced oppression just for being who they are.
- Gay and lesbian immigrants have faced discrimination based on sexual orientation, as well as other immigration-related factors.
- Immigration policy has a profound impact on:
  - Undocumented immigrants who are more vulnerable to exploitation if they are not heterosexual
  - Immigrants seeking political asylum based on sexual orientation
  - Anyone who may be HIV positive
  - U.S. citizens and immigrants who are part of a binational couple
  - Transgender immigrants who may face harassment
  - Any gay or lesbian immigrant dependent on their employer or family for immigration status

WORKSHOP MENU

Activity:	Time:
Welcome, workshop orientation	10 minutes
Opening: Our Shared Circle	15 minutes
Review Objectives/Ground Rules	15 minutes
*Act Like A Lady, Act Like A Man	45 minutes
Who's In, Who's Out?	30 minutes
Xenophobia, Homophobia, and More...	30 minutes
*Looking At Our Stories: Testimonies of LGBT Immigrants	40 minutes
Closing: Head, Heart, Feet	15 minutes

*core exercises

Total Time: 3 hours and 20 minutes

Tips for Facilitators

Using the LGBT and Immigrant Rights Module: A Few Words for Facilitators

Out of all the BRIDGE modules, we've found that facilitators face more challenges using this module. Many facilitators in immigrant rights work have less experience in discussing LGBT issues, and some organizations may not view LGBT issues as valid or important. The discussion of LGBT rights is limited in the immigrant rights movement, and we encourage facilitators to use this tool as widely as possible. Here are a few things to keep in mind for this module:

- Be sure to set the tone for a respectful space for the trust and participation of all. A good opening is particularly important, with focus on icebreakers and ground rules.
- Take into account the diversity of participants and range of feelings about LGBT issues, but make it clear that you, as the facilitator, are an ally to gay and lesbian issues.
- Frame this workshop as a serious issue. There is room for laughter in all education processes, but participants may deal with their own discomfort and cause disruption by laughing, or making inappropriate jokes. This is a teaching opportunity—you can address these moments by revisiting the ground rules, by emphasizing that homophobia is a form of oppression, or by explaining the effects of such homophobia—such as the incidence of hate crimes against LGBT people.
- Make sure LGBT folks who are participants are not singled out as token "representatives," where they have the burden of educating the whole group about LGBT issues, or their personal experience as a LGBT person. Rather, it is the group's responsibility as a whole to participate in the learning experience.
- If possible, gather information to gauge the group's experience in dealing with LGBT issues before you facilitate this workshop. For example, has the group had any prior workshops on LGBT issues, or is this the first formal discussion on the topic? What is the motivation to cover this subject? This information will help you gauge if you need to do some work with the group prior to some of the activities in this module, such as discussing common definitions like "lesbian," "gay," etc. with the group. (A fact sheet with definitions is provided at the end of the module.)
- Consider the possibility of holding this workshop with only non-LGBT identified participants. This can avoid the risk of endangering the safety of LGBT community members, and also ensure that you don't unfairly place a burden on LGBT community members to educate the whole group. One way to determine if you should do so is to ask LGBT community members if they are wiling to

attend as you are planning the workshop.
- Consider adapting small group discussions to large group discussions, particularly in a group where small group discussions without facilitation could create an unsafe environment for participants.
- This workshop deals most directly with issues of homophobia and heterosexism, and less with transphobia. If don't have experience with these issues and if you want to focus a training on transgender issues, it may be helpful to gain outside training or contact a local resource before raising the discussion with your organization.
- Address people's homophobia when it happens: don't let it derail the whole process. Anticipate ways to quickly defuse homophobic comments. You may want to include some of these phrases in your introduction:
  - We may have strong feelings because of our religious beliefs or our upbringing, but in this space it's important that we are respectful of each other.
  - We're all learning about assumptions we've take for granted all our lives. For example, just last week I learned that (example of something you've learned recently)
  - While we have the right to disagree another's opinions and beliefs, we need to respect these differences. We may not discriminate against, or be violent with, another person just because they are different than we are.
  - Acknowledge that stereotypes are a reality of our lives, but today perhaps we can dispel a few of them and look at how people who are not heterosexual in our own immigrant communities face particular challenges and prejudice.
  - Like other systems of oppression, such as racism and sexism, homophobia and heterosexism is a force that hurts people just for who they are.

immigrant rights and LGBT rights

Opening: Our Shared Circle

WHY DO IT?
- To use as an icebreaker, establish trust, and to get people moving
- To demonstrate to the group that there are shared values in the room

TIME 15 minutes

MATERIALS NEEDED none

DIRECTIONS
1. Form a large circle, with all participants standing inwards.
2. Go around the circle, and ask participants to quickly state their name and organization.
3. Explain to the group that they will be doing a quick activity to learn about each other. Explain that you will be reading a list of statements to the group. If the statement applies to them, they should step into the circle until the next statement is read. If the statement doesn't apply to them, they should remain in place.

Here is a sample list of statements (statements should go from more light hearted ones to more reflective statements, with the final statement something that everyone can agree with):
- I love chocolate.
- I am wearing glasses.
- I have a pet.
- I have a white shirt on.
- I have moved from one place to another in my life.
- I was born in another country.
- I have family that lives in another country.
- I can speak more than one language.
- I have worked at a minimum wage job.
- I have faced some kind of discrimination because someone had a negative idea about who I am.
- I believe that my rights, just like everyone else's, should be respected.

SOURCE the authors

immigrant rights and LGBT rights   module 5

Act Like A Lady, Act Like a Man

WHY DO IT?
- To talk about how messages about gender and sexual orientation are shaped very early on in our lives from our society, cultures, families, and communities.
- To discuss the meaning of stereotypes, and how they take power away from groups of people.
- To discuss how people who don't fit inside society's expectations of gender and sexuality--what it means to be an "acceptable" man or woman, are stereotyped.

TIME 45 minutes

MATERIALS NEEDED
- Copies of "women and men" handout (looks like the signs on restrooms) for each participant
- easel paper, markers, tape
- sticky notes, basket

FACILITATOR PREP
- Draw an outline of a large figure in a dress and the words "Act like a lady" on one piece of easel paper, and an outline of a figure in pants and the words "Act like a man" on another.

DIRECTIONS
1. Introduce the exercise by explaining that we will be looking at how messages from our society, cultures and families shape our understanding of sexual orientation and gender. From the time we are children, we pick up certain messages about what it means to "act like a lady," or "act like a man."
2. Pass out the "women and men" handout (looks like the signs on restrooms) to each participant. What messages have we heard about what it means to act like a proper lady or a proper man? Ask participants to write these messages on their handouts—messages for ladies in the figure that is wearing a dress, and messages for men in the figure that is wearing pants. (5-10 minutes)

Some examples we've heard:

ACT LIKE A LADY	ACT LIKE A MAN
Wear a dress	Wear pants
Stay home and take care of family	Work outside the house
Emotional	Not Emotional, except anger
Learn to cook	Play sports

national network for immigrant and refugee rights | 193

immigrant rights and LGBT rights

3. Go around the room, and ask each participant to name one statement they wrote on what it means to "Act like a lady." Write each statement on the easel paper.

4. Go around the room once again, and ask each participant to name one statement they wrote on what it means to "Act like a man." Write each statement on the easel paper.

5. Briefly discuss the statements on the paper with the group. Are there any other statements not on the paper?

6. Pass out two sticky notes to each participant, and put the basket in the middle of the room. Ask the group to think about the statements on the easel paper. What are women called when they don't fit into these stereotypes? What are men called when they don't fit into these stereotypes? Ask participants to write down one word for women and one word for men on a sticky note, and put it in the basket.

7. Write "Harmful Words and Stereotypes" at the top of a piece of easel paper. After all participants have put their notes in the basket, pass around the basket and ask each person to take out two notes. Go around the room and ask each person to read the words on their sticky note, and to put it up on the easel paper. (Some examples of words we have heard include: "fag," "pansy," "dyke," "maricón," "tomboy," "butch," etc.)

8. After the group has read the words, process the activity. Ask:
   - How did you feel when we went around and read the words?
   - What do these words have in common?
   - What are the effects of these words on people?
   - What is the purpose of these words in larger society?
   - Think back to the original statements we wrote about what it means to be a "proper lady" or a "proper man." Are there any ways you don't fit into the statements?

After the group has discussed these questions, review the teaching points.

TEACHING POINTS

- Stereotypes of what it means to "act like a woman" or "act like a man" hurt everyone, and they keeps everybody from being who they fully are.
- Men and women who don't seem to fit in the "act like a woman" or "act like a man" category are often stigmatized as being gay or lesbian, even if they may not be.
- People who are gay or lesbian may or may not fit the "act like a lady" or "act like a man" expectations. Some lesbians wear dresses, some gay men play sports. There is not one way to "tell" if someone is gay or lesbian based on these columns.

immigrant rights and LGBT rights   module 5

- Transgendered people may not fit into the "act like a lady" or "act like a man" categories, and they may not consider themselves gay or lesbian either.
- Many of these words represent stereotypes about gender and sexual orientation in our society. A stereotype is a generalization used to characterize a whole group of people. This generalization is usually negative and is used to take power away from that group.
- Just as stereotypes about women can be used to take power away from women, or people of color, stereotypes about sexual minorities are used to take power away from them.

CHALLENGES

- Some parts of this exercise, particularly the part where participants read the stereotypes out loud may cause some discomfort for participants, who may react in several ways—by cracking jokes, laughing, exchanging looks, etc. You may want to preclude this by reminding the group that the topic is a serious issue, and that stereotypes are hurtful and no laughing matter.

SOURCE authors, developed with Moira Bowman, Western States Center

E. Cho

handout

Insert Act like a Lady, Act Like a Man

In this exercise, we will be thinking about the messages we have heard about what it means to be a "proper lady" or a "proper man."

In the figures below, write down the messages you have heard about what it means to be a "proper lady" in the figure wearing a dress, and the messages you have heard about what it means to be a "proper man" in the figure wearing pants.

BRIDGE: Building a Race and Immigration Dialogue in the Global Economy
www.nnirr.org

module **5**

immigrant rights and LGBT rights

Who's In, Who's Out?

WHY DO IT?
- To illustrate the need for solidarity between people regardless of differences
- To give examples of why a struggle for human dignity means that no one should be left behind
- To begin exploring how immigrant rights organizations can work in solidarity with LGBT people
- To energize the group with a physical and fun activity

TIME 30 minutes

MATERIALS NEEDED none

FACILITATOR PREP Facilitator Prep:
- Review (and even rehearse) the theatrical "raids" scenario ahead of time
- This activity works best with a co-facilitator to model the activity, and to assist in some of the scenarios.

DIRECTIONS
1. Ask participants to stand up together in an open space in the classroom. Explain that we will use this theatrical exercise to explore the need to build solidarity with different groups of people.
2. Ask participants to act as if they are working in a factory (choose one that works with the context of your group: i.e. garment factory, assembly line, etc.)
3. Announce to your group, in a quick and excited voice:

   "Quick! There's been an immigration raid in our workplace! Quick!
   Everyone hide!"

   Wait until everyone has hidden—behind chairs, tables, other furniture in the room. Then announce:

   "Oh, no! They have arrested us all. Now they are putting us in their vans
   in groups of five. Quick, everyone get into a group of five."

   Wait until everyone has gotten into a group of five (there may be some odd numbers, which is fine), and announce:

   "Unfortunately, everyone in our factory was deported because we had not
   been organized."

national network for immigrant and refugee rights
www.nnirr.org

immigrant rights and LGBT rights

4. Announce to your group:

> "Now, we will pretend we are in another factory down the street from the last factory. We are all hard at work, especially because we heard about what happened in the other factory."

Wait until all of the participants are pantomiming their work. Then, announce to the group:

> "Oh, no! There's an immigration raid in this factory, too! Quick, everybody hide! Be very quiet!"

Wait until everyone has hidden—behind chairs, tables, other furniture in the room. Then announce:

> "Oh, no! They have arrested us all. Now they are putting us in their vans in groups of three. Quick, everyone get into a group of three."

Wait until everyone has gotten into a group of three (there may be some odd numbers, which is fine), and announce:

> "Now we are all in the detention center. Wait—do you hear the chanting outside? It sounds like—I think there is a crowd outside telling Immigration to let us out! Wait—it looks like the community groups, churches, and unions have worked together to get us out! Ok, they are letting us go!"

5. Ask the group to stand still, and close their eyes. Read the following monologue aloud, in a slower and quieter tone:

> "Imagine that we are all back to work in the factory. Thanks to the great organizing of our community, we've even got a raise. We can finally pay our bills, and more. Now imagine that immigration officers have come back to our factory. They are raiding our factory again, and putting us all into buses. They are putting us into detention cells–it is cold, and people are scared. But wait—the door opens, and the officer is letting all of us go—except three of your friends. You have been let go because your husband or wife is a U.S. citizen, or your son petitioned for you. You ask the officer why they are not letting your friends go—it turns out that they are deported because they don't have the same protections because they are gay and lesbian."

Wait for a few moments, and then ask participants to open their eyes.

immigrant rights and LGBT rights

6. Process the activity with the group. Ask:
   - How did this exercise make you feel? What did you notice?
   - How did this exercise relate to the experience of your community?
   - How did organizing strengthen you?
   - What would you do in the last situation?

VARIATION As an added step, you may want to ask participants to do a quick role play. Ask participants to imagine a homophobic incident, or any other type of discriminatory incident. What would you say? What would you do?

SOURCE the authors

E. Cho

immigrant rights and LGBT rights

Homophobia, Xenophobia, and More...

WHY DO IT?
- To introduce participants to the concepts of homophobia, transphobia, sexism, and xenophobia and how they intersect
- To explore some history about immigration policy's impact on lesbian, gay, bisexual, and transgendered people

TIME 30 minutes

MATERIALS NEEDED
- A copy of "Moments in LGBT History" handout, cut into five slips (one for each example)
- Easel paper, markers, tape

DIRECTIONS

1. Explain to the group that we will be revisiting some themes raised in previous activities. Write the following words on separate sheets of easel paper: *xenophobia, sexism, homophobia, transphobia*.

2. Ask participants to help define each word. Offer these common definitions for each word:

    Xenophobia: *fear or hatred of foreigners or immigrants*
    Sexism: *discrimination, stereotypes, and actions used to take power away from women*
    Homophobia: *discrimination, stereotypes, and actions used to take power away from lesbians, gays, and bisexuals*
    Transphobia: *discrimination and stereotypes used to take power away from people whose gender identity may not match their biological body*

3. Explain to the group that we will be looking at a few moments in immigration history. Pass out the four examples in the "Moments in LGBT Immigration History" handout to four participants at random.

4. Ask these four participants to read each of their slips aloud. After each of the four facts is read, ask the group to think about and discuss the example. How is the example a case of xenophobia? How is it a case of sexism? Homophobia? Transphobia? How are these forms of oppression linked to each other? How has immigration policy over the years affected LGBT immigrants?

CHALLENGES
- Keep a focus on a group dialogue, to ensure that it doesn't turn into a dialogue where LGBT participants have to educate heterosexuals in the room

SOURCE authors, developed with Moira Bowman, Western States Center

handout

Moments in LGBT Immigration History

1. In 1875, Congress passed the *Page Law*, the first immigration law that prohibited immigrants considered to be undesirable—including convicts, contract laborers, and specifically, Asian women thought to be prostitutes. Immigration officials focused most of their efforts on keeping Chinese women from immigrating to the U.S., saying those who didn't have the protection of a man "might become a prostitute."

2. In 1917, Congress passed the *Immigration Act of 1917*, which required all immigrants to pass a literacy test. The test was designed to keep large numbers of southern and eastern Europeans out of the U.S., because they were not considered "ideal Americans." The *Immigration Act of 1917* also banned "Psychopaths, Inferiors, and 'people with abnormal sexual instincts'" from coming to the U.S. Lesbian and gay immigrants were officially excluded from coming to the U.S. until 1990.

3. In 1969, police raided a gay bar in New York called the Stonewall Inn. The Stonewall Riots that happened on the night of the raid marked a new phase in the LGBT liberation movement. One of the customers at the Stonewall Inn that night, however, was an immigrant man who later committed suicide rather than be deported for being gay. If people didn't admit that they were gay when they entered the U.S., but were later caught by the INS, they could be deported for perjury - lying to cover up their sexuality.

4. The Border Patrol often used stereotypes to decide who was gay or lesbian. If a Border Patrol agent suspected an immigrant of being gay or lesbian, they could either immediately exclude them or send them to a psychiatrist for a deportation hearing. For example, in 1979, two Mexican men were detained for carrying cosmetics in their luggage.

SOURCE

Eithne Luibheid, *Entry Denied: Controlling Sexuality At the Border*, 2002, and Bill Ong Hing, *Defining America Through Immigration Policy*, 2004.

immigrant rights and LGBT rights

Making the Stories Fit: Testimonies of LGBT Immigrants

WHY DO IT?
- To examine some specific cases of challenges faced by current LGBT immigrants
- To discuss ways that the immigrant rights movement can better support the rights of LGBT people

TIME 40 minutes

MATERIALS NEEDED
- Copies of small group handouts for participants (note: there are five sets of testimonies)

DIRECTIONS

1. Divide the participants into five small groups. Give each small group a testimony to read and discuss.
2. Small groups will read and discuss the testimony of a LGBT immigrant. (20 minutes)
3. Reconvene the small groups, and ask each group to briefly give a summary of their group's story, and to name three ways that immigrant rights groups can better support the rights of LGBT people.

TEACHING POINTS

Immigration policy has a profound impact on:
- Undocumented immigrants who are more vulnerable to exploitation if they are not heterosexual
- Immigrants seeking political asylum based on sexual orientation
- Anyone who may be HIV+
- U.S. citizens and immigrants who are part of a binational couple
- Transgender immigrants who may face harassment
- Any gay or lesbian immigrant dependent on their employer or family for immigration status

VARIATION Consider discussing one or two of the testimonies in a large group setting, particularly in a group where small group discussions without facilitation could create an unsafe environment for participants.

SOURCE the authors

handout

testimonies

Sushmila's Story

Sushmila is a 23-year old immigrant from India who came to the U.S. on an H1-B* visa three years ago. She works in a computer software company. She is a lesbian and she is in a relationship with another woman, but nobody at work knows it.

Sushmila usually gets to work at 7:30 in the morning and leaves at 9 or 10 at night. When she got hired, her employer agreed to put in an application to sponsor her green card. She feels she has to work extra hard to make sure her employer is impressed enough to keep her on. Her boss knows it, too. He often gives her extra assignments and has never offered to pay her for overtime. Sushmila is afraid to even ask about taking a vacation, because she doesn't want her boss to think she is a complainer and not file for her green card.

Sushmila is afraid of her boss for other reasons. He is always making jokes about gay people, and once she heard him call gay men "sick and perverted." One night when she was working late, he made sexual advances towards her. Sushmila politely told him she had a lot of work to do, but he keeps harassing her.

One day, some of Sushmila's friends invited her to a Gay Pride parade. She decided to go, but later regretted it. She and her friends appeared on the 6 o'clock news as part of the parade. Sushmila felt sick to her stomach. What if her boss watched the news that night and found out she was a lesbian?

Work is the only way Sushmila can get a green card. Even though her father became a permanent resident before she was 21, he refused to sponsor her unless she agreed to marry a man from India. Her parents stopped talking to her when they found out she was a lesbian.

Discuss with your group:
   What are the immigration policies that impacted Sushmila?
   How would Sushmila's story been different if she were not a lesbian?
   What did you relate to in Sushmila's story?
   What are some ways that the immigrant rights movement can better support the rights of LGBT people?

* A H1-B visa allows immigrants with special skills, such as "high tech" or computer skills to live and work in the U.S. Employers, not immigrants themselves, apply for H1-B visas, and if an immigrant loses their job, they also lose their visa.

handout

testimonies

Yelena's Story

Yelena is a 43-year old immigrant woman from Russia who worked in a factory outside of Moscow. She is a lesbian and was first involved in gay and lesbian organizations in her home country. When she came to the U.S., she applied for asylum based on her "political opinion," but she didn't put in the application that one of the reasons she was afraid of the Russian government was because she was a lesbian. In fact, she was afraid to tell immigration officials that she was a lesbian, because she thought they might think she was a bad person or deport her based on that. Even so, her application was denied and she was put in deportation proceedings.

Then Yelena found out that immigration officials had granted asylum to some gay and lesbian immigrants like her who feared persecution BECAUSE of their sexual orientation. When she went before the judge, she told him that she was involved in gay organizations, that she had been targeted by the Russian mafia, and that when she went to get help from the police, they forced her into a mental institution.

Immigration officials fought her case, saying that Russia no longer had problems with human rights violations, and that the Russian government was just trying to treat what it thought was a mental illness, not necessarily prosecute her based on race or religion. The judged ruled against Yelena.

Several hundred gay and lesbian immigrants have won asylum based on sexual orientation. But most of those who have won their cases have been able to provide concrete evidence of persecution of gay people in their home country. Gay men have won most asylum cases because lesbians often can't provide this kind of documentation. When they are punished or targeted by the police, it is often recorded as "violence against women" or not recorded at all. It is hard to document some of the physical and sexual violence that lesbians face, because it sometimes comes from within their own families.

Yelena thinks she lost her case because she couldn't afford a fancy lawyer to help get police records and documents from Russia. She also thinks the INS might have approved her case if she were, say, a doctor rather than a factory worker.

Discuss with your group:

What are the immigration policies that impacted Yelena?
How would Yelena's story been different if she were not a lesbian?
What did you relate to in Yelena's story?
What are some ways that the immigrant rights movement can better support the rights of LGBT people?

testimonies

José's Story

José was arrested in a workplace raid at a factory in New Jersey. When the INS arrested him, he had been in the U.S. for seven years.

In El Salvador, Jose had been abused and teased by others and was attacked several times because he was gay. In one case, the attacker was a police officer. José was rejected by his family and had moved away from his hometown to get away from family members who had threatened to kill him when they found out he was gay. In the cities, José experienced raids on gay bars, where gay people are arrested and jailed simply because of their sexual orientation.

Eventually José came to work in the U.S. as an undocumented immigrant. He had hoped that life for a gay man would be easier in the U.S., and like many immigrants, he hoped to earn good money. Instead, he found himself working long hours in a factory with a boss that threatened to call the INS if the workers ever complained. One day, the INS did show up, and took Jose and other undocumented workers to a detention center.

Before José was arrested, he had learned that he was HIV positive. Not only did he potentially have a life-threatening disease, but he knew that the U.S. has banned anyone who is HIV positive from legally immigrating. The only way to get a waiver for this is if you are a spouse or unmarried child of a U.S. citizen or permanent resident. José had no family in the U.S., except his Mexican boyfriend, Manuel. José's family in Honduras wouldn't speak to him. Now he was sick and would probably be deported back to Honduras, where he would face danger from police and have no one to care for him.

José had a very good attorney, who told him something amazing. Even though the U.S. bans anyone who is HIV+ from entering the country, once you are here, you can apply for asylum based on the fact that you are HIV+. Even though it didn't make any sense to José, he decided to give it a try. But then his lawyer told him the bad news: in order to apply for asylum, you have to do it within one year of entering the U.S. But José had been in the U.S. seven years. He was stuck.

But José was lucky. In 1998, a judge made a special exception to José filing late. The judge ruled that José didn't know he could apply for asylum within one year, and that he was afraid to tell anyone--including a lawyer or an immigration official--about his sexual orientation or his HIV status. The judge also said that the persecution of people with HIV in Honduras, as well as the persecution of gay men, made his claim for asylum a strong one. But José's case is exceptional. Most judges would not have given him a second chance.

handout

jose's testimonies

Discuss with your group:
- What are the immigration policies that impacted José?
- How would José's story been different if he were not a gay man? If he were not HIV+?
- What did you relate to in José's story?
- What are some ways that the immigrant rights movement can better support the rights of LGBT people?

Note: José's story is based on a true story account in the Fall 1998 Newsletter of the Lesbian and Gay Immigration Rights Task Force.

handout

testimonies

Carmen's story

Carmen is a 35-year-old transsexual woman from Mexico. From a very young age, she knew that she was a girl, not a boy, even though she was born into a male body. For her whole life, she faced discrimination and abuse from people in her family, neighborhood, school, and work. At the age of 30, she began to undergo hormone therapy to transition into a female body. That year, she was beaten so badly by a group of men on the street that she had to spend 20 days in the hospital.

After the attack, Carmen decided to immigrate to the United States because she thought that it would be safer, even though she didn't have papers. Once she arrived in the U.S., however, she was picked up during an immigration raid and put into a detention center. Her problems in the detention center began almost immediately. While she was well into a medical process to become a woman, she was placed in the men's quarters, where she faced harassment by guards and other detainees.

Shortly after, Carmen was transferred out of the men's dormitory to an isolation unit, where she was detained by herself. However, her guard forced her to undress in front of him, and he beat and raped her while she tried to defend herself. She reported it to the authorities of the detention center, and was sent to the clinic. A week later, the same guard snuck into the clinic and raped her once again. Then immigration officials told Carmen that she could either be put into a mental institution, a prison, or deported back to Mexico.

Carmen, however, was luckier this time. An investigation of the detention center stopped her deportation. She was later able to sue the detention center, and the guard who attacked her was convicted of sexual assault. After her lawsuit, many other women at the detention center came forward and told their own stories about assault and abuse from guards.

Discuss with your group:
What are the immigration policies that impacted Carmen?
How would Carmen's story been different if she were not transsexual?
What could you relate to in Carmen's story?
What are some ways that the immigrant rights movement can better support the rights of LGBT people?

Note: Carmen's account is based on a true story, reported in a report by the Women's Commission for Refugee Women and Children, "Behind Locked Doors: Abuse of Refugee Women in the Krome Detention Center," October 2000.

testimonies

Alfred and Brian's Story

Alfred is an immigrant from China. Brian was born and raised in the U.S. They met through friends and began a relationship six years ago. They have both agreed that they want to be life partners, but as gay men they cannot have a legally recognized marriage.

Alfred is undocumented, and wants to be able to stay in the U.S. so he can be with Brian. They live together, have two dogs and a cat, and have a network of friends that are like a family. But with each new law that gets passed against immigrants, Alfred and Brian are getting very nervous. Alfred works in a restaurant where he is paid in cash. But if he loses his job, he may not be able to find another one that pays as well since he doesn't have a green card.

Alfred and Brian sat down to talk about their options. "Why don't we move to China?," Brian said. Alfred said, "Are you crazy? My parents don't know I'm gay. They have a wife picked out for me back home. I can't bring you back with me. We can't live there and openly have a relationship."

Another option was for Alfred to go back to China. But that would mean breaking up, and neither of them wanted to do that. They talked about trying to find a woman that Alfred could marry so he could get his green card. But if the INS ever found out Alfred was gay, he could be fined, jailed, and deported for life. And the woman would be punished too. Besides, Alfred couldn't imagine pretending to be married to someone else when he loves Brian. He would have to pretend he was someone he wasn't, and he certainly couldn't go to gay events anymore. What if the INS recognized him and realized his marriage was a fake?

Alfred and Brian were stuck. They loved each other, but their love couldn't help them get a green card.

Discuss with your group:

What are the immigration policies that impacted Brian and Alfred?
How would this story have been different if Brian and Alfred could get married?
What could you relate to in Brian and Alfred's story?
What are some ways that the immigrant rights movement can better support the rights of LGBT people?

immigrant rights and LGBT rights

module 5

Closing: Head, Heart Feet

WHY DO IT?
- To close out the day's activities
- To evaluate the day's activities

TIME 15-30 minutes

MATERIALS NEEDED
- Easel paper, markers, tape
- Pens for all participants
- Small strips of paper and tape or sticky notes

DIRECTIONS

1. Ask a participant draw the image of a person as big as possible on a piece of easel paper, with emphasis on the head, heart, and feet. This time, this person is a reflection of the group, and it has feelings, organs, and emotions. It's not just a doll full of stereotypes!

2. Hand out three slips of paper or sticky notes to each participant.

3. Ask participants to identify three things: a new idea, a feeling, and one idea for action that they gained from the workshop, and to write it each on a slip of paper/sticky note. It could be expressed in words, as a headline, or as a drawing.

   a. One note should reflect something they thought=head
   b. One note should reflect something they felt=heart
   c. One note should reflect something they plan to do=feet

4. Ask participants, one at a time, to select one of their three strips of paper and put it on the corresponding part of the paper person. If time permits, or it's a small group, you could ask them to share all three.

VARIATIONS

You can ask participants to draw their own head, heart, and feet on a piece of paper, and record new ideas they learned on the head, new feelings on the heart, and new action ideas or skills on the feet. They can then tell the group about one of the things they've learned and they can hand in their drawings/evaluations or post them on the wall as they share so there's a "people quilt" at the end of the evaluation.

SOURCE adapted with permission from *Education for Changing Unions*, by Bev Burke, Jojo Geronimo, D'Arcy Martin, Barb Thomas, and Carol Wall, with Marsh Sfeir.

BRIDGE Fact Sheet

Glossary of Terms: LGBT and Immigrant Rights*

Bisexual: People who form primary loving and sexual relationships with both men and women. Many people avoid this term because of its implication that there are only two sexes/genders to be sexually attracted to and thus reinforces the binary gender system.

Biphobia: The fear, hatred, distrust of bisexual people and their ability to have sexual, emotional, and spiritual relationships with someone of any sex.

Gay: Someone who is primarily and/or exclusively attracted to members of their own sex or gender. In certain contexts, this term is used to refer only to those who identify as men.

Gender: Cultural and societal understandings of what "maleness" or "femaleness" means (as opposed to sex, the biological or physical identification of male or female)

Gender identity: How we see ourselves—some of us as women, as men, or some as a combination of both, or some as neither.

Heterosexual/Straight Person: A person who is primarily and/or exclusively attracted to members of a gender or sex which is seen to be "opposite" or other than the one with which they identify or are identified.

Heterosexism: The societal/ cultural, institutional, and individual beliefs and practices that assume hetrosexuality is the only natural, normal, acceptable sexual identity

Homophobia: The fear, hatred or intolerance of gays, lesbians, or queer-identified people in general. This can be manifested as an intense dislike or rejection of such people, or violent actions against them.

Homosexual: A person who is primarily and/or exclusively attracted to members of what they identify as their own sex or gender. Because the term can have connotations of disease and abnormality, some people do not like to identify as homosexual. Others do not feel that it accurately defines their chosen identity.

Intersex: An anatomical variation from typical understandings of male and female genetics. The physical manifestation, at birth, of genetic or endocrinological differences from the cultural norm. Also a group of medical conditions that challenge standard sex designations, proving that sex, like gender, is a social construct. Intersex and transgender folks share some overlapping experiences and perspectives, but the terms are not synonymous, and the issues are not the same. "Intersex" or "intersexual" is used today in favor of the term "hermaphrodite".

Lesbian: Women who form primary loving and sexual relationships with other women. Some women may also use the term "gay" to describe themselves.

LGBT: Lesbian, Gay, Bisexual, and Transgender. Also seen as: GLBT, GLT, etc.

BRIDGE Fact Sheet

Sex: Refers to a person's biological identity as male or female (as opposed to "gender," which speaks to cultural and societal understandings of maleness or femaleness)

Transgender: This term has many definitions. It is frequently used as an umbrella term to refer to all people who deviate from their assigned gender or the binary gender system, including intersex people, transsexuals, cross-dressers, transvestites, gender queers, drag kings, drag queens, two-spirit people, and others. Some transgendered people feel they exist not within one of the two standard gender categories, but rather somewhere between, beyond, or outside of those two genders. The term can also be applied exclusively to people who live primarily as the gender "opposite" to that which they were assigned at birth. These people may sometimes prefer the term "transsexual".

Transphobia: A reaction of fear, loathing and discriminatory treatment of people whose gender identity or gender presentation (or perceived gender or gender identity) does not match, in a socially accepted way, the sex they were assigned at birth. Transgendered people, intersexuals, lesbians, gay men & bisexuals are typically the targets of transphobia.

Transsexual: People whose sense of themselves as male or female is different from their birth or biological sex. Sometimes transsexual people hormonally and/or surgically change their bodies to more fully match their gender identity.

Queer: An umbrella identity term encompassing lesbians, questioning people, gay men, bisexuals, non-labeling people, transgendered folks, and anyone else who does not strictly identify as heterosexual. "Queer" originated as a derogatory word. Currently, it is being reclaimed by some people and used as a statement of empowerment. Some people identify as queer to distance themselves from the rigid categorizations of "straight" and "gay". Some transgendered, lesbian, gay, questioning, non-labeling, and bisexual people, however, reject the use of this term due its connotations of deviance and its tendency to gloss over and sometimes deny the differences between these groups.

Xenophobia: Literally, a fear or hatred of strangers, and this term is usually used to refer to fear or hatred of immigrants and foreigners.

* These are common understandings of these words, but are working definitions, as political movements change their vocabulary with changes in political circumstances and growing awareness.

BRIDGE Fact Sheet

Historical Exclusion of LGBT Immigrants to the United States

1875 Page Law ends the arrival of Chinese women immigrants based on the fear that Asian immigrants would begin to form families in the U.S.

1920 "Ladies Agreement" ends the arrival of Japanese and Korean picture brides. European women are also affected—they were banned from entry if they could not show that either a man or a job was available.

1917 Entry of "constitutional psychopathic inferiors" were banned

1918 Manual for the Mental Examination of Aliens explained "constitutional psychopathic inferiors" as:

"the moral imbeciles, the pathological liars and swindlers, the defective delinquents, many of the vagrants and cranks, and persons with abnormal sexual instincts"

1950 Gays become the target of a Congressional Subcommittee on immigration, which recommended that "classes of mental defectives (who are excludable) should be enlarged to include homosexuals and other sex perverts.

1965 Immigration and Nationality Act significantly altered eligibility to enter the United States. The act stressed family reunification and awarded _ of immigration slots to relatives. "Family" is based on strictly heterosexual and nuclear ties. Law explicitly bans lesbians and gays as "sexual deviates."

1969 Stonewall Riots, which marked a new phase in the LGBT liberation movement, take place in New York City, where gays fight off police during a raid on the Stonewall Inn. One of the customers at Stonewall Inn on the night of the raid is an immigrant man who committed suicide rather than be deported for being gay.

1974 The American Psychiatric Association ruled against classifying homosexuality as a mental illness.

1979 Two Mexican nationals who were suspected of being homosexuals are detained because cosmetics are found in their luggage.

1980 INS announces new policy on homosexuality: If an immigrant admitted that s/he was homosexual to an INS inspector, s/he is excluded from entering the U.S. If a homosexual person denied that s/he was homosexual, but was later found out, s/he could be deported for perjury (lying under oath).

1990 Congress lifts blanket exclusion of gays and lesbians.

1993 Congress places ban on immigrants who are HIV+.

1994 Gays and lesbians qualify as a particular social group for purposes of US asylum law.

SOURCE Eithne Luibheid, "Entry Denied: Controlling Sexuality at the Border," University of Minnesota Press, 2002.

immigrant rights and LGBT rights module 5

Resources

Organizations:

Al-Fatiha Foundation: foundation for LGBT Muslims. www.al-fatiha.org. PO Box 33532, Washington DC, 20033. 202-319-0898

Audre Lorde Project: Center for Lesbian, Gay, Bisexual, Two Spirit and Transgender People of Color Communities. www.alp.org. 85 South Oxford Street, Brooklyn, NY 11217-1607. Telephone: (718) 596-0342

International Gay and Lesbian Human Rights Commission. www.iglhrc.org. 1375 Sutter Street, Suite 222, San Francisco, CA 94109, 415-561-0633.

Lesbian and Gay Immigration Rights Task Force. www.lgirtf.org. 350 W. 31st St. Suite 505, New York, NY, 10001. 212-714-2904.

LLEGÓ (LATINO/A LESBIAN & GAY ORGANIZATION) www.llego.org. 1420 K Street, NW Suite 200, Washington, DC 20005, 202.408.5380

SALGA: South Asian Lesbian and Gay Association, www.salganyc.org. PO Box 1491, Old Chelsea Station, New York, NY 10113. Tel: 212-358-5132.

Trikone: LGBT people of South Asian descent. www.trikone.org. PO Box 14161, San Francisco, CA 94414/ 415-487-8778.

Publications:

Sasha Khokha and Eithne Luibheid, "Xenophobia and Homophobia: Lesbian, Gay, Bisexual, and Transgendered Immigrants in the U.S.," *From the Borderline to the Colorline: A Report on Anti-Immigrant Racism in the U.S.*, NNIRR, 2001.

Kumashiro, Kevin. *Troubling Education: Queer Activism and Anti-Oppressive Pedagogy*. Routledge Palmer Press, 2002.

Luibheid, Eithne. *Entry Denied: Controlling Sexuality at the Border*, University of Minnesota Press, 2002.

immigrant women's leadership

immigrant women's leadership

module 6

OVERVIEW

The goals of this workshop are to:
- Discuss immigration policy's specific impact on women
- Honor important women in our lives
- Explore how migration has changed women's roles in their families and communities, particularly over generations
- Learn how sexism affects women in personal and political realms, including within social justice organizations
- Brainstorm ways that immigrant rights organizations and women's organizations can better support immigrant women's leadership

WHAT WILL WE BE TALKING ABOUT?

In this workshop, we will think about the following questions:
- Who are some important women in our lives?
- How have women's roles in families and communities changed due to migration and over the generations?
- How has immigration policy specifically affected women?
- How does sexism impact immigrant women's leadership and participation in organizing?
- What are some ways that we can better support immigrant women's leadership?

NOTE TO FACILITATORS

This module is designed for mixed-gender audiences, although it is also effective with single-gender groups. It is primarily intended for groups whose primary focus is immigrant and refugee rights, and have less experience addressing gender or women's leadership. This module can be used with the other sections of the BRIDGE curricula or as a stand-alone module.

immigrant women's leadership

Backgrounder: The State of Immigrant Women in the U.S.

Immigrant women in the U.S. are not a homogeneous group; they come from diverse situations and regions throughout the world, but are linked through the process of migration. Over the past forty years, the number of women migrants have increased dramatically, reflecting the growing number of migrants worldwide and the changing conditions of migration. For example, in 1960, there were 35 million women in migration. By the year 2000, the number of women migrants increased to over 85 million. Women now constitute over half of all new immigrants coming to the U.S. each year.

Over the last twenty-five years, globalization has also contributed to changes that have significantly increased women's burden of both paid and unpaid labor. As real wages decline, more women are forced into the paid labor force, usually without any reduction in their share of household and family responsibilities. Women have increasingly become a large part of migration, and women migrants often work in the "3-D's" dirty, dangerous, and demeaning jobs segregated by gender.

Once in the U.S., immigrant women face particular obstacles as workers due to immigration status, language, and/or citizenship, in addition to factors of discrimination based on gender and/or race. Immigrant women often lack adequate health care—both for economic reasons, as well as for fear of losing immigration status or being deported for accessing health programs. Almost one out of every five immigrant women live in poverty, and immigrant women, on average, earn less than their U.S.-born counterparts.

Anti-immigrant groups have taken particular aim at immigrant women and their children, portraying them as the cause for overpopulation, poverty, and even environmental degradation. These arguments color public policy debates that concern women, especially around issues such as access to health and social services.

Women play a central role in organizing efforts for immigrant rights in the U.S. Their contributions, however, are often under-appreciated and unrecognized, and at times, our own organizations can replicate sexism, racism, and other forms of oppression. This module offers tools to create a process where groups can discuss ways to better support the work of immigrant women in our movement.

immigrant women's leadership

module 6

SUMMARY POINTS
- The roles and responsibility of women often change over generations and due to conditions of migration, which can be an opportunity for both tension and growth.
- Immigrant women are often specifically impacted by policies aimed at restricting immigrant rights.
- Immigration policy has a profound impact on:
  - Women's access to health care, child care, employment rights
  - Women's vulnerability to domestic violence and abuse
  - Women who may face abuse from law enforcement officials
- In addition to facing gender discrimination at work or from the government, women also can face sexism in their families or within social justice organizations

WORKSHOP SETUP

Exercise:	Time:
Welcome, introduction to workshop	10 minutes
Opening Activity: Honoring Women in Our Lives	20 minutes
Review Objectives and Ground Rules	10-15 minutes
*Our Roots and Branches: Three Generations of Women in Our Family	35 minutes
*Step In, Step Out	50 minutes
Focus on Immigrant Women's Rights	45 minutes
*Dismantling Gender Inequality in Organizing	40 minutes
Closing: Postcards to Ourselves	10-15 minutes
Evaluation	10 minutes

*core exercises

Total Time: 3 hours and 50 minutes

immigrant women's leadership

Opening: Honoring Women in Our Lives

WHY DO IT?
- To use as an introduction and icebreaker
- To honor and reflect on the influence of women in our lives

TIME 20 minutes

MATERIALS NEEDED
- Matches (enough for each participant, and an ashtray to collect used matches)

FACILITATOR PREP
- For safety reasons, you may want to check for a fire extinguisher or smoke ventilation in your room

DIRECTIONS

1. Explain to participants that to open the day's activities, we will introduce ourselves and honor an important woman in our lives.

2. Pass around the matches, one for each participant. Ask each participant to:
   - Light the match
   - Say your name (and organization)
   - Say the name of a woman that is important in your life
   - Explain briefly why this woman is important in your life

The only condition of this exercise is that you can only talk for as long as the match is burning; once it goes out, you have to stop and move onto the next person.

SOURCE the authors

Eunice Cho

immigrant women's leadership

module 6

Our Roots and Branches: Three Generations of Women In Our Families

WHY DO IT?
- To reflect on how the role of women has changed in own families over generations, and due to migration
- To set the groundwork for moving from personal stories to a larger discussion about how sexism and gender discrimination shapes our lives

TIME 35 minutes

MATERIALS NEEDED
- Copies of the "Our Roots and Branches" handout, enough for each participant
- Copies of the small group discussion questions
- Markers, pens, or other art supplies

FACILITATOR PREP
- Write up questions for partners to discuss on the easel paper

DIRECTIONS

1. Explain to participants that this exercise will examine the changes in women's lives in three generations of our families: ourselves, our mothers, and our grandmothers.

2. Distribute a copy of the "Our Roots and Branches" handout to each participant.

3. Review the handout with participants, and ask them to draw or write the answers on their "family tree." (10-15 minutes)
   - On the ROOTS, write your grandmother's name. What work did she do? Where did she live?
   - On the TRUNK, write your mother's name. What work did she do? Where did she live?
   - On the BRANCHES, write your name. What work do you do? Where do you live?

4. Once everyone has finished their picture, ask them to pair up with someone they don't know. Then each pair should spend fifteen minutes sharing their pictures and stories with each other, and reflecting on the following questions (10 minutes):
   1. How is the work of women in each generation different? How is it similar?
   2. How has immigration changed the role of women in your family?
   3. How do you think the leaves – the children of the next generation – will have different lives from the women who came before them?

national network for immigrant and refugee rights
www.nnirr.org

immigrant women's leadership

5. Reconvene the large group. Ask for a few volunteers from the partners to briefly share something they learned or noticed through their conversation. (10-15 minutes)

TEACHING POINTS
- Women's work often changes over the generations, including differences in culture and economic needs due to migration; but in many ways, stay the same.
- The roles and responsibilities of women often change over generations and due to conditions of migration, which can be an opportunity for tension and growth.

VARIATIONS
- This activity can be extended for more than 35 minutes, with more in-depth discussion and sharing of women's history.

CHALLENGES
- You may want to note at the start of the exercise that the women we choose to list as our "mothers" or "grandmothers" may not necessarily be our "birth" mothers; and also that participants may not necessarily know all the answers to the questions, which can be the result of migration, cultural loss, and other factors.

SOURCE adapted from *WedGE: Women's Education in the Global Economy* by Miriam Ching Louie with Linda Burnham, Women of Color Resource Center and American Friends Service Committee, *Facilitator's Guide for Women's Workshops on Women, Poverty, and Economic Power*.

handout

Our Roots and Branches

In this activity, we will examine the changes in women's lives in three generations of our families: ourselves, our mothers, and our grandmothers.

- On the ROOTS, write your grandmother's name. What work did she do? Where did she live?
- On the TRUNK, write your mother's name. What work did she do? Where did she live?
- On the BRANCHES, write your name. What work do you do? Where do you live?

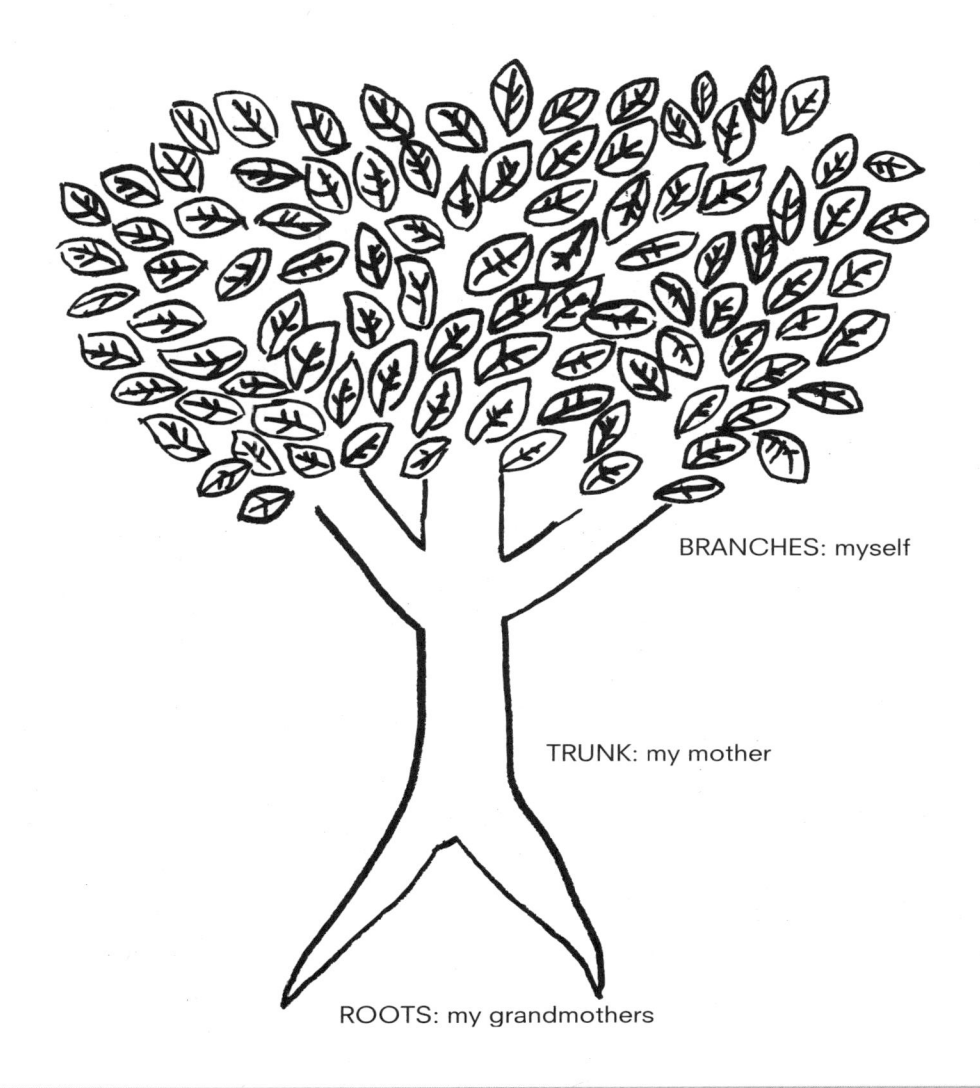

BRANCHES: myself

TRUNK: my mother

ROOTS: my grandmothers

national network for immigrant and refugee rights | 221
www.nnirr.org

immigrant women's leadership

Step In, Step Out

WHY DO IT?
- To show the pervasiveness of sexism and violence against women
- To illustrate how violence against women affects women regardless of age, nationality, etc.
- To highlight some of the personal experiences of people in the training group as a way to reflect on broader social issues

TIME 50 minutes

MATERIALS NEEDED
- Easel paper, markers, tape
- Small group discussion questions on easel paper, or copies of small group discussion questions for participants

FACILITATOR PREP
- Review the "step in/step out" statements for the exercise, and change or adapt to your group's needs if necessary.

DIRECTIONS

1. Explain to participants that:
    - The purpose of this exercise is to highlight some of the ways our gender shapes our experience.
    - Some of this exercise will reflect on the mistreatment of women. This does not mean that men haven't been mistreated too or that all men are "guilty" of mistreating women.

You may want to predict some reactions ("Some of you may feel embarrassed, others angry, etc.) Reiterate the ground rules for the group.

2. Ask the large group to stand and form a circle, which will create the space for the exercise. Explain the rules of the exercise:
    - The facilitator will be reading a number of statements – some of which have to do with gender. If the statement applies to you, you should "step in" the circle. If the statement doesn't apply, remain on the outside. For example, if "I have brown eyes," or "I think all children should have free health care," etc.
    - Remind participants that the group is sharing responsibility for each other, and that people need to be supportive and respectful of where people choose to stand. People may choose not to step in or out on certain statements, even if the statement applies to them.

immigrant women's leadership

module 6

Step In, Step Out

- Ask people to pay attention to their own reactions during this exercise, but that we will not be speaking during the exercise, which should be done in SILENCE.

3. Begin reading the list of statements. They start with warm-up statements, and move on to more challenging ones. You may want to pause a bit between each statement. (20 minutes)

- I love chocolate.
- I speak more than one language.
- I am an immigrant.
- My parents were immigrants.
- I am an only child.
- I have sons.
- I have daughters.
- I have been discriminated against because of my race.
- My parents treated my brothers better than me.
- People have commented on my accent when I speak.
- I have felt unsafe walking alone at night.
- There have been times when I felt my needs came second because of my gender.
- I have been told that I'm too aggressive.
- I have felt limited about which careers I could follow because of my gender.
- I have been whistled at or yelled at in public in a way that made me uncomfortable.
- There have been times when I have not spoken up because of my gender.
- I have been verbally or physically abused by a man.
- I have been called a bitch, whore, or a slut.
- I have tried to change my appearance or have worn uncomfortable clothing in order to please a man.
- There have been times when I worried I didn't appear strong or tough enough.
- I have been forced to fight when I didn't want to.
- I have been sexually harassed.
- I have held back tears when I felt like crying inside because I didn't want to look weak.

national network for immigrant and refugee rights | 223

immigrant women's leadership

- I have stopped myself from hugging, showing affection, or touching another man because I was worried about how it might look.
- I am a woman who has not spoken up at times when I was afraid of how a man would react to what I had to say.
- I have been expected to take full responsibility for birth control.
- I have been afraid of men's anger.

4. Briefly process this exercise with the group. How did this exercise make you feel?

5. After several people have shared their reactions, ask the group to divide into gender separate groups. Depending on the number/gender of participants, this can include:
   Group(s) for women
   Group(s) for men
   A mixed or non-gender specific group (in order to create a safer space for transgender participants)

6. Ask each group to reflect on the following questions in their small group discussions. These questions are available as a handout. (20 minutes)
   1) How did the exercise make you feel?
   2) What did you notice about who stepped in and who stepped out on the various statements?
   3) What was a statement that had a strong impact for you? Why?
   4) How does violence against women affect us as individuals and as a community?

After your discussion, come up with a creative symbol of the ideas/feelings that this exercise brought up for you. (This could be a drawing, a poem, a human statue, etc.) Mention the statements that most spoke to you.

7. Reconvene the large group, and have the small groups share their "creative symbol" from their discussions. Then process the exercise with the following questions:
   - What statements did it seem like people connected to the most?
   - After your discussions, would you have changed whether you stepped in/out for any of the statements?
   - How does gender inequality and violence against women affect us as a community?

immigrant women's leadership

module 6

TEACHING POINTS
- Sexism affects everyone in our community, including women and men.
- Sexism can affect us in different ways, due to other differences in power and privilege (such as race, immigration status, class, etc.)

CHALLENGES
- Be sure to set the content of this exercise, and to give participants the option to pass. This exercise may make some women vulnerable by sharing their experiences in front of men. Some men may respond with guilt or embarrassment, or defensiveness.
- We have found that this exercise works better with a woman facilitator.

SOURCE adapted with permission from Hugh Vasquez and Isoke Femi, the Todos Institute, No Boundaries: A Manual for Unlearning Oppression and Building Multicultural Alliances

Eunice Cho

handout

Small Group Discussion Questions: Step In, Step Out

Before you start, pick someone in your group to keep the discussion going, and someone to write down key thoughts that come up in your discussion.

1. How did the exercise make you feel?
2. What did you notice about who stepped in and who stepped out on the various statements?
3. What was a statement that had a strong impact for you? Why?
4. How does violence against women affect us as individuals and as a community?

After your discussion, come up with a creative symbol of the ideas/feelings that this exercise brought up for you. (This could be a drawing, a poem, a human statue, etc.) Mention the statements that most spoke to you.

immigrant women's leadership

module 6

Focus on Immigrant Women's Rights

WHY DO IT?
- To build on personal experiences of gender discrimination discussed in earlier exercises
- To discuss the ways that gender inequality and sexism affect immigrant women's lives
- To help groups who may have less experience applying a gender framework to consider a new perspective.

TIME 45 minutes

MATERIALS NEEDED
- easel paper, markers, tape
- handout or easel paper with discussion questions for small groups

FACILITATOR PREP
- You may want to consider a few topics for the group to discuss, given the group's area of focus. You may also want to think of a few less-familiar topics for your group.

DIRECTIONS

1. Explain to the group that this exercise will be an opportunity to look more closely at issues faced by immigrant women. With the group, generate a list of topics that the group would like to address, and have the group choose their top 3-4 topics with a show of hands. (10 minutes)
Some topics that we have used include:
   - Workplace issues
   - Health care
   - Lack of papers/undocumented status
   - Education

2. Divide the large group into 3-4 small groups, each for a topic decided by the large group. Participants may want to choose which group they join, according to topic. Distribute the small group discussion questions, easel paper, and markers to the groups, and review the questions with the large group.

3. Small groups should discuss their questions, and develop a presentation for the large group. (20 minutes)

4. Reconvene the large group and have each small group present their discussion, by providing one answer to each question. Depending on time, you can allow for some discussion, but the main point of this exercise is to give exposure on how using a gendered perspective can help us in our organizing and policy work.

immigrant women's leadership

TEACHING POINTS
- Immigrant women are often specifically impacted by policies aimed at restricting immigrant rights.
- Immigration policy has a profound impact on:
  - Women's access to health care, child care, employment rights
  - Women's vulnerability to domestic violence and abuse
  - Women who may face abuse from law enforcement officials

SOURCE the authors

Eunice Cho

handout

Small Group Discussion Questions: Focus on Immigrant Women's Rights

Before you start, pick someone in your group to keep the discussion going, and someone to record your group's discussion on a large sheet of paper.

1. What is the impact of this issue on your community?
2. What is the impact of this issue on immigrant women in particular?
3. What are some ways that communities are/can address this issue?

If you don't know the answers to these questions, try not to guess—instead, think about some questions you need answered or information you need to answer the questions.

When you are done, pick one person to present your group's discussion to the large group. Pick only one answer to each question.

immigrant women's leadership

Dismantling Gender Inequality in Organizing

WHY DO IT?
- To talk about how sexism and gender inequality impacts our organizations
- To identify specific problems and concrete solutions to sexism and gender inequality in our work

TIME 40 minutes

MATERIALS NEEDED
- Easel paper, markers, tape
- Slips of paper/large sticky notes and pens for each participant
- Basket

DIRECTIONS
1. Explain to the group that in this exercise, we will build on the previous discussions to talk about how we can address sexism and gender oppression in an important part of our lives—our organizations and our work. Remind participants of ground rules. Ask participants that if they choose to share information about their organization, they should choose to share it in a way that maintains confidentiality.

2. (**Optional**) To frame the topic, you may want to read a few examples of sexism faced by women organizers in social justice work, or provide your own:

> *Jing has been involved in an organizing campaign for immigrant workers, even though she works a full-time job at a restaurant, and takes care of her three children and her elderly parents. When her organization comes forward with a position that she and other women in the group disagrees with, they are told that it is too late to change the position, and that they should have shown up to the meeting where the decision was made, even though the group has never provided child care for the women.*

> *Nafeez is a young woman who works for an immigrant advocacy group. While she has an advanced degree in international relations and has organized many campaigns in her community, the points she raises in staff meetings are ignored, until her male supervisor repeats them, and gets credit for his "great ideas." She ends up doing the bulk of the copying, mailing, and typing of meeting notes instead of the organizing work she was hired to do.*

> *Luz has put in many hours organizing a huge rally and press conference with the community, spending long evenings in the office and the*

immigrant women's leadership

module 6

weekends. During the rally, all the speakers are men. After the rally and event, the men go off to do media interviews, while she and the other women are left to clean up by themselves.

3. Write the following statement on the board:
One example of sexism/gender inequality that happens in my organization is when:
This could be reflected in areas such as:
- Who makes the decisions in your organization and how
- Who has the power and controls resources
- Who has leadership
- Attention to family and child care issues
- Who does what work (who does the dishes? Photocopying?)
- What types of issues get more attention/resources
- Whose ideas are valued more
- Who talks in meetings

4. Give participants a slip of paper and ask them to complete the statement, and to write it down (neatly, because other people will be reading them!) Ask participants to put their paper in the basket.
Here are a few examples we have seen:
One example of sexism/gender inequality that happens in my organization is when: the young women stay the latest every day, and get less credit for their work.
One example of sexism/gender inequality that happens in my organization is when: Our board members are mostly men—in an organization that is for immigrant women!

5. Once all of these responses are in the basket, pass the basket. Ask participants to pick out a slip of paper and read it out loud to the whole group. Participants should hold onto the piece of paper they read.

6. Divide the large group into small groups. Give each group easel paper and markers to record their discussion. Each group should discuss the examples on their slips of paper. The group should then brainstorm some solutions for each example. (20 minutes)
For example, if the problem is: "Women clean up at my office all the time," a solution could be: "Develop a chore wheel to rotate tasks among all the staff. Build a way to make men accountable to sharing the work."

national network for immigrant and refugee rights

immigrant women's leadership

7. Reconvene the large group. Ask each group to report back to the rest of the group. They should share 2 problems and 2 solutions they came up with.

CHALLENGES
- Participants may feel uncomfortable openly discussing examples of organizational inequality, particularly if this workshop is done within an organization. Stressing ground rules and also reminding the group that the purpose of the exercise is not to blame a specific person or organization, but to help us all learn and think about possible solutions. If a concrete situation of gender inequality does arise between members of the same organization, it can be helpful to agree that the organizations or persons involved should have a specific meeting to address it.
- If participants fear reprisal, create an environment where they can choose to make general statements rather than identify specific organizations.
- Some examples of sexism will undoubtedly also raise questions of other oppressions and privileges. It is important to point out that sexism—like all forms of oppression—is intertwined with other forms of oppression and privilege.

SOURCE the authors

Eunice Cho

immigrant women's leadership

Closing: Postcards to Ourselves

WHY DO IT?
- To evaluate the day's events
- To use as a closing activity
- To provide for some "follow up"—participants will receive a reminder of their experience a few days after the workshop

TIME Time: 10-15 minutes

MATERIALS NEEDED
- Postcards (enough for all participants)
- Pens
- Stamps

DIRECTIONS
1. Ask each participant to go around the circle and share one sentence that describes what s/he learned at today's workshop.
2. Pass out postcards and ask each person to write a postcard to her/himself. They should write something concrete they plan to do to address something they learned about in the training, and address the postcard to themselves. Tell them you will mail out the postcards.
3. Ask everyone to come together in a circle and thank the group. Honor their participation and sharing in the training.
4. Don't forget to mail out the postcards!

SOURCE the authors

John Minardi

immigrant women's leadership

Resources

Organizations:

ANDOLAN: Organizing South Asian Workers. Andolan_organizing@yahoo.com. PO Box 2087, Long Island City, NY 11102. Tel: 719-390-7264.

Asian Immigrant Women Advocates. www.aiwa.org. 310 8th St. Suite 301, Oakland, CA 94607. Tel: 510-268-0192.

Asian and Pacific American Health Forum. www.apiaf.org. 942 Market St., Suite 200, San Francisco, CA 94102. Tel: 415-954-9988.

Asian Women's Shelter. www.sfaws.org. 3543 18th Street, Box 19, San Franscisco, CA 94110. Tel: 415-751-7110

Campaign for Migrant Domestic Women's Rights, c/o the Institute for Policy Studies. http://www.ips-dc.org/campaign/index2.htm. 733 15th Street, NW Suite 1020, Washington, DC 20005. Tel: 202-234-9382

Center for Women's Global Leadership. www.cwgl.rutgers.edu. Douglass College, Rutgers, The State University of New Jersey, 160 Ryders Lane, New Brunswick, NJ 08901. Tel: 732-932-8782

Coalition to Abolish Slavery and Trafficking. www.castla.org. 5042 Wilshire Blvd., #586, Los Angeles, CA 90036. Tel: 213-365-1906

Domestic Workers United. www.domesticworkersunited.org. c/o CAAAV: Organizing Asian Communities, 2437 Valentine Ave., Bronx, NY10458. Tel: 718-220-7391 x 11.

Family Violence Prevention Fund. www.fvpf.org. 383 Rhode Island St. Suite #304, San Francisco, CA 94103-5133. Tel: 415-252-8900

Fuerza Unida. 710 New Laredo Hwy., San Antonio, TX 78211. Tel: 210-927-2294.

Haitian Women for Haitian Refugees. 319 Maple St. Brooklyn, NY 11225. Tel: 718-735-4660.

Incite! Women of Color Against Violence. www.incite-national.org. (National group.) P.O. Box 6861, Minneapolis, MN 55406. Tel: (415) 553-3837.

La Mujer Obrera, PO Box 3975, El Paso, TX 79923. Tel: 915-533-9710.

Lideres Campesinas/Farmworker Women's Leadership Network. 611 S. Rebecca St., Pomona, CA 91766. Tel: 909-865-7776.

Manavi (South Asian women's organization). www.research.att.com/~krishnas/manavi/. PO Box 3103, New Brunswick, NJ 08901. Tel: 732-435-1414.

Mujeres Unidas y Activas. 3543 18th Street #23, San Francisco, CA 94110. Tel: 415-261-8140.

National Network To End Violence Against Immigrant Women, c/o National Immigration Project of the National Lawyer's Guild. 14 Beacon St. Suite 602, Boston, MA 02108. Tel: 617-227-9727.

NOW Legal Defense and Education Fund, Immigrant Women's Program. www.nowldef.org. 1522 K Street, N.W. Suite 550, Washington, DC 20005. Tel: 202-326-0044.

Refugee Women's Network. www.riwn.org. 4151 Memorial Dr. Suite 103-F. Decatur, GA 30032. Tel: 414-299-0180.

immigrant women's leadership

module 6

Sakhi. www.sakhi.org. P.O.Box 20208, Greeley Square Sation, New York, NY 10001-0006. Tel: 212-714-9153.

Women of Color Resource Center. www.coloredgirls.org. 1611 Telegraph Ave. #303, Oakland, CA 94612. Tel: 510-444-2700.

Women's Commission for Refugee Women and Children. www.womenscommission.org. 122 East 42nd St. 12th Floor, New York, NY 10168. Tel: 212-551-3088.

Women Watch Afrika. 4281 Memorial Dr. Suite 1, Decatur, GA 30032. Tel: 404-292-0069.

Books and Publications:

Disposable Domestics: Immigrant Women Workers in the Global Economy. By Grace Chang, published by South End Press. This book highlights the unrewarded work immigrant women perform as caregivers, cleaners, and servers in the context of the broader need for jobs with justice and dignity for all—and shows how these women are actively resisting the exploitation they face. Available at www.southendpress.org.

Doméstica: Immigrant Workers Cleaning and Caring in the Shadows of Affluence. By Pirette Hondagneu-Sotelo. This book highlights the voices, experiences, and views of Mexican and Central American women who care for other people's children and homes, as well as the outlooks of the women who employ them in Los Angeles.

Hands That Shape The World: A Report on the Conditions of Immigrant Women in the U.S. Published by the National Network for Immigrant and Refugee Rights. This report reviews the state of immigrant women living in the U.S. five years after the 1995 World Conference on Women in Beijing, China. Available at www.nnirr.org.

Sweatshop Warriors: Immigrant Women Workers Take on the Global Factory. By Miriam Ching Yoon Louie, published by South End Press. This book highlights the voices of the pioneers of the growing anti-sweatshop movement: immigrant women workers! Available at www.southendpress.org.

WedGE: Women's Education in the Global Economy. Published by the Women of Color Resource Center. A popular education workbook increases understanding of how women around the globe are affected by the global economy and how they are organizing to defend their rights. Available at www.coloredgirls.org.

Whose Safety? Women of Color and the Violence of Law Enforcement. Published by American Friends Service Committee and the Committee on Women, Population, and the Environment, Philadelphia, May 2001. This comprehensive research report documents how women of color, both immigrant and U.S-born, face violence and the abuse of authority from law-enforcement agencies--from local police to the prison system to INS raids. Available for download at www.cwpe.org.

Finding Common Ground I: The Changing Demographics of Race and Migration

The Changing Demographics of Race and Migration

OVERVIEW

The goals of this workshop are to:
- Explore the racial and ethnic make-up of our communities
- Discuss changes in the demographic make-up of our communities, and more broadly in the U.S.
- Place local demographic changes and tensions within a broader historical context of racism, nationality and class oppression, and other systems of injustice
- Identify and examine areas of tension within communities, and discuss possible solutions
- Explore how different communities have used these changes as opportunities for new learning, organizing, leadership development, coalition-building, and solidarity

WHAT WILL WE BE TALKING ABOUT?

In this workshop, we will think about the following questions:
- Who makes up our community? Who is visible? Who is less visible?
- What is the racial and ethnic make-up of our community, and how does it compare to the past?
- Who holds power in our communities?
- What are areas of tension between groups in our communities? What are some solutions to these tensions?
- How have other communities worked to build coalitions and solidarity between different groups?

NOTE TO FACILITATORS

This module works best with groups where participants have a shared context and are engaged in a process of building a relationship, such as a workplace, neighborhood, campaign, organizing drive. Certain activities, such as the "The Ten Chairs," "Share Squares," and "Building on Success Stories," also work well in settings where participants are less familiar with each other.

Because this module addresses divisions and conflicts within communities, we strongly advise facilitators and participants to first use at least one of the following modules before proceeding with this one: (1) History 101; (2) Introduction to Race, Migration and Multiple Oppressions; or (3) Globalization and Workers Rights. These modules provide participants with some "root cause" analytical tools critical to processing some of the conflicts they'll be identifying and addressing in this module.

Backgrounder:
The Changing Demographics of Race and Migration

New Census figures show that recent immigration is changing the racial character of the U.S. Migrants from Latin America, Asia, the Caribbean, the Middle East, and Africa comprise the majority of newcomers to the U.S. Today, 85% of arriving migrants are people of color. The Immigration Act of 1965 ended quotas that limited migration from Asia and Latin America. This marked the beginning of the transformation of both the racial composition of newly-arriving immigrant groups and the racial makeup of many communities in the U.S.

Immigration is one component of a demographic shift taking place in the U.S. The Census recently projected that by 2050, Latinos, African Americans, Asian Pacific Americans, and Native Americans/Indigenous peoples will make up at least 50% of the total U.S. population. Since the 1990s, immigration has fanned out from traditional destinations (California, New York, Texas, Illinois, New Jersey and Florida) to include states in the Southeast, Midwest, and Rocky Mountain regions of the country.

Although the civil rights movement movements forced the end of legalized racial discrimination, actual racism and economic disparity continue to divide US society today. Newcomers walk right into this polarization. Today, immigrants face *racial discrimination*, as well as *nationality discrimination* and *xenophobia* because of their accent, national origin, religion, or other features that "mark them" as foreign-born. Demographic change in many communities can result in conflict between newer immigrants and more established groups. U.S.-born citizens and earlier arrivals sometimes see more recent immigrants as jeopardizing access to jobs, social services, and public space.

While hurt by racism, immigrants may also adopt racist and xenophobic attitudes and practices against other groups. Similarly, U.S.-born people of color and whites may adopt racist and xenophobic beliefs and practices against immigrants. Due to restrictive immigration policy, immigrants often have far fewer avenues to express their interests, obtain needed services, or find redress for wrongdoings committed against them on an equal basis. Yet many immigrants share common interests and issues with other groups, and alliances between new immigrants and established residents can help to solve common issues. Alliances work best when all parties share concrete goals, put interests and differences out on the table, and make a strong investment in a process to create mutually beneficial solutions.

the changing demographics of race and migration

module 7

SUMMARY POINTS

- Demographic change in many communities can result in conflict between newer immigrants and more established groups.
- Change in our communities can be a source of tension, or an opportunity for change.
- Tensions between newer immigrant communities and other communities take place within a framework of historical economic inequality and institutionalized racism.
- Tension between groups is a relationship—without a relationship, there is no context for change for finding common ground.
- Alliances work best when all parties share concrete goals, put interests and differences out on the table, and make a strong investment in a process to create mutually beneficial solutions.

WORKSHOP MENU

Exercise:	Time:
Welcome, introduction to the workshop, review goals	10 minutes
Opening/Introductions: Share Squares	20 minutes
Review Objectives/Ground Rules	10 minutes
*Mapping Our Community	50 minutes
*Identifying and Discussing Tensions in our Community	60 minutes
The Ten Chairs: Race, Migration, and Wealth in U.S. History	40 minutes
*Building on Success Stories	50 minutes
Closing: Our Common Circle	10 minutes
Evaluation	5-10 minutes

*core exercises

Total: 4 hours, 15 minutes

the changing demographics of race and migration

Opening: The Share Squares

WHY DO IT?
- To use as an introduction and a fun icebreaker
- To introduce themes of shared experience to the group

TIME 20 minutes

MATERIALS NEEDED
- Copies of the "Share Squares" handout
- Pens for all participants
- Small prizes for "winners" (optional)

DIRECTIONS

1. Explain to the group that this activity will be a chance for everyone to meet one another and to begin to find out more about each other.

2. Distribute the handout to all participants. Ask participants to look over it carefully, and to think about which statements in the squares apply to them.

3. Review the rules of the activity:
   a. The object is to meet and introduce yourself to other participants—and to get as many people to sign your sheet as possible.
   b. You can only sign squares that are true about you.
   c. You can only sign another person's sheet once.
   d. Don't feel pressured to share personal information if you don't want to; and don't pressure other participants to do so either.

4. Have participants mingle and fill out their sheets for about 10 minutes. Then determine a winner, based on who collected the most signatures.

5. Choose a few of the comments on the "squares," and ask for a show of hands of participants who signed or could have signed that square. Ask a participant to explain a bit about why s/he signed the square. (You can start with a light-hearted one, such as, "I am wearing socks," and move onto more serious statements, such as "I have experienced racism.")

TEACHING POINTS
- Participants in this group have a lot of similarities, some of which can only be discovered by sharing information with each other.
- There are also a lot of differences within the group, which can be a source of strength through diversity.

SOURCE We have seen this activity in many places, although we especially drew from Education for Changing Unions, by Bev Burke, Jojo Geronimo, D'Arcy Martin, Barb Thomas, and Carol Wall, with permission.

handout

share squares

instructions

- The object is to meet and introduce yourself to other participants—and to get as many people to sign your sheet as possible.
- You can only sign squares that are true about you.
- You can only sign another person's sheet in one square.
- You can sign your name in one of your squares.

I have lived under a corrupt government	I wear glasses	I have lived in another country	I have experienced racism	I am the grandchild of immigrants
I can speak more than one language	I am an immigrant or refugee	I have been hurt at work	I live in a democracy	I am wearing a shirt made in another country
I can vote in U.S. elections	I need a vacation	I am wearing socks	I have been unemployed	I have participated in a protest or rally this year
I have one or more children	I live in a community with problems of poverty	I have moved from one town to another	I can hop up and down and clap at the same time (prove it!)	I am the child of immigrants
I have been wrongfully pulled over by the police	I like chocolate	I have worked a minimum wage job	I have one or more grandchildren	I am a union member

national network for immigrant and refugee rights
www.nnirr.org

the changing demographics of race and migration

Mapping Our Community

WHY DO IT?
- To open up a conversation about the shared space (physical and political) between different groups of people
- To examine different visions of our "common ground," or shared community
- To examine the way we perceive power in the community—who is visible and who is less visible

TIME 50 minutes

MATERIALS NEEDED
- Easel paper, tape
- Markers, crayons, or other art supplies

FACILITATOR PREP
- Before the workshop, try to learn as much as possible about the participants and their relationship to one another. This can help you to frame the discussions, and to suggest a specific community space, such as a workplace or neighborhood, to focus on during the activity.

DIRECTIONS

1. Explain to participants that this activity will lead us to think about the communities where we live and work.

2. Divide participants into small groups of 4-5 participants.

3. Distribute the handout to all participants, and review the instructions. Give each small group a large piece of easel paper, markers, or other art supplies. Each group will be responsible for drawing a mural of their community—the people, landmarks, or whatever else can be found where they live.

4. Small groups will complete drawings of their community. (20-25 minutes)

5. Reconvene the group, and ask each small group to present their drawing, and to briefly explain who is in the drawing. Applaud the efforts of each group, and place all of the diagrams on the wall, next to each other.

6. Discuss with the large group:
   - What were some of the similarities in all of the drawings?
   - What are some of the differences between the drawings?
   - Who are the people that are visible in all of these drawings? Are there any people that are not visible in these drawings that we should add? Why do you think they were not visible?

the changing demographics of race and migration — module 7

7. You may want to review these Teaching Points:
- These are all visions of our shared community, our "common ground."
- We all have different visions of our community, but there are also many similarities in what we see.

CHALLENGES
- This activity works well in situations where participants can visualize a shared physical or geographic space where they interact, such as a common work place, a major street where activity takes place, or a large-scale version of their city.

SOURCE the authors

Michelle Yamashita

handout

Mapping Our Community

For this activity, your group will draw a mural/map of your communities. After you are finished, pick 1-2 people to present it to the whole group.

Before you start to draw, think about the following:
- Who are the people in my community/neighborhood?
- What do people do when they are in my community/neighborhood?
- What does my community/neighborhood look like?

When you are finished, pick 1-2 people to present your mural to the large group.

the changing demographics of race and migration

module 7

Identifying and Discussing Tensions in our Community

WHY DO IT?
- To open space to dialogue about changing demographics within local communities
- To identify tensions and conflicts, as well as opportunities to build bridges across race, nationality and other divisions

TIME 60 minutes

MATERIALS NEEDED
- copies of small group discussion handout
- easel paper, markers, tape

DIRECTIONS
1. Explain to the group that this activity will further explore our community—who makes up the community, and some sources of tension.
2. Divide the large group into smaller groups of 4-6 participants.
3. Distribute the "Identifying and Discussing Tensions in Our Community: Small Group Discussion Questions" handout to all participants, and review the instructions. Give each small group a large piece of easel paper, markers, and pens.
4. Ask each small group to discuss the questions in their handout. (30 minutes)
5. Bring the large group back together. Ask each group to quickly present three major themes that came out of their discussion.
6. Process the small group discussions with the large group. Place the easel paper (from the small group discussions) on the wall. As a group, go through the questions one at a time, looking at the different groups' responses for each question. Discuss with the group:
   - Did anything in your discussion surprise you? If so, what?
   - Did you notice any patterns or similarities in the discussions?
   - How would you change your "community murals" after this discussion?

VARIATIONS
- This activity is also useful to examine tensions beyond immigrant and non-immigrant groups. For example, if participants are all members of one ethnic or racial community, it may be useful to also explore tensions between:
  - Between/inside different national origin groups
  - Between/inside different generations of the same race/ethnic group

SOURCE the authors

handout

Identifying and Discussing Tensions in Our Community
Small Group Discussion Questions

Before you start, pick someone in your group to keep the discussion going, and someone to record your group's discussion on a large sheet of paper. Review these questions, and answer these questions together as a group.

1. Who are the people in your community? What ethnic and racial groups are present in your community? Has this been true in the past, or has it changed recently?

2. What are some specific examples of tensions between immigrants and non-immigrants in your community? What about tensions between different ethnic/racial groups in your community?

3. Who benefits from these tensions? How are they involved in creating these tensions?

4. Who are the different groups that are affected in some way by this problem? What do you have in common with them?

5 What can you do to address these tensions? What will you do?

After your group is finished with the discussion, pick one person to report back to the group on *three major themes* that emerged from your discussion.

the changing demographics of race and migration

module 7

The Ten Chairs:
Race, Migration, and Wealth in U.S. History

WHY DO IT?
- To illustrate the changing demographics of race and immigration in the community
- To illustrate inequalities in the distribution of wealth in the U.S.
- To energize a group and have them move physically

TIME 40 minutes

MATERIALS NEEDED
- 10 chairs, or 10 spots marked on the floor with masking tape
- Easel paper, markers, and tape
- About 40 sheets of paper for "immigration and race" signs (this works best if you use 4 different colors of paper, 10 sheets each)

FACILITATOR PREP
Facilitator Prep:
- Read the following "Ten Chairs: Immigration and Race Statistics" fact sheet.
- Copy "Where Do Immigrants Come From?" statistics onto easel paper.
- Line up 10 chairs at the front of the room, or mark 10 spots on the floor with masking tape.

DIRECTIONS

1. Assemble the group. Explain that this is an exercise to look at how the demographics of race and immigration have changed during the last forty years, and also to examine the distribution of wealth in the U.S. today.

2. Ask for ten volunteers to come forward. Explain that each person will represent one tenth of the total population in the U.S. at a certain period in time, and together, the group will illustrate the racial makeup of the U.S. Also explain that this is a very rough illustration of the U.S. population, and that many communities may not be visible in this exercise.

3. Announce to the group that they will look at racial demographics in the year 1900. (Refer to the facilitator guide for this exercise for the statistics.) Hand out the first set of "immigration and race" signs to the 10 participants sitting in the chairs, and have participants look around: this is roughly what the U.S. racial makeup looked like in 1900. Then read off the easel for "Immigration and Race Statistics" and "Where Do Immigrants Come From?" for the year 1900.

4. Repeat step 3: hand out "immigration and race" signs and read off the easel for the years 1960, 1980, and 2000, with a new group of volunteers each time.

the changing demographics of race and migration

5. Briefly discuss with the large group:
   - Did anything about this activity surprise you? If so, what?
   - What are some of the reasons that racial demographics have changed? What are some of the policies that have led to this?
   - The "numbers" that we dramatized were based on U.S. Census figures. Are there ways the U.S. Census can give an inaccurate picture of racial demographics in our communities? (check facilitator's guide for more information on this subject)

6. Now explain that the group will be examining the division of wealth in the United States. Wealth is "what you have in the bank and what you own, minus your debts." Explain that each person still represents 10% of the U.S. population, and each chair represents 10% of wealth in the U.S. If wealth were to be evenly distributed, there would be one person for each chair. Ask the 10 volunteers to sit down in their chairs.

7. Pick one volunteer, preferably one who had held a sign for "white," and designate her/him as the "wealthiest 10% of the U.S." The rest of the group is the "bottom 90% of the U.S.") Explain to the group that we will look at the true picture of the division of wealth in the U.S. In 1998, the top 10% owned 71% of all wealth (ask one volunteer to stretch across seven chairs), while the remaining 90% owned 29% (ask nine volunteers to squeeze onto three chairs.)

8. Process the activity with the large group. Ask:
   - Did the exercise on wealth inequality surprise you? If so, how?
   - How did the person in the top 10% feel? How did the bottom 90% feel?
   - How does the information about the distribution of wealth affect how you view the demographic change in the U.S.? How does this information affect how you would shape your campaigns?

TEACHING POINTS
- Tensions between newer immigrant communities and other communities take place within a framework of historical economic inequality and institutionalized racism.

FACILITATOR TIP This exercise works particularly well after a group has completed the "History of Immigration 101" module.

SOURCE the authors; wealth activity adapted with permission from "Closing the Racial Wealth Divide," United for a Fair Economy.

Facilitator's Guide to Ten Chairs: Immigration and Race Statistics

Shifting Categories: Changes in U.S. Census Racial Classification:

The history of census taking has always been a politically biased process. Different groups have been put into different categories at different times. From 1790 until 1970, the U.S. Census identified race by the following categories: White, Black, American Indian, Eskimo and Aleut; Asian and Pacific Islander and Other Race. The population of Hispanic origin was first identified comprehensively in the 1970 census. Prior to this, the "Mexican" category was used once as a separate racial category (in the 1930 Census). This category was later eliminated in 1940 when "Mexican" was revised and included with the "White" population. The 2000 Census also marked change: Asians and Pacific Islanders were counted in separate categories, and for the first time, the Census tracked figures for people who considered themselves of multiple racial background.

Immigration and Race Statistics:

These statistics are based on U.S. Census figures for 1900, 1960, 1980, and 2000. We have chosen these dates because they provide a good gauge of demographic change due to changes in immigration policy. 1900 marks a period where European immigration to the U.S. was at a high point (before the passage of restrictive immigration legislation in the 1920s.) 1960 provides a good benchmark to compare demographic changes after the passage of the 1965 Immigration Act, which eliminated racial quotas to immigration. 1980 and 2000 show the growing demographic change within the U.S., also reflecting changes in the way that the U.S. Census Bureau determined racial categories, particularly for "Hispanics."

Writing out the chart:
For the first set of "immigration and race signs," you should write:

"1900: white" on nine sheets of paper; and "1900: African American" on one sheet of paper.

1900:
- 87.9% of the U.S. population was considered white*
- 11.6% of the U.S. population was considered African American
- 0.3% of the U.S. population was considered Native American/Indigenous
- 0.1% of the U.S. population was considered Asian/Pacific Islander

Facilitator Overview

For the second set of "immigration and race signs," you should write:
"1960: white" on nine sheets of paper; and "1960: African American" on one sheet of paper.

1960:
- 88.6% of the U.S. population was considered white
- 10.5% of the U.S. population was considered black
- 0.3% of the U.S. population was considered Native American/Indigenous
- 0.5% of the U.S. population was considered Asian/Pacific Islander

For the third set of "immigration and race signs," you should write:
"1980: white" on eight sheets of paper; "1980: African American" on one sheet of paper. On the last sheet of paper, write: "1980: Hispanic, Asian/Pacific Islander/Native American."

1980:
- 79.6% of the U.S. population was considered white and not Hispanic
- 11.7% of the U.S. population was considered black
- 0.6% of the U.S. population was considered Native American/Indigenous
- 1.5% of the U.S. population was considered Asian/Pacific Islander
- 6.4% of the U.S. population was considered Hispanic

For the fourth set of "immigration and race signs," you should write:
"2000: white" on seven sheets of papers; "2000: African American" on one sheet of paper, "2000: Hispanic" on one sheet of paper. On the last sheet of paper, write: "2000: Hispanic, African American, Asian, Pacific Islander, Native American, Other."

2000:
- 75.1% of the U.S. population was white, not Hispanic
- 12.3% of the U.S. population was black
- 0.1% of the U.S. population was considered Native American/Indigenous
- 3.6% of the U.S. population was considered Asian
- 1% of the U.S. population was considered Pacific Islander/Native Hawaiian
- 12.5% of the U.S. population was considered Hispanic
- 5.5% of the U.S. population was considered of an "other" racial background

BRIDGE: Building a Race and Immigration Dialogue in the Global Economy
www.nnirr.org

Racial Wealth Gap in the U.S.

Here are a few key facts on the racial wealth gap in the U.S.:

- In 1998, the median net worth for Hispanic, African American, Asian and other minority families was $16,400. That was less than one-fifth the $94,900 median net worth for non-Hispanic white families.
— Yochi Dreazen, "USA: Racial Wealth Gap Remains," *Wall Street Journal*, March 14, 2000.

- From 1995 to 2001, typical families of color saw their net worth (assets minus debts) fall 7% ...while typical white families' net worth grew 37% to $120,900.
— Ana Aizcorbe, Arthur B. Kennickell, and Kevin B. Moore, *Recent Changes in U.S. Family Finances: Evidence from the 1998 and 2001 Survey of Consumer Finances*, 2001.

E. Cho

BRIDGE Fact Sheet

Where Have Immigrants Come From?

1900   13.6% of the U.S. population was born outside the U.S.
   86.0% of all immigrants were from Europe
   11.4% of all immigrants were from Northern America (including Mexico)
   2.6% of all immigrants were from other areas

1900: Top Ten Sending Countries: Germany, Ireland, Great Britain, Canada, Sweden, Italy, Poland, Russia, Poland, Norway, Austria.

1960   6.9% of the U.S. population was born outside the U.S.
   75% of all immigrants were from Europe
   9.8% of all immigrants were from Northern America (including Mexico)
   9.4% of all immigrants were from Latin America
   5.1% of all immigrants were from Asia
   0.7% of all immigrants were from other areas

1960: Top Ten Sending Countries: Italy, Germany, Canada, United Kingdom, Poland, Soviet Union, Mexico, Ireland, Austria and Hungary.

1980   6.2% of the U.S. population was born outside the U.S.
   39.0% of all immigrants were from Europe
   6.5% of all immigrants were from North America
   33.1% of all immigrants were from Latin America
   19.3% of all immigrants were from Asia
   2.1% of all immigrants were from other areas

1980: Top Ten Sending Countries: Mexico, Germany, Canada, Italy, United Kingdom, Cuba, Philippines, Poland, Soviet Union, Korea.

2000   10.4% of the U.S. population was born outside the U.S.
   15.3% of all immigrants were from Europe
   2.5% of all immigrants were from Northern America
   51.0% of all immigrants were from Latin America
   25.5% of all immigrants were from Asia
   5.7% of all immigrants were from other areas

2000: Top Ten Sending Countries: Mexico, China, Philippines, India, Cuba, Vietnam, El Salvador, Korea, Dominican Republic, Canada.

BRIDGE Fact Sheet

SOURCES:

"Profile of the Foreign-Born Population in the United States: 2000," U.S. Census Bureau, 2001.

Hobbs, Frank and Nichole Stoops. "The Foreign Born Population in the United States: 2000," US Census Bureau, 2002.

Gibson, Campbell J. and Kay Jung. "Historical Census Statistics on Population Totals By Race, 1790 to 1990, and By Hispanic Origin, 1970 to 1990, For The United States, Regions, Divisions, and States." US Census Bureau. Washington D.C., 2002.

Gibson, Campbell J. and Emily Lennon. "Historical Census Statistics on the Foreign-born Population of the United States: 1850-1990". U.S. Bureau of the Census. Washington D.C., 1999.

the changing demographics of race and migration

Building on Success Stories

WHY DO IT?
- To use case studies shared by immigrant rights and racial justice organizations to analyze problems, and sharpen analysis and problem-solving skills
- To discuss strategies for problem solving
- To explore any problem-solving approaches that might be applicable to those participants' communities

TIME 50 minutes

MATERIALS NEEDED
- Copies of small group handouts
- Easel paper, pens, markers, tape

FACILITATOR PREPARATION
- Check the suggested discussion questions at the end of each Success Story. Make any changes you need to ensure that the questions are relevant for your group

DIRECTIONS

1. Explain to participants that this exercise will examine different scenarios faced by community groups in Los Angeles, Atlanta, and New York, including:
   - Intervening in conflicts
   - Taking pro-active steps of inclusion, collaboration and coalition building
   - Initiating recruitment, education, leadership development and organizing among several different nationalities and ethnicities (both within a single organization and within a coalition of organizations)
   - Developing the tools and resources necessary to promote immigrant leadership

2. Divide participants into three small groups. Distribute small group discussion questions.
3. Ask small groups to read and discuss their case study. (30 minutes)
4. Reconvene the large group, and ask each group to briefly give a summary of their group's story, and different strategies that organizers in the case studies used to overcome challenges. Then discuss with the large group:
   - What are some ways of resolving conflict or coalition-building that you would like to use?
   - Do you think that your organization/union/church should be working with different race and nationality groups? If so, break down the steps through which such a process could take place. What can you and other members do to get the ball rolling on this?

SOURCE the authors

handout

Building on Success Stories
Small Group Scenarios/Discussion Questions

Latino Day Laborers & Jewish Residents Reach Agreement, Los Angeles

For over the past 25 years, the corner of Beverly and La Jolla—in the parking lot of a local paint store, had served as the place where mostly Mexican and Central American day laborers gathered to look for work. While the old owner of the paint store didn't mind having day laborers in his lot, things changed after he sold the store. The new owners kicked the day laborers out, and had to stand on the street corners to look for work.

A few of the neighborhood residents, who were mostly elderly and Jewish, called the police to complain. Although the day laborers stood on public property and had committed no crime, the police officers began to harass and arrest the workers. Threatened with more arrests, the workers began to organize with the Day Laborer Leadership Program of the Coalition for Humane Immigrant Rights of Los Angeles (CHIRLA).

First, CHIRLA organizers went door to door to talk with the different residents. In these neighborhood visits, they found out some surprising information. They discovered that the residents held a wide variety of opinions on the day laborers, and that the two women who most frequently called the police did not speak for all the residents. Some residents had even hired the day laborers in the past. The organizers also found that while most of the residents in the neighborhood were Jewish seniors, many younger Asians and Russians had moved into the neighborhood. Some of the older residents were feeling threatened by this change.

Next, CHIRLA and the workers talked to the local police—a new captain who was more open to working out solutions—and to the paint store owner. Together, they decided that the day laborers could meet in a lot across the street from the paint store. But residents opposed to the deal said "No way!" Finally, CHIRLA and the workers decided to hold a community meeting. Before the community meeting, CHIRLA held meetings with the workers, and they discussed stereotypes about the Jewish residents. The process took a long time, but at the end, workers agreed that many of the stereotypes were not valid.

The community forum was well attended, with over 70 participants. The organizers arranged for simultaneous interpretation through headsets, and the police agreed to send a beat cop to the meeting to observe. The dialogue gave workers the opportunity to respond to how residents treated them. Participants agreed that workers could continue to meet across the street from the paint store. Workers agreed not to litter and to keep the alley clean. Workers pledged to stay in their designated area and leave space for people to move through.

Building on Success Stories: Day Laborers & Residents, con't...

Mayron, an organizer, expressed satisfaction with the lasting results of the dialogue. "Every time I go by the corner the guys are still there. They're still in the designated area and sticking to agreements."

Discussion Questions:
1. Who are the groups involved in this situation? Why did the day laborers and CHIRLA staff find it necessary to work with other groups? What were some of the ways they began to work with other communities?
2. Who were the decision-makers in the situation? What did the workers and organizers do to work with them in this situation?
3. What were some of the challenges that the workers and organizers faced? What were some of the strategies they used to overcome these challenges?
4. Are you and your community experiencing any conflicts or problems where you could visualize using some of the methods in this story? If so, how? If not, why not?

After your group is finished, choose 1-2 people to report back to the large group a quick description of your case study, and the strategies that the groups used to overcome the challenges.

CHIRLA: Coalition for Humane Immigrant Rights Los Angeles, www.chirla.org.

handout

Reaching Out To Newcomers through the Brown/Black Alliance in Atlanta, GA

Like many other places in the U.S. South, Atlanta has drawn increasing numbers of Latinos and other immigrants and refugees since the mid-1990s. While the majority of new Latino immigrants come from Mexico, the community also includes people from Venezuela, Argentina, Columbia and other countries. Some African American organizations took initiative to learn about and reach out to the expanding Latino community.

Project South, a community membership popular education and action organization with roots in the African American freedom struggle, made these links, especially through its Youth Council. Project South's Christi Ketchum recalled, "We'd seen the tensions build up around jobs and limited resources. We knew the history of divisions, so we believed in bringing the two cultures together to learn about each other."

African American youth conducted strong outreach to bring Latinos to its annual Summer Institute in 2001, which featured an hour-long play by Sueño Latino, a drama group that on youth issues. The play portrayed the array of problems impacting the community, including substance abuse, domestic violence, punitive immigration laws, police brutality, and mistreatment of immigrant youth.

After the groups got some experience working together, the two African American groups (Project South and Alternative Roots), and the two Latino groups (Sueño Latino and Somos), jointly approached the Community Foundation of Georgia for resources to continue to work together.

The groups have spent time together sharing foods, stories, cultures, and staging events. Christi says that it takes a lot of time and patience to work together in the collaborative. Project South and Alternative Roots are the organizations that have been around longer, and they have some staff to help push along the program. As newer groups, Sueño Latino and Somos do not. Sueño Latino produced and performed another play for Atlanta's 2003 Juneteenth celebration, which commemorated the day slaves in Texas finally learned they were free.

"As a movement-building organization, we've got to be broad based," says Christi. "We can leave no one behind. Everyone has got to be brought to the table. Everyone has got to participate. We cannot go on without you. The communicating, the understanding, the learning never stops. It keeps on happening down through the generations."

Reaching Out To Newcomers, con't...

Discussion Questions:
1. Who are the groups involved in this situation? Why did they find it necessary to work with other groups? What were some of the ways they began to work with each other?
2. What were some of the challenges that the groups faced? What were some of the strategies they used to overcome these challenges?
3. Do you see opportunities in your city where different communities or different sections within an ethnic group could work in closer collaboration with each other? What issues or ways could the different communities work together?
4. What does it take to work together as equals in this situation? What kinds of inequalities, differences, and misunderstandings can come up? How can they be addressed?

After your group is finished, choose 1-2 people to report back to the large group a quick description of your case study, and the strategies that the groups used to overcome the challenges.

Project South, 9 Gammon Ave. Atlanta, Georgia 30315. Tel: 404.622.0602, www.projectsouth.org.

Organizing Immigrant Domestic Workers Across Nationalities, Languages & Cultures in New York

Domestic workers in New York City represent a huge workforce of immigrant women with very diverse backgrounds. They come from many different ethnic and racial backgrounds, and speak many languages. But they all face similar issues in their work, including problems such as long hours, low wages, isolation, lack of vacation time and health care.

In 2000, Domestic Workers United was formed, representing a number of community groups who worked within their own communities to organize domestic workers—including workers who are Caribbean, Haitian, Filipina, Tibetan, Malaysian, Indonesian, and South Asian. While many of the groups had previously worked to target individual abusive employers, they began to feel that this strategy was limited. Groups had gotten familiar with each other through supporting one another's rallies and campaigns over the years. Together, they believed that any real change in the domestic work industry could only happen if the entire workforce was united and organized around one standard of dignity, justice and human rights for all. Today, Domestic Workers United is predominantly comprised of Caribbean immigrant women, and led by a Steering Committee of Asian and Caribbean domestic workers. DWU engages in efforts to build power among all domestic workers to transform the domestic work industry of New York City to one where workers rights and dignity are respected.

Working together successfully across race and nationality lines required a focus on political education. DWU's Nanny's Training Course offered job skills and leadership training for nannies. In the course, workers participate in workshops in CPR and child psychology along with sessions on the impact of globalization on the home countries of immigrant communities. Looking at diverse experiences together, where certain common themes and patterns can be drawn out, helps to build unity and consciousness of one another's stories.

DWU also emphasizes leadership development. The leaders in the group try to represent different leadership styles and cultures, and to reflect the membership in terms of style/personality, language and immigration status. Also, the group has created social spaces to build across race and nationality lines, through retreats, parties, dinners and other informal spaces. DWU holds most of their meetings in English. Because DWU does not have any Spanish-speaking organizers, and has not yet come into contact with Latino organizations focused on organizing domestic workers, it hasn't yet built a large membership of Latina workers.

handout

Organizing Immigrant Domestic Workers, con't...

Discussion Questions:
1. Why did the women in this story find it necessary to organize across ethnic and racial lines? What helped them to do this? What were some of the challenges?
2. What were some of the strategies that DWU used to overcome these challenges?
3. Is the membership of your organization, union, church, etc. cross-racial or cross-nationality, or both? What are the main racial and nationality and language groups of your organization? Is your organization/union/church made up principally of a single group? Do you believe that it should be serving other racial and nationality groups as well?
4. What are the special needs and contributions of each group involved in your organization? How are these needs and contributions addressed? Are some addressed while others are not?

After your group is finished, choose 1-2 people to report back to the large group a quick description of your case study, and the strategies that the groups used to overcome the challenges.

Domestic Workers United, www.domesticworkersunited.org. c/o CAAAV, 2437 Valentine Ave., Bronx, NY 10458. Tel: 718-220-7391 x 11.

the changing demographics of race and migration — module 7

Closing: Our Common Circle

WHY DO IT?
- To demonstrate and appreciate the participants' shared experience
- To provide a sense of closure for the day

TIME 5-10 minutes

MATERIALS NEEDED none

DIRECTIONS

1. Ask the group to form a large circle, standing and facing inwards.
2. Explain to the group that you will be reading off a list of statements. Ask participants to take a step forward if they agree with the statement.
3. Read the statements to the group, and have everyone step forward. (The object of this exercise is to read statements that everyone could agree with.) Continue until everyone in the group is standing very close to each other, and have a group hug, celebratory yell, or other ways to express thanks to the group.

Here is a sample list of statements:
- I learned something new today.
- I found out something new about someone I didn't know so well.
- I have some new ideas about my work.
- I want to work with other people in my community.
- I want to work with people outside my community.
- I appreciate this group!

SOURCE the authors

Michelle Yamashita

the changing demographics of race and migration

resources

Organizations:

Domestic Workers United, www.domesticworkersunited.org. c/o CAAAV, 2437 Valentine Ave., Bronx, NY 10458. Tel: (718) 220-7391 x 11.

Highlander Center, www.highlandercenter.org. 1959 Highlander Way, New Market, TN 37820. Tel: (865) 933-3443

Incite! Women of Color Against Violence. www.incite-national.org. (National group.) P.O. Box 6861, Minneapolis, MN 55406. Tel: (415) 553-3837.

Institute for Multiracial Justice, www.multiracialjustice.org. 522 Valencia Street, San Francisco, CA 94110. Tel: (415) 701-9501.

Labor/Community Strategy Center, www.thestrategycenter.org. 3780 Wilshire Blvd., Suite 1200, Los Angeles, CA 90010. Tel: (213) 387-2800.

National Organizer's Alliance, www.noacentral.org. 715 G Street SE. Washington, DC 20003. Tel: (202)543-6603. If your current work (or the majority of your work—whether paid or unpaid—for the past 5 years) is to build democratic structures and leadership to empower people to gain social, economic and environmental justice, join NOA as a member! Check out their website for membership information.

MIWON: Multiethnic Immigrant Workers Organizing Network. MIWON is a coalition of the Garment Worker Center, Pilipino Worker Center, CHIRLA: Coalition for Humane Immigrant Rights Los Angeles, and KIWA: Korean Immigrant Worker Advocates. MIWON's focuses on leadership development and civic participation of immigrant workers from different communities to improve workplace and living conditions. Visit www.garmentworkercenter.org, www.kiwa.org, and www.chirla.org for more information.

Poverty & Race Research Action Council (PRRAC), www.prrac.org. 3000 Connecticut Ave., N.W., Suite 200, Washington, DC 20008. Tel: (202) 387-9887

Project South: Institute for the Elimination of Poverty and Genocide, www.projectsouth.org. 9 Gammon Ave. Atlanta, Georgia 30315. Tel: (404)622-0602.

Southeast Regional Economic Justice Network, www.rejn.org. P.O. Box 240, Durham, NC 27702. Tel: (919)683-4310.

Women of Color Resource Center. www.coloredgirls.org. 1611 Telegraph Ave. #303, Oakland, CA 94612. Tel: (510) 444-2700.

the changing demographics of race and migration module 7

Educational Resources and Publications:

Colorlines Magazine: Race, Culture, Action. Quarterly magazine. Available at www.colorlines.com.

The Energy of a Nation: Immigrants in America, a video and study guide. Produced by Minnesota Advocates for Human Rights. Available at www.mnadvocates.org.

From the Borderline to the Colorline: A Report on Anti-Immigrant Racism in the United States. Produced by the National Network for Immigrant and Refugee Rights. This report provides an in-depth picture of the nature of anti-immigrant racism in the U.S. today. Through personal testimony and frontline analysis, it details key issues impacting immigrant and refugee communities -- from trafficking, enforcement, and detention centers, to policy, legislation, and social rights. Available at www.nnirr.org.

Grantmakers Concerned with Immigrants and Refugees (GCIR). www.gcir.org. This website features in-depth statistics, resources, and information on immigration in the U.S. and internationally.

The New Americans: Building Bridges: Deepening Understanding Between Long-Term Residents and New Immigrants. Study guide to documentary series, The New Americans. Available at www.activevoice.net/New-Americans.shtml.

Finding Common Ground II:
Transforming Conflict in Community Organizing

transforming conflict in community organizing module 8

WHY DO IT? The goals of this workshop are to:
- Reflect upon our different conceptions and styles of conflict
- Challenge our current understandings of conflict
- Identify how our approaches to conflict can improve when we are able to place problems in a wider context

WHAT WILL BE TAKING ABOUT In this workshop, we will think about the following questions:
- How do we manage conflict in our lives? In our community?
- What are some other ways that we can see conflict?
- Why is it so important to reframe conflict and put it in a wider context?
- What are the resources that our community has developed to deal with conflict?

NOTE TO FACILITATORS Because this module addresses divisions and conflicts within and between communities, we strongly recommend that facilitators and participants use introductory BRIDGE modules that examine larger social and political contexts before engaging this one. Introductory modules include: "Immigration History 101," "Globalization, Migration, and Workers' Rights," "Introduction to Race, Migration, and Multiple Oppressions," as well as "Common Ground I."

This module, unlike other BRIDGE modules, has not been tested in community-based settings, and is less developed than the other modules. Feedback from community members, as well as the significance of the topic encouraged us to include this module in BRIDGE, even in this rough form. We encourage your feedback to improve and expand upon it.

transforming conflict in community organizing

Backgrounder: Conflict Transformation as a Tool for Community Building

Conflict is a part of all human relations, and a part of everyday life. For those who work to build social and racial justice in communities, conflict is often a very common outcome. In the course of testing out BRIDGE in different settings, we heard repeated requests for a tool to address conflict within communities and organizations. As a result, we developed this module as a tool for organizers to be more intentional in dealing with conflict. While conflict often stirs up unpleasant emotions and reactions for everyone involved, moments of conflict can also become important learning opportunities. As social justice activists, we need to practice what we preach within our own organizations, so when conflict happens within our organizations or movements, we need to develop ways to address it in a constructive way. Conflict transformation can become an important tool to increase our own capacity as organizations, communities, and individuals to fight for justice.

Engaging in conflict transformation can address local challenges that can lead to the development of new alliances. Conflicts that our communities experience at the local level take place within a wider social and historical context of oppression and exclusion, as well as resistance and struggle for survival and liberation. For example, what appears at the local level as competition for jobs or services has the potential to be redefined as common ground in the struggle for shared human rights. Examples of this include hostility between African Americans and immigrant communities, tensions within communities between U.S.-born or permanent residents and undocumented immigrants, as well as conflict within our own organizations. Learning to integrate our values and visions of social justice with conflict resolution is not only a matter of personal, psychological, organizational, and political survival. It's also a critical part of resistance and movement building.

Without an intentional approach to conflict resolution, we can reproduce the methods and values of dominant cultures, focusing on only "winning" or "losing," or overpowering and destroying our opponents. In many cases, conflict occurs within our own organizations, communities, and movements, and when handled badly, results in a collective loss.

Several strategies towards conflict resolution find that reframing conflict is itself an essential starting point to conflict transformation and peace building. In this module, we offer a few activities and discussion questions to begin examining the way in which we understand or define conflict. This module does not, however, provide a full orientation to mediation skills, nor does it address a valid critique of the growing mediation-for-profit industry, which can often disempower survivors from access to avenues for justice.

transforming conflict in community organizing — module 8

SUMMARY POINTS

- Local tensions and conflict often take part within a context of larger inequalities.
- Conflict is one facet of relationships in society. Conflict can only occur when there is a relationship; it often erupts in situations where awareness of injustice is present.
- Understanding how we view conflict within our own lives, within our organizations, and more broadly is useful in transforming conflict.
- Conflict is not an anomaly—it is inevitable, we need to expect conflict! We need concrete strategies to integrate conflict transformation as a part of our organizing efforts.
- Conflict transformation can be one tool to establish a relationship based on equality and mutual respect.
- Our communities have developed different ways of viewing conflict, and have also developed resources and limitations on how to address conflict. These resources and limitations are often shaped by our communities' privileges and oppressions.

WORKSHOP MENU

Activity:	Time:
Welcome, introduction to the workshop, review of summary points	10 minutes
Review Objectives/Ground Rules	10 minutes
*Opening: Naming Conflict	30 minutes
*Visualizing Personal Experiences of Conflict and Steps to Conflict Transformation	90 minutes
Changing the Script: Visualizing Solutions to Conflict	90 minutes
Closing: Naming Conflict Transformation	15 minutes
Evaluation	10 minutes

*core exercise

Total Time: 4 hours

transforming conflict in community organizing

A FEW WORDS FOR FACILITATORS

This module offers a few activities and discussion questions to begin examining the way in which we understand or define conflict, but does not provide a full orientation to mediation skills.

In what kinds of situations is this module useful?

This module can be used as part of a process for participants to understand conflicts that may develop between different ethnic communities and/or between different sectors of a single ethnic community. This module is useful for situations when participants are not engaged in an intense conflict, but want to address how conflict works in their lives. The session/ module is designed to discuss and practice some concrete exercises for conflict resolution.

In what kinds of situations would this module NOT work?
- When a conflict is too polarized to permit a respectful dialogue, or a situation that would require a more formal mediation/conflict resolution.
- When groups are unable to make commitments to build the long-term relationships necessary to implement lasting measures
- The facilitators cannot put sufficient time and energy into the necessary preparation and follow through

transforming conflict in community organizing module 8

Opening: Naming Conflict

WHY DO IT?
- To use as an introduction and opening activity
- To frame the day's activities around the topic of conflict
- To begin investigating different conceptions of conflict

TIME 30 minutes

MATERIALS NEEDED
- Easel paper, markers, tape
- Slips of paper or sticky notes and pens (enough for all participants)

DIRECTIONS

1. Explain to the group that this activity will explore our common understandings of conflict.

2. Distribute a slip of paper or sticky note to each person. Ask participants to find a partner, preferably someone they don't know. If there is an odd number of participants, form one group of three.

3. Ask participants to briefly introduce themselves to each other, and then to brainstorm words and phrases that come to mind when they think about conflict. How do you name conflict in your culture/ language? (Some words that come to mind include: *problemas, fracas, blowout, mess, desmadre,* (Spanish) *dajia,* (Mandarin Chinese) *jontu* or *tujaeng* (Korean), *chingazo* (Spanish), etc.) (5 minutes)

4. After partners have brainstormed, ask participants to think of one word that they generated in their discussion, and to write it on their slip of paper.

5. Reconvene the large group. Ask everyone to place his or her post-it up on a large piece of butcher paper and then sit down. Go around the room and ask each person to introduce her/himself, and to name the word or brief phrase that they posted, and to explain what the word means to them.

6. Discuss the activity with the large group.
   - What did you notice about the words that were generated?
   - What were the similarities between the words?
   - What were the differences between the words? Are there any specific cultural, ethnic, gender, race, or nationality dimensions to the way we view conflict?

transforming conflict in community organizing

7. Review teaching points with the group.

TEACHING POINTS
- Conflict, as a concept, is often charged with negative meanings, such as disorder, disharmony, chaos, anger.
- Many cultures also view conflict as an opportunity to bring about something positive. A common example is how the Chinese word for "crisis"--*weiji*--contains both the characters for "danger" and for "opportunity."
- Conflict is only one type of a broad spectrum of relationships that we have with other people, and can be transformed into something that benefits everyone.

SOURCE the authors, adapted from John Paul Lederach, *Beyond Prescription: New Lenses for Conflict Resolution Training Across Cultures*

transforming conflict in community organizing   module 8

Visualizing Personal Experiences of Conflict and Steps to Conflict Transformation

WHY DO IT?
- To explore our personal experiences with conflict
- To examine different styles of dealing with conflict and identify our own individual styles
- To examine the concepts of interests and demands

TIME 90 minutes

MATERIALS NEEDED
- Paper, pens, markers, crayons and other art supplies (enough for all participants)
- Easel paper, markers, tape
- Copies of handout for all participants

FACILITATOR PREP
- Review the handout thoroughly before conducting this module

DIRECTIONS

1. Explain to the group that this exercise will be a chance to explore the role of conflict in our lives, and to think about the different styles of handling conflict.

2. Ask everyone to arrange their chairs so that they are not touching any of the other participants. Then ask participants to close their eyes, to breathe deeply, and to relax in their chairs. Lead them through a visualization exercise (we provide the following one here as an example.) (5 minutes)

   Close your eyes, and relax.
   Feel your body get heavy, from your legs, your arms, and your chest.
   Take a few deep breaths. Breathe deeply into your belly, so that you can feel your stomach rise when you breathe in, and fall when you breathe out.

   Remember a conflict that you were involved in.
   Who was involved? Picture that person.
   What did the other person want? Think about what the other person wanted.
   What did you want? Think about what you wanted in that situation.
   How did the conflict turn out? Did it turn out in a good way?
   Slowly open your eyes, and bring your attention to the present moment.
   Look at the floor—what color is the floor?
   Look at the wall—what color is the wall?

transforming conflict in community organizing

3. Distribute a piece of paper and a pen to all the participants. Ask participants to quietly find a place where they can draw a picture of what they visualized. It can be any picture that helps "tell the story" of what happened and who was involved. (10 minutes)

4. Ask participants to find a partner, and to share their drawing with their partner. Groups should answer the following questions when sharing their drawing: (20 minutes)
   - Who was involved in the conflict?
   - What did you want in the conflict?
   - What did the other person/group want in the conflict?
   - What was the outcome of the conflict?
   - What did you like about the way you resolved this conflict? What didn't you like about the way you resolved this conflict?

5. Reconvene the large group. Briefly process the exercise with participants. How did the visualization make them feel?

6. Distribute the handout to participants. Review the contents of the handout with participants by defining the difference between needs and demands, the difference of styles and outcomes to conflict management, and the steps needed for conflict resolution.

   Discuss with the large group:
   - What are the advantages for each style of conflict resolution?
   - What are the disadvantages for each style of conflict resolution?
   - Are there other styles in addition to the four we've talked about that you want to add to the list?
   - What are some factors that may influence our individual styles of handling conflict?
   - Do you use the same style of resolving conflict for most situations? Why do you think you do this?
   - How does inequality in power affect the different strategies that we bring to resolving conflict? (Factors affecting power inequality can include immigration status, race, class, gender, age, sexual orientation, and other forms of inequality or privilege.)

transforming conflict in community organizing — module 8

7. Ask participants to think about the conflict that they had envisioned earlier in the exercise. Ask each participant to name one thing that they would do differently in the conflict, based on the discussion that they have had today.

8. Review the teaching points with the large group.

TEACHING POINTS

- There are several styles of resolving conflict, which include: avoidance, accommodation, confrontation, and compromise. One strategy doesn't always apply to all situations; different styles work in different contexts.
- There are several outcomes of conflict, which include: I win, you lose; you win, I lose; I lose, you lose; I win, you win.
- We have developed different ways of viewing conflict, sometimes shaped by the different contexts of privilege or oppression.
- Different communities have developed many resources to address conflict.
- Conflicts are successfully resolved when the needs of both parties are met.

SOURCE the authors. We also drew the four basic methods of dealing with disputes, especially around race, from conflict resolution methods used by high school students and staff.

handout

Conflict Transformation in Community Organizing

Needs are: key, fundamental, underlying principles
Demands are: your position—what you want to bargain for

Four Styles of Handling Conflict:
- Avoidance: Avoid conflict at all costs; or denial that there is a problem
- Accommodation: Accommodate the demands of the other group to avoid conflict or negotiation
- Confrontation: Demand that the other party take your needs into account, demand a change
- Compromise: Both parties come to the table with their demands, but also make offers as well

Four Outcomes of Handling Conflict:
- I lose, you win: My needs are not met while the other person's are fully met
- I win, you lose: The conflict is only resolved when I come out on top and the other person comes out on the bottom
- I lose, you lose: The conflict results in neither of us having our needs met
- I win, you win: I assert my rights and respect your needs, so the conflict is resolved in a way that benefits both of us

handout

Some steps for transforming conflict between community members:

1. Allow people to name the problem, express how it has impacted them personally and as a community.

2. Explore the historical or larger context of the conflict.

3. Listen to how the problem has impacted the other side and recognize the humanity and rights of the other side.

4. Acknowledge your own role in the conflict.

5. Search for shared experiences that you have with the other side, such as shared hurts and suffering, cultural or spiritual sources of understanding and support, common humanity, etc.

6. Recognize the connections and interdependence between communities.

7. Determine what's appropriate for your situation. Is it building a short term, task-oriented solution to defuse a dangerous conflict or a more long term alliance to address deeper levels of interests?

8. Work together to elaborate win/win solutions that are mutually beneficial to all parties.

9. If necessary, develop a formal agreement to capture the spirit of the unity people reach.

10. Identify mechanisms and parties who will be responsible for convening another dialogue or problem-solving process to resolve any conflicts that may arise in the future in a mutually positive way.

11. Figure out the ways to publicize and mobilize people in the broader community in order to implement the agreement or new understanding.

transforming conflict in community organizing

Changing the Script: Visualizing Solutions to Conflict

WHY DO IT?
- To allow participants to collectively visualize different solutions to conflict
- To use theater and role-playing techniques to develop creative problem-solving tools for conflict transformation

TIME 90 minutes

MATERIALS NEEDED none

FACILITATOR PREP
- You may find it useful to familiarize yourself with Augusto Boal's work, Theater of the Oppressed and his technique of "Forum Theater," on which this activity is based.

DIRECTIONS

1. Explain to the group that this exercise will be a way to examine conflicts that we have experienced, and to visualize different solutions as a group through theater exercises.

2. Ask participants to think a conflict in the community, or between different community groups for which they would like to develop some solutions. The conflicts could be based on one of the scenarios from the earlier exercise. Explain that the large group will pick one example of a conflict upon which to focus, act out, and develop solutions. Ask for a few volunteers who are willing to share their situation with the rest of the group. After a few participants have shared their scenarios, have the whole group decide, through a show of hands, which scenario that they would like to work on during the activity. Be sure to thank the volunteers for taking a risk and sharing their example of conflict.

3. After the group has decided on the scenario that they would like to work on, ask the following questions:
   - Who are the main characters in this scenario?
   - What are the causes of this conflict?
   - How is the conflict resolved in this case?

4. "Take One:" pick volunteers to act out the scene as it happened in front of the large group, and lead volunteers through a dramatization of the conflict.

transforming conflict in community organizing — module 8

5. Divide the large group into 2-3 small groups. Ask small groups to meet for 10 minutes to develop strategies and solutions to transform and resolve the conflict, and then present it as a skit. The only condition is that all of the solutions must be realistic—something within the realm of possibility when the conflict took place. There is no "magic" in our drama—for example, a large gust of wind cannot suddenly appear and sweep one of the people away.

6. "Take Two!" Reconvene the large group. Ask a participant to briefly recap the original conflict. Then ask each small group to act out their skits.

7. After the dramas are completed, process the activity with the large group.
    - What were some helpful hints for conflict resolution?
    - What are some actions that hinder conflict resolution?
    - What are some actions that might both help and hinder conflict resolution?

SOURCE the authors, inspired by Augusto Boal's *Theater of the Oppressed*

transforming conflict in community organizing

Closing: Naming Conflict Transformation

WHY DO IT?
- To reflect on the day's theme of conflict resolution
- To envision successful resolutions to conflict
- To provide a sense of closure for the day in a creative, shared experience

TIME 15 minutes

MATERIALS NEEDED
- Slips of paper or sticky notes and pens (enough for all participants)
- Sticky notes from the opening exercise
- Easel paper and markers

FACILITATOR PREP
- Write the words "conflict" and "conflict transformation" on two large pieces of easel paper. Place the paper or sticky notes from the opening exercise on the piece of easel paper that says "conflict."

DIRECTIONS

1. Distribute a slip of paper or a sticky note and pen to all participants.
2. Explain to participants that since the day's activities began with words connected with "conflict," we will close the day's activities thinking about the "opposite of conflict."
3. Ask participants to briefly think of a word that has an opposite meaning than the word conflict, and to write it down on their paper. (Some examples include: resolution, peace, agreement, etc.)
4. Gather the group into a large circle. In the middle of the circle, place the large pieces of easel paper with the words "conflict" and "conflict transformation."
5. Go around the circle, and ask each participant to read their statement aloud, and then place their sticky note on a place the easel paper that says "conflict transformation."
6. Thank the group for their participation.

SOURCE the authors

Additional Thoughts on Conflict Transformation

But what if...

> *"We're already in the middle of a conflict, and we can't wait until there is a training on mediation!"*

This module is not intended to diffuse conflict, but here are some tips to consider in establishing a constructive context for conflict resolution:

- Working with members from all interested parties, identify who needs to be in the room to name the problem and think of solutions. It may be most helpful to identify people who occupy mid-level positions in organizations, such as field organizers or community leaders. They may be more familiar with the concrete context and challenges of the conflict, and have developed strong relationships with members at the base. As this process unfolds, however, commitment from and incorporation of formal organizational leadership will become essential.

- Determine whether there are a sufficient numbers of people from both sides willing to invest time and commitment to resolve the conflict.

- Conduct outreach and in-depth investigation before the largermeeting. Solicit opinions on the problem from all those involved, and encourage people to become involved in the process and participate in a meeting to voice their opinions and to help create solutions. Especially if the situation is highly polarized, the investigation team needs to learn how each of the different sets of impacted parties view the conflict and its history of development.

- After outreach and initial investigation has been completed, share what has been learned among the facilitators' team in order to propose a agenda that will incorporate the priority issues of the different parties and prepare for the meeting.

- Take any extra preparation steps necessary to propose an agenda that will help participants break through negative stereotyping and mutual recriminations to encourage active listening and engagement.

- Recognize that different parties will have different needs to "come to terms with the past" and deepen sharing of the impacts of a problem instead of figuring out how to move forward. As necessary, facilitators can give participants the opportunity to reach consensus about how much of the process needs to be "slowed down" to deal with reflection and summation of the conflict's history, or "speeded up" to deal with next steps and action plans.

- If the discussion becomes extremely muddled or frustrating for participants, don't be afraid to call time out for the facilitators to caucus and develop a revised agenda proposal for how the discussion could proceed more effectively. Facilitators can gauge whether participants need to take a break or if they want to

Additional Thoughts on Conflict Transformation

talk in small groups. Small group discussions allow each participant to check in and offer any suggestions they want to report back to the larger group.
- Sometimes participants can take positive steps to develop closer relations through focusing on a common task, need or problem without necessarily focusing on the tension or conflict. Goodwill built through those small acts can in turn nourish the overall process.
- When non-English speaking immigrants are involved in a conflict with English speakers, take the necessary steps to conduct simultaneous interpretation of activities as part of your preparation. Failure to do so will put immigrant participants at a severe disadvantage, and deny English-speaking participants access to important information from immigrant participants.

What skills do you need on your facilitation team?

The optimal situation would be for the facilitator's team to include a person from the same ethnicity, migration status, and gender from each of the key parties in the dispute, who have some understanding of and connection to the issues. The Centre for Conflict Resolution in Cape Town, South Africa includes in its training manual for community mediators a number of basic skills that have proved helpful in resolving community and family conflicts, some of which are summarized below. If your team includes or can develop a majority of the following skills, you're off to a great start! These skills include:

- Commitment to the reconciliation process
- Good communication skills to draw people out and not to allow a few individuals to dominate the discussion, including the facilitators!
- Conciliation, facilitation, and mediation skills
- Ability to use positive paraphrasing and summary statements to calm rhetoric and facilitate constructive communication
- Ability to identify the main parties and stakeholders and analyze the situation
- Ability to help people recognize and challenge stereotypes
- Ability to recognize and have the group address any specific language, social and cultural factors that may influence the process
- Ability to minimize and avoid being manipulated by one side or the other
- Ability to help people reach mutually agreeable, sustainable solutions
- Humor, patience and tolerance
- Ability to distinguish between each party's formal stated position vs. its actual interests or needs. Interests are deeper needs or concerns that are vitally important to the parties. Questioning and digging down into interests yields

Additional Thoughts on Conflict Transformation

fertile ground for creating solutions by getting to the core issues of what people really want. For example, a group of workers may have a large list of demands,, but a primary need for economic security and respect. By examining and addressing peoples' core interests and needs instead of looking at more surface issues of demands and positions, different parties can find the seeds of a mutually beneficial resolution.

Is there a role for religion and spirituality in this process?
Yes! While at times, religion has been used to justify oppression and inflame intolerance and violence, teachings in many different religions advocate respect and acceptance of "the other", forgiveness, and peace. Those seeking peace in many conflicts have found shared expression of different faiths and rituals to be a comforting and powerful means to bring them closer together. If you can call on priests, imams, pastors, elders, rabbis, monks, nuns, etc. from different faiths involved in the conflict to lend support or give suggestions for relevant prayers and rituals, by all means do so. You may also want to be careful to honor all different faiths—including those who are agnostics or atheists—in a respectful and equitable way.

What role does racial, class, gender, and cultural difference play in conflicts?
Racial, class, gender, and cultural differences can make conflicts between different groups even more challenging than when disputes break out between members of the same background. For example, different communities value different types of communication, such as eye contact, touching, bluntness, informality, joking, voice tone and volume, and varied forms of address according to age, gender and social positions. The more diverse the group is, the more time you will need to adapt the process to ensure that everyone is on board. Finding creative ways for the different parties to learn about and listen to other cultures can provide an avenue to develop friendships across the old divisions.

Resources

Curriculum and Training Guides:

Centre for Conflict Resolution, African Case Studies Manual for Conflict Resolution Training (Rondebosch, South Africa: University of Cape Town). This manual teaches students conflict resolution methodology through processing ten case studies of conflicts in several African countries at http://ccrweb.ccr.uct.ac.za/training_material/casestudies.pdf.

www.restorativejustice.org. This website provides training manuals, articles, and resources on the model of restorative justice. Restorative Justice is a systematic response to wrongdoing that emphasizes healing the wounds of victims, offenders and communities. Practices and programs reflecting restorative purposes will respond to crime by: identifying and taking steps to repair harm; involving all stakeholders, and transforming the traditional relationship between communities and their governments in responding to crime.

Works Cited and Further Reading:

Augusto Boal, *Theater of the Oppressed*, (New York: Theater Communications Group, 1979).

Augusto Boal, *Legislative Theater: Using Performance to Make Politics,* (London and New York: Routledge Press: 1998).

Bev Bruke, Jojo Geronimo, D'Arcy Martin, Barb Thomas, and Carol Wall, *Education for Changing Unions*, (Toronto: Between the Lines Press, 2000).

Equipo Maíz, *Vamos a Jugar Otra Vez: Juegos y Dinámicas para la Educación, no. 2* (El Salvador, C.A.: Asociacion Equipo Maiz, 2000).

Robert Evans and Alice Frazer Evans with Ronald Kraybill, *Peace Skills: Manual for Community Mediators*, (San Francisco: Jossey Bass Press, 2001).

Lederach, John Paul, *Beyond Prescription: New Lenses for Conflict Resolution Training Across Cultures* (Syracuse: Syracuse University Press, 1994).

Mohammed Abu-Nimer (ed.), *Reconciliation, Justice, and Coexistence* (Lanham, Boulder, New York, Oxford: Lexington Books, 2001).

Linda Singer, *Settling Disputes: Conflict Resolution in Business, Families, and the Legal System* (New York: Harper Collins, 1994).

section three
appendix/resources

Additional Resources:

Curriculum Guides and Tools for Popular Educators:

Rick Arnold, Bev Burke, Carl James, D'Arcy Martin, and Barb Thomas. *Educating for a Change.* Toronto, Between the Lines Press, 1996. To order, visit www.btlbooks.com.

Bev Burke, Jojo Geronimo, D'Arcy Martin, Barb Thomas, and Carol Wall. *Education for Changing Unions.* Toronto, Between the Lines Press, 2002. To order, visit www.btlbooks.com.

Nancy Flowers with Marcia Bernbaum, Kristi Rudelius-Palmer, and Joel Tolman. *The Human Rights Education Handbook: Effective Practices for Learning, Action, and Change.* Minneapolis: Human Rights Resource Center, University of Minnesota, 2000. To order, visit www.hrusa.org.

Paulo Friere. *Pedagogy of the Oppressed.* Continuum Press, 2000 (reprint edition).

Paulo Friere and Ira Shor. *Pedagogy for Liberation.* Bergin and Garvey Press, 1987.

Paulo Friere. *Pedagogy of Freedom: Ethics, Democracy, and Civic Courage.* Rowman and Littlefield Press, 2000.

Highlander Center. *A Very Popular Economic Education Sampler.* Highlander Research and Education Center, 1997. To order, visit www.highlandercenter.org.

bell hooks. *Teaching to Transgress: Education as the Practice of Freedom.* New York: Routledge Presss, 1994.

Myles Horton, with Judigh Kol and Herbert Kohl. *The Long Haul: An Autobiography.* New York: Doubleday Press, 1990.

Miriam Ching Louie with Linda Burnham. *WEdGE: Women's Education in the Global Economy: A Workbook of Activities, Games, Skits and Strategies for Activists, Organizers, Rebels and Hell Raisers.* Women of Color Resource Center, 2000. To order, visit www.coloredgirls.org.

Minnesota Advocates for Human Rights. *The Energy of a Nation: Immigrants in America, A Video and Study Guide.* Minnesota Advocates for Human Rights, 1995. To order, visit www.mnadvocates.org.

New Mexico State University, Center for Latin and Border Studies. *Border Studies Curriculum: 20 Ready-To-Use Lesson Plans for the Secondary Classroom.* Available at www.nmsu.edu/~bsc/.

Project South. *Popular Education for Movement Building: A Project South Resource Guide, Volume 2.* Project South: Institute for the Elimination of Poverty and Genocide, 2001. To order, visit www.projectsouth.org.

Hugh Vasquez and Isoke Femi. *No Boundaries: A Manual for Unlearning Oppression and Building Multicultural Alliances.* Todos Institute, 1993. To order, call 510-444-6448.

Videos on Immigrant and Refugee Rights:

Border Crossings/Cruzando Fronteras documents the impact of the Border Patrol on the civil rights of community members in Southern Arizona. Produced by Heather Lares, Pan Left Productions. 30 minutes. Subtitled in English/Spanish. To order, visit www.nnirr.org.

La Ciudad/The City presents four vignettes depicting the struggles of Latin American immigrants in New York City. Beautifully shot in black and white, the separate stories - "Bricks," "Home," "The Puppeteer" and "Seamstress" - are connected by images from a studio photographer shooting portraits of the people in his community. Produced by David Riker. 83 minutes, 2001. Subtitled in English/Spanish. Facilitator's guide, written by Francisco Argüelles Paz y Puente, available in English and Spanish at http://www.pbs.org/itvs/thecity/resources.html. To order, contact Zeitgeist Films at 212-274-1989.

Echando Raices/Taking Root: Immigrant and Refugee Communities in California, Texas, and Iowa includes stories and reflections from immigrants and refugees are woven together with scenes of community life and a vibrant musical score. Includes a facilitator's discussion guide. Produced by the American Friends Service Committee. 60 minutes, 2002. Available in English and Spanish options. To order, visit www.takingroot.org.

Journey to Durban: Migrant Rights at the UN World Conference Against Racism follows the Immigrant Rights Working Group, a delegation of over 50 immigrant and refugee rights community leaders from the United States as they travel to Durban and work with other migrant and refugee rights organizers from around the world. The video documents the resulting work and accomplishments of an international group of immigrant and refugee rights organizers and activists at this conference, and projects the hopes and challenges that lie ahead. Produced by Peek Media and the National Network for Immigrant and Refugee Rights. 26 minutes, 2003. To order, visit www.nnirr.org.

The New Americans is a seven-hour PBS miniseries that focuses on the search for the American dream through the eyes of immigrants and refugees from Nigeria, India, the Dominican Republic, and Palestine. Filmed between 1998 and 2002, the series follows these newcomers before they leave their homelands and into their first years in America. The miniseries is also available in shorter, thematically-arranged versions for educators, and has a series of facilitators guides available for educators and organizers. Produced by Kartemquin Films. 7 hours, 2004. To order, visit http://www.pbs.org/independentlens/newamericans/.

New World Border is a film documenting the rise of human rights abuses along the US-Mexico border since the implementation of border walls (such as Operation Gatekeeper) that have been erected in populated areas throughout the border region during the last decade. This documentary includes interviews with immigrant rights organizers, testimony from immigrants, analysis of 'free trade' policies, and discusses current efforts to build a vibrant movement for immigrant rights." Produced by Peek Media. 28 minutes, 2001. To order, visit www.nnirr.org.

Raids and Rights: INS Activity in Washington. This video chronicles the impact of INS raids in a rural community, and efforts to fight back. Produced by Heather McRae Woolf, Sassafras Productions. 14 minutes. Subtitled in English/Spanish. To order, visit www.nnirr.org.

The Sixth Section tells the story of Grupo Unión, an extraordinary transnational union created by a community of Mexican immigrants living and working in Upstate New York. Through their collective efforts they have raised tens of thousands of American dollars to rebuild their Mexican hometown on Boqueron, Puebla. This revealing documentary sheds new light on an unexplored phenomenon driving the global economy and poignantly demonstrates how today's twenty-first century immigrants are redefining the "American Dream." Produced by Alex Rivera. 26 minutes, 2003. To order, visit www.pbs.org/pov/thesixthsection.

Los Trabajadores/The Workers. Through the words of immigrant workers and the families they've left behind, Los Trabajadores/The Workers tells the stories of workers at an Austin, Texas day labor site. It places their struggles and contributions in the context of the City's economic development, and reveals the impact of globalization on their lives. Produced by Heather Courtney. 48 minutes, 2002. To order and to see a discussion guide, visit www.daylabormovie.com.

Trade Secrets: The Hidden Costs of the FTAA. The FTAA would extend NAFTA to the rest of the Western Hemisphere, except for Cuba, including 31 more countries and another 400 million people. Scheduled for completion by 2005, it would be the most far-reaching free trade agreement ever negotiated. Trade Secrets examines in clear, concise language how NAFTA and FTAA impact workers' rights, the environment, and our democracy. Includes a viewer's discussion guide. Produced by Casey Peek and Jeremy Blasi, and the UC Berkeley Labor Center. 16 minutes, 2003. To order, visit http://henningcenter.berkeley.edu/projects/tradesecrets.html.

UPROOTED: Refugees of the Global Economy documents how the global economy has forced people to leave their home countries. UPROOTED presents three stories of immigrants who left their homes in Bolivia, Haiti, and the Philippines after global economic powers devastated their countries, only to face new challenges in the United States. These powerful stories raise critical questions about U.S. immigration policy in an era when corporations cross borders at will. Nominated for a 2002 Emmy Award! Produced by the National Network for Immigrant Rights with the Interfaith Coalition for Immigrant Rights. 28 minutes, 2002. Bilingual with English/Spanish subtitles. To order, visit www.nnirr.org.

Well Founded Fear. This documentary looks at the process of granting political asylum to the United States. Who deserves it? Who gets it? Who decides? Entering the closed corridors of the U.S. Immigration and Naturalization Service (INS) the filmmakers uncover a world where American ideals about human rights collide with the nearly impossible task of trying to know the truth. Facilitator's guide is available. Produced by Michael Camerini and Shari Robertson. 119 minutes, 1999. To order, visit http://www.pbs.org/pov/pov1999/wellfoundedfear.

Organizational Contacts

ANDOLAN: Organizing South Asian Workers
PO Box 2087,
Long Island City, NY 11102
Tel: 719-390-7264

Arab Women's Solidarity Association,
P.O. Box 95760 Seattle, WA 98145
www.awsa.net

Asian American Legal Defense and Education Fund
99 Hudson St., 12th Fl.
New York, NY 10013
Tel: 212-966-5932
www.aaldef.org

Asian Immigrant Women Advocates
310 8th Street Suite 301
Oakland, CA 94607
Tel: 510-208-7290
Fax: 510-268-0194
www.aiwa.org

Asian and Pacific American Health Forum
942 Market St., Suite 200
San Francisco, CA 94102
Tel: 415-954-9988
www.apiaf.org

Asian Women's Shelter
3543 18th Street, Box 19
San Franscisco, CA 94110
Tel: 415-751-7110
www.sfaws.org

Audre Lorde Project
85 South Oxford Street
Brooklyn, NY 11217-1607
Tel: (718) 596-0342
Fax: (718) 596-1328
www.alp.org

Bay Area Immigrant Rights Coalition
310 8th St. Suite 303
Oakland, CA 94607
Tel: 510-839-7598

Border Action Network
PO Box 384
Tucson, AZ 85702
Tel: 520-623-4944
www.borderaction.org

Border Network for Human Rights
611 S. Kansas
El Paso, TX 79901
Tel: 915-577-0724
Fax: 915-577-0370

CAAAV: Organizing Asian Communities
2473 Valentine Ave.
Bronx, NY 10458
Tel: 718-220-7391
Fax: 718-220-7398
www.caaav.org

Campaign for Migrant Domestic Women's Rights, c/o the Institute for Policy Studies
733 15th Street, NW Suite 1020,
Washington, DC 20005
Tel: 202-234-9382
http://www.ips-dc.org/campaign/index2.htm

Center for Immigrant Families
2710 Broadway, 2nd Fl.
New York, NY 10025
Tel: 212-521-3011

Center for Women's Global Leadership
Douglass College, Rutgers, The State University of New Jersey
160 Ryders Lane,
New Brunswick, NJ 08901
Tel: 732-932-8782
www.cwgl.rutgers.edu

Centro Juan Diego
8812 S. Commercial
Chicago, IL 60617
Tel: 773-731-0109
Fax: 773-731-0119

Coalición de Derechos Humanos
PO Box 1286
Tucson, AZ 85702
Tel: 520-770-1373

Organizational Contacts

Coalition to Abolish Slavery and Trafficking
5042 Wilshire Blvd., #586
Los Angeles, CA 90036
Tel: 213-365-1906
www.castla.org.

Detention Watch Network
700 Light St.
Baltimore, MD 21230
Tel: 410-230-2700
www.lirs.org

Domestic Workers United, c/o CAAAV
2437 Valentine Ave., Bronx, NY 10458.
Tel: 718-220-7391 x 11.
www.domesticworkersunited.org.

Family Violence Prevention Fund
383 Rhode Island St. Suite #304
San Francisco, CA 94103
Tel: 415-252-8900
www.fvpf.org

Farmworker Association of Florida
815 S. Park St.
Apopka, FL 32703
Tel: 407-886-5151

Filipino Civil Rights Advocates
310 8th St. Suite 308
Oakland, CA 94607
Tel: 510-465-9876

Haitian Women for Haitian Refugees
335 Maple St.
Brooklyn, NY 11225
Tel: 718-735-4660

Highlander Center
1959 Highlander Way
New Market, TN 37820
Tel: 865-933-3443 x 242
Fax: 865-933-3424
www.highlandercenter.org

Illinois Coalition for Immigrant and Refugee Rights
36 S. Wabash Ave. Suite 1425
Chicago, IL 60603
Tel: 312-332-7360
www.icirr.org

Immigrant Worker Freedom Ride Network
1219 28th St., NW, Washington, DC 20007
Tel: 202-661-4204
www.iwfr.org

Incite! Women of Color Against Violence
P.O. Box 6861, Minneapolis, MN 55406. Tel: (415) 553-3837.
www.incite-national.org.

Institute for Multiracial Justice
522 Valencia Street, San Francisco, CA 94110.
Tel: 415-701-9501
www.multiracialjustice.org

International Gay and Lesbian Human Rights Commission
1375 Sutter Street, Suite 222
San Francisco, CA 94109
Tel: 415-561-0633
www.iglhrc.org

Just Act
333 Valencia Street, Suite 325
San Francisco, CA 94103
Tel: 415-431-4204
Fax: 415-431-5953
www.justact.org

Korean Immigrant Workers Association
3465 W. 8th St.
Los Angeles, CA 90005
Tel: 213-378-9050
www.kiwa.org

La Mujer Obrera
PO Box 3975
El Paso, TX 79923
Tel: 915-533-9710

Labor/Community Strategy Center
3780 Wilshire Blvd., Suite 1200
Los Angeles, CA 90010.
Tel: 213-387-2800.
www.thestrategycenter.org

La Raza Centro Legal
474 Valencia St. Suite 295
San Francisco, CA 90005
Tel: 415-575-3500

Organizational Contacts

Lesbian and Gay Immigration Rights Task Force
350 W. 31st St. Suite 505
New York, NY, 10001
Tel: 212-714-2904
www.lgirtf.org

Líderes Campesinas/ Farmworker Women's Leadership Network
611 S. Rebecca St.
Pomona, CA 91766
Tel: 909-865-7776

LLEGÓ
1420 K Street, NW Suite 200
Washington, DC 20005
Tel: 202-408-5380
www.llego.org

Manavi
PO Box 3103
New Brunswick, NJ 08901
Tel: 732-435-1414
www.research.att.com/~krishnas/manavi/

Massachusetts Immigrant and Refugee Advocacy Coalition
105 Chauncy St. #901
Boston, MA 02111
www.miracoalition.org

Migration Policy and Resource Center at Occidental College
1600 Campus Road
Los Angeles, CA 90041
Tel: 323-259-1407
Fax: 323-259-2734

Mujeres Unidas y Activas
3543 18th St. #23
San Francisco, CA 94110
Tel: 415-626-2128
www.mujeresunidas.net

National Asian Pacific American Legal Consortium
1140 Connecticut Ave NW, Suite 1200
Washington, DC 20036
Tel: 202-296-2300
www.napalc.org

National Center for Human Rights Education
PO Box 311020
Atlanta, GA 31131
Tel: 404-344-9629
Fax: 404-346-7517
www.nchre.org

National Day Laborer Organizing Network
2533 W. Third St., Ste. 101
Los Angeles, CA 90057
Tel: 213-353-1336
Fax: 213-353-1344

National Network To End Violence Against Immigrant Women, c/o National Immigration Project of the National Lawyer's Guild
14 Beacon St. Suite 602
Boston, MA 02108
Tel: 617-227-9727

National Network for Immigrant and Refugee Rights
310 8th St. Suite 303
Oakland, CA 94607
Tel: 510-465-1984
www.nnirr.org

National Korean American Service and Education Consortium
900 S. Crenshaw Blvd.
Los Angeles, CA 90019
Tel: 323-937-3703
www.nakasec.org

National Mobilization Against Sweatshops
PO Box 130293
New York, NY 10013
Tel: 718-625-9091
www.nmass.org

National Organizers Alliance
715 G Street SE
Washington DC 20003
Tel: 202-543-6603
Fax: 202-543-2462
www.noacentral.org

Pineros y Campesinos Unidos Noroeste (PCUN)
300 Young St.
Woodburn, OR 97071
Tel: 503-982-0243
www.pcun.org

Organizational Contacts

Poverty & Race Research Action Council (PRRAC)
3000 Connecticut Ave., N.W.,
Ste. 200, Washington, DC 20008.
Tel: 202-387-9887
www.prrac.org

Project South
9 Gammon Ave.
Atlanta, Georgia 30315
Tel: 404-622-602
Fax: 404-622-618
www.projectsouth.org

Proyecto Libertad
113 N. 1st St.
Harlingen, TX 78550
Tel: 956-425-9552

Refugee Women's Network
4151 Memorial Dr. #204A
Decatur, GA 30032
Tel: 404-296-3967
Fax: 404-296-9118
www.riwn.org

Sakhi
P.O. Box 20208
Greeley Square Station
New York, NY 10001
Tel: 212-714-9153
www.sakhi.org.

SALGA: South Asian Lesbian and Gay Association
PO Box 1491
Old Chelsea Station
New York, NY 10113
Tel: 212-358-5132
www.salganyc.org

Services, Immigrant Rights, and Education Network
778 N. 1st St. Suite 202
San Jose, CA 95112
Tel: 408-286-5680
www.siren-bayarea.org

Southeast Regional Economic Justice Network
PO Box 240
Durham, NC 27702
Tel: 919-683-4310
Fax: 919-683-4310
www.rejn.org

Sweatshop Watch
310 8th St. Suite 303
Oakland, CA 94607
Tel: 510-834-8990
www.sweatshopwatch.org

Trikone
PO Box 14161
San Francisco, CA 94414
Tel: 415-487-8778.
www.trikone.org

UC Berkeley Center for Labor Research and Education
2521 Channing Way # 5555
Berkeley, CA 94720
Phone: (510) 642-0323
Fax: (510) 642-6432
www.laborcenter.berkeley.edu

Western States Center
PO Box 40305
Portland, OR 97240
Tel: 503-228-8866x110
Fax: 503-228-1965
www.westernstatescenter.org

Women of Color Resource Center
1611 Telegraph #303
Oakland, CA 94612
Tel: 510-444-2700
Fax: 510-444-2711
www.coloredgirls.org

Women Watch Afrika
4281 Memorial Dr. Suite 1
Decatur, GA 30032
Tel: 404-292-0069

Bridge Glossary

245(i): A provision of immigration law, now expired, which allowed people on the verge of gaining their immigration status to remain in the U.S. Without this option, immigrants returning to their home countries to process their paperwork could be prevented from returning to the U.S. due to new three and ten year bars.

AEDPA: The Anti-Terrorism and Effective Death Penalty Act, passed in 1996, allowed the U.S. government to use secret evidence to accuse immigrants of terrorist acts. This legislation also eliminated a waiver that allowed permanent residents convicted of crimes to avoid deportation and implemented "summary exclusion" of asylum seekers.

Ally: Someone who advocates for and supports members of a community other than their own, reaching across differences to achieve mutual goals. Also refers to a member of a dominant group who works to end a form of oppression that gives her/him privilege. For example, an ally could be a white person who works to end racism, a heterosexual person who works to fight homophobia.

Asylum seeker: A migrant in the United States or at a port of entry who is found to be unable or unwilling to return to his or her country of nationality, or to seek the protection of that country because of persecution or a well-founded fear of persecution. Persecution or the fear thereof must be based on the individual's race, religion, nationality, membership in a particular social group, or political opinion.

Backlog: Accumulated applications from people who meet the requirements to immigrate to the United States but are waiting for visas to become available. Depending on the family relationship (i.e., parent, spouse, children, sibling) to a U.S. citizen or permanent resident, as well as the country of origin, the wait can be very lengthy—sometimes as long as twenty years. The backlog accumulates in part because there is an annual limit on the number of these visas that can be issued per country and overall.

Biphobia: The fear, hatred, distrust of bisexual people and their ability to have sexual, emotional, and spiritual relationships with someone of any sex.

Bisexual: People who form primary loving and sexual relationships with both men and women. Many people avoid this term because of its implication that there are only two sexes/genders to be sexually attracted to and thus reinforces the binary gender system.

Bureau of Border and Transportation Security (BTS): Primary bureau under the Department of Homeland Security that is responsible for immigration, transportation, and customs. BTS absorbed the enforcement units of the Immigration and Naturalization Service, such as the

Border Patrol and investigative agents of INS.

Bureau of Citizenship and Immigration Services (BCIS): Bureau under the Department of Homeland Security that administers services such as immigrant and nonimmigrant sponsorship; adjustment of status; work authorization and other permits; naturalization of qualified applicants for U.S. citizenship; and asylum or refugee processing.

Bureau of Immigration and Customs Enforcement (BICE): Bureau under the Department of Homeland Security that is responsible for immigration enforcement in the interior, raids at the workplace, and is responsible for detention and removal, the Student and Exchange Visitor Information System (SEVIS), and Special Registration.

Capital: Resources such as factories and equipment used to produce other goods and services; the cash that is invested in business.

Chicana/Chicano: Person of Mexican descent in the U.S.

Civil rights: The right to be equal to anyone else in society. Civil rights are a human right.

Cultural rights: These rights include the right to freedom of religion, to speak your own language, and maintain a distinct cultural identity. Cultural rights are a human right.

Department of Homeland Security: The Department of Homeland Security (DHS) was created in 2003, and took over the responsibilities of the Immigration and Naturalization Service (INS.) See also: Bureau of Citizenship and Immigration Services (BCIS), and Bureau of Immigration and Customs Enforcement (BICE), and Bureau of Border and Transportation Security (BTS.)

Deregulation: A reduction in government regulation of industries that could diminish profits, including environmental laws and legislation that protects worker safety.

Developing Country: One of many terms used to refer to nations of the "South," primarily former colonies that remain impoverished by a global economy dominated by Northern industrial nations. Other terms include "Third World" and "less developed countries." There is much debate about the appropriateness of all of these terms.

Disability: A form of social oppression, caused by disadvantages or restrictions of activities when society takes little or no account of people who have physical impairments, excluding them from participation in the mainstream of social activities. (Nasa Begum, "Disabled Women and the Feminist Agenda, Feminist Review, Spring 1992)

Economic Justice- A conviction that economic policies must result in benefits that are distributed equally across income and racial lines; that jobs created by state and local tax incentives must go to local people and taxpayers; and that the health, natural resources, and the culture of the community must be protected.

Economic rights: The right to have an economy that meets people's economic needs, such as the right to a living wage, and the right to organize labor unions. Economic rights are a human right.

Employer Sanctions: The first federal law that criminalized the hiring of undocumented workers, and required employers to verify workers' documents. This policy has been criticized for causing more discrimination and for undermining workers' rights.

Environmental Justice: The right to a safe, healthy, productive, and sustainable environment; equal enforcement of environmental regulations; and a movement to protect communities of color and poor communities from environmental hazards.

Environmental Racism: Racial discrimination in environmental policy-making, enforcement of regulations and laws, and targeting of communities of color for toxic waste disposal and siting of polluting industries; and the history of excluding people of color from the leadership of the environmental movement.

Free Trade: This term is often used to describe capitalism in general, referring to the fact that goods, services, and labor are bought and sold in an open market. The reality is that under capitalism, markets can be controlled through government regulation, concentration of industry in a few hands (monopolies, cartels), and such illegal activities such as price fixing, discrimination, etc.

Gay: Someone who is primarily and/or exclusively attracted to members of their own sex or gender. In certain contexts, this term is used to refer only to those who identify as men.

Gender: Cultural and societal understandings of what "maleness" or "femaleness" means (as opposed to sex, the biological or physical identification of male or female.)

Gender bias: Socially and culturally based ideas and practices that shape women and men's different status and opportunities.

Gender identity: How we see ourselves—some of us as women, as men, or some as a combination of both, or some as neither.

Global North: A term used to label wealthier countries (including the United States, Canada, Australia, and Western European Nations). Most nations in the Global North gained much of their wealth through colonialism, and continue to benefit from exploitation of countries in the Global South through unequal trade and economic practices.

Global South: A term used to label poorer countries, located in Asia, Africa, Latin America, and the Caribbean. The majority of the world's population lives in the Global South.

Globalization: A term used to refer to the expansion of economies beyond national borders, in particular, the expansion of production by a firm to many countries around the world, i.e. globalization of production, or the "global assembly line." This has given transnational corporations power beyond nation-states, and has weakened any nation's ability to control corporate practices and flows of capital, set regulations, control balances of trade and exchange rates, or manage domestic economic policy. It has also weakened the ability of workers to fight for better wages and working conditions from fear that employers may relocate to other areas.

Green Card: "Green Card" is identification issued by the U.S. Bureau of Immigration and Citizenship Services to non-U.S. citizens who have been granted the right to live and work in the U.S. permanently. Green cards are so-named because they were originally green in color.

H-1 B visa: A provision of immigration law that allows companies to hire "skilled" foreign workers to work in the U.S. under temporary visas. These visas are linked to employment, so employers have the power to fire and hire workers and grant them legal immigration status, further increasing the vulnerability of an immigrant worker.

Heterosexual/Straight Person: A person who is primarily and/or exclusively attracted to members of a gender or sex which is seen to be "opposite" or other than the one with which they identify.

Heterosexism: The societal/ cultural, institutional, and individual beliefs and practices that assume hetrosexuality is the only natural, normal, acceptable sexual identity.

Homophobia: The fear, hatred or intolerance of gays, lesbians, or queer-identified people in general. This can be manifested as an intense dislike or rejection of such people, or violent actions against them.

Homosexual: A person who is primarily and/or exclusively attracted to members of what they identify as their own sex or gender. Because the term can have connotations of disease and abnormality, some people do not like to identify as homosexual. Others do not feel that it accurately defines their chosen identity.

Human Rights: Human rights are those rights that are considered universal, inalienable, indivisible and interconnected for all people, recognized with the UN's passage of the Universal Declaration of Human Rights. Every person has the same human rights, and human rights can never be taken away from a person. No person's human rights are more important than another person's, and all human rights are equally important. Human rights include civil, cultural, economic, political and social rights.

"Illegal Immigrant:" The term used by anti-immigrant forces to refer to undocumented or out-of-status immigrants who are not granted authorization by the U.S. government to live or work in the United States.

Immigrant: Any individual from one country living in another country.

Immigration and Naturalization System (INS): Until 2003, the INS was the U.S. department responsible for immigration services and enforcement. See also: Department of Homeland Security.

Indigenous peoples: The original inhabitants of an area.

Informal Economy: Economic activities that take place outside the framework of corporate, public, and private sector establishments. Features include small size of operation, reliance on family labor and local resources, low capital investments, labor-intensive technology, limited barriers to entry, high degree of competition, unskilled workforces. Informal businesses usually do not comply with established regulations governing labor practices, taxes, and licensing. This absence of regulation can affect the status of workers, working conditions, and form of management. Sometimes called the "underground" or "secondary economy."

Institutionalized oppression: The systematic, pervasive, and routine mistreatment of various groups of people who are disadvantaged by imbalances of power in society. This mistreatment occurs in social institutions, such as economic, political, educational, judicial systems. Unequal access to health care, housing, employment, and discriminatory policing and profiling are examples of institutionalized oppression.

Internally Displaced Persons: People who are forcibly uprooted from their homes by violent conflicts, gross violations of human rights and other traumatic events, but who remain within the borders of their own countries.

International Monetary Fund: Founded in 1944 at the Bretton Woods Conference by the western industrial powers, the IMF administers and coordinates exchange rate policies and provides member states with financing to enable them to balance their trade payments. Today, the IMF acts as a financial policeman over the developing world, pushing for trade liberalization, debt payments, and privatization.

Intersex: An anatomical variation from typical understandings of male and female genetics. The physical manifestation, at birth, of genetic or endocrinological differences from the cultural norm. Also a group of medical conditions that challenge standard sex designations, proving that sex, like gender, is a social construct. Intersex and transgender folks share some overlapping experiences and perspectives, but the terms are not synonymous, and the issues are not the same. "Intersex" or "intersexual" is used today in favor of the term "hermaphrodite".

Leadership training: Training grassroots leaders through political and organizational skills development to plan, implement, and critically evaluate an organization's work.

Legal Permanent Resident: An immigrant in the United States with legal residency with the government's authorization to live and work. The Department of Homeland Security also defines this person as a "Permanent Resident Alien."

Legalization: term of providing legal permanent residency to undocumented immigrants. See also amnesty.

Lesbian: Women who form primary loving and sexual relationships with other women. Some women may also use the term "gay" to describe themselves.

LGBT: Lesbian, Gay, Bisexual, and Transgender. Also seen as: GLBT, GLT, etc.

Maquila/ Maquiladora: Spanish term for foreign-owned plants that operate in Mexico, Central America, and the Caribbean, using local labor to assemble goods for the U.S. and other foreign markets. The politics of U.S. and regional governments encourage U.S. businesses to transfer production to Latin American subsidiaries or subcontractors.

Migrant: People who move from their place of origin, within a country, or across borders. International migrants include settlers who stay permanently, contract workers for a limited period of time, professionals, and undocumented workers. In the U.S., "immigrant" is often used to describe people who move across borders, while "migrant" often refers to workers who move seasonally to work in different areas (for example, farm workers.)

Monetary policy: The use of interest rates and money supply changes to control the business cycle. During recessions, the Federal Reserve Bank often lowers interest rates to stimulate more spending; during inflationary periods, the Federal Reserve Bank usually raises interest rates.

Nativism: Intense dislike and opposition to a minority group perceived to be "foreign."

Naturalization: The act of changing one's citizenship from one country to another. Generally, legal permanent residents may apply to become naturalized United States Citizens five years after residing in the United States as permanent residents. Other requirements include: (1) good moral character for the five years preceding application for naturalization (usually interpreted to mean serious criminal convictions); (2) the ability to ready and write in English; and (3) permanently residing in the US (and not being outside more than six months) for the five years preceding application.

Neo-liberalism: "Neo-liberalism" is a set of economic policies that have recently become widespread. Neo-liberalism supports an extreme of privatization and deregulation, cutting of public expenditures for social services, and allows the freedom of movement for capital, goods and services.

NGO: (Non governmental-organizations) - An international organization made up of persons other than states. "Non-profit," or "community based organization" is the terminology most used in the U.S.

Network building: Building alliances among organizations that share common political perspectives and concerns.

Oppression: the systematic and institutionalized mistreatment, exploitation, and exclusion of people who are members of a certain group.

People of Color: A term used to refer to nonwhite people, used instead of the term "minority," which implies inferiority and disenfranchisement. The term emphasizes common experiences of racial discrimination or racism.

Political rights: Political rights include the rights to take part in the government of one's country, such as the rights enshrined in the U.S. Bill of Rights, which include voting rights, freedom of speech, etc. Political rights are a human right.

Popular Education: A form of social change education with roots in Latin America. Popular education starts with the experience of oppressed people, links new knowledge and information with what they already know, and leads to action through this knowledge towards social change.

Privatization: The sale of state-owned enterprises, goods and services to private investors. This includes banks, key industries, railroads, toll highways, electricity, schools, hospitals and even fresh water. Although usually done in the name of greater efficiency, which is often needed, privatization has mainly had the effect of concentrating wealth even more in a few hands and making the public pay even more for its needs.

Profits: The difference between a firm's costs and the income gained from the sale of its products and services, most often generated by labor.

Queer: An umbrella identity term encompassing lesbians, questioning people, gay men, bisexuals, non-labeling people, transgendered folks, and anyone else who does not strictly identify as heterosexual. "Queer" originated as a derogatory word. Currently, it is being reclaimed by some people and used as a statement of empowerment. Some people identify as queer to distance themselves from the rigid catagorizations of "straight" and "gay". Some transgendered, lesbian, gay, questioning, non-labeling, and bisexual people, however, reject the use of this term due its connotations of deviance and its tendency to gloss over and sometimes deny the differences between these groups.

Racism: The institutionalized and day-to-day mistreatment of people of color. This mistreatment takes on many forms including economic, social, and physical violence.

Refugee: Any person who is outside his or her country of nationality who is unable or unwilling to return to that country because of persecution or a well-founded fear of persecution. Persecution or the fear thereof must be based on the alien's race, religion, nationality, membership in a particular social group, or political opinion. People with no nationality must generally be outside their country of last habitual residence to qualify as a refugee. Refugees are subject to ceilings by geographic area set annually by the President in consultation with Congress and are eligible to adjust to lawful permanent resident status after one year of continuous presence in the United States.

Remittances: The money that migrant and immigrant workers send to their families living in their countries of origin. Remittances often contribute substantially to the economy of developing countries.

Student and Exchange Visitor Information System (SEVIS): government process that collects information and monitors international foreign students and visitors in the United States.

Sex: refers to a person's biological identity as male or female (as opposed to "gender," which speaks to cultural and societal understandings of maleness or femaleness).

Social rights: These rights include the right to food, shelter, education, health care, and social services. Social rights are a human right.

Stereotype: Negative messages about specific groups of people that allows mistreatment of people, granting a whole system of privileges to one sector of the population at the expense of another.

Temporary Protected Status (TPS): A status allowing residence and employment authorization to nationals of foreign states for a period of not less than six or no more than 18 months, when such states have been appropriately designated by the attorney general because of extraordinary and temporary conditions in such state(s).

Third World: Nations of Latin America, the Caribbean, Africa, Asia, and the Middle East. This term is often used for developing nations that were colonized and exploited by the nations of the "first world," i.e. Western Europe, Japan, and the U.S. According to this framework, which arose in a political context that no longer exists, the second world included the socialist nations of Eastern Europe and the Soviet Union.

Trafficking: the United Nations defines trafficking in persons as "the recruitment, transportation, transfer, harboring or receipt of persons, by means of the threat or use of force or other forms of coercion, of abduction, of fraud, of deception, of the abuse of power or of a position of vulnerability or of the giving or receiving of payments or benefits to achieve the consent of a person having control over another person, for the purpose of exploitation. Exploitation shall include, at a minimum, the exploitation of the prostitution of others or other forms of sexual exploitation, forced labour or services, slavery or practices similar to slavery, servitude or the removal of organs."

Transgender: This term has many definitions. It is frequently used as an umbrella term to refer to all people who deviate from their assigned gender or the binary gender system, including intersex people, transsexuals, cross-dressers, transvestites, gender queers, drag kings, drag queens, two-spirit people, and others. Some transgendered people feel they exist not within one of the two standard gender categories, but rather somewhere between, beyond, or outside of those two genders. The term can also be applied exclusively to people who live prmarily as the gender "opposite" to that which they were assigned at birth. These people may sometimes prefer the term "transsexual".

Transphobia: A reaction of fear, loathing and discriminatory treatment of people whose gender identity or gender presentation (or perceived gender or gender identity) does not match, in a socially accepted way, the sex they were assigned at birth. Transgendered people, intersexuals, lesbians, gay men & bisexuals are typically the targets of transphobia.

Undocumented Immigrant: An immigrant who has entered the United States without authorization or someone who has overstayed the stated amount of time on their visa/paperwork. Often referred to by anti-immigrant groups as "illegal alien."

White Supremacy: White supremacy is a historically based, institutionally perpetuated system of exploitation and oppression of continents, nations and peoples of color by white peoples and nations of the European continent; whiteness and the construction of all races based on shifting definitions and categories.

World Bank (The International Bank for Reconstruction and Development): Founded in 1944 at the Bretton Woods Conference between dominant "free world" powers, the World Bank was also known as the International Bank for Reconstruction and Development (IBRD). It was established to coordinate with several regional banks in the long-term development of nations. In recent years it has joined with the International Monetary Fund (IMF) in imposing loan conditions that promote "free market" policies and restructuring.

Xenophobia: hatred or fear of strangers and foreigners.

Sources:

American Friends Service Committee, "Immigration Reform: A Glossary." Philadelphia: AFSC, April 2004. Reprinted with permission. From http://www.afsc.org/immigrants-rights/policy/glossary.htm.

Bev Burke, Jojo Geronimo, D'Arcy Martin, Barb Thomas, and Carol Wall. *Education for Changing Unions.* Toronto: Between the Lines Press, 2002. Reprinted with permission.

Miriam Ching Louie and Linda Burnham, *WEDGE: Women's Education in the Global Economy.* Berkeley, CA: Women of Color Resource Center, 2000. Reprinted with permission.

National Network for Immigrant and Refugee Rights, "Legalization Then and Now: An 80-Year History," *Network News,* Summer 2000.

Pamela Sparr, *Global Economics—Seeking a Christian Ethic.* Washington, DC: Women's Division, United Methodist Church, 1993. Reprinted with credit.

Hugh Vasquez and Isoke Femi. *No Boundaries: A Manual for Unlearning Oppression and Building Multicultural Alliances.* Todos Institute, 1993. Reprinted with permission.

About the Authors:

Francisco "Pancho" Argüelles Paz y Puente, born in Mexico, has lived in the U.S. since 1997. He has organized and taught popular education extensively in rural communities throughout Central America and the U.S. for the past 20 years. Pancho received a B.A. in Pedagogy and participated in the student movement at the Universidad Nacional Autonoma de Mexico (UNAM). He began to work as a popular educator in 1983 with Guatemalan refugees in Chiapas. He co-founded the Universidad Campesina in Esteli, Nicaragua, and then returned to Mexico to coordinate a research collective on Poverty and the Environment. From 1994-1996, he coordinated "Caminemos Juntos," a rural development project in the mountains of Central Mexico. He is a board member of NNIRR, and worked as the organizer for the Immigrant Community Organizer Working Group (ICO) of the National Organizer's Alliance (NOA) from 2000-2003.

Eunice Hyunhye Cho is the BRIDGE Project Coordinator at the National Network for Immigrant and Refugee Rights. She coordinates the organization's education programming. She co-coordinated NNIRR's campaign to bring grassroots immigrant rights leaders to the UN World Conference Against Racism, and co-authored and edited *"From the Borderline to the Colorline: A Report on Anti-Immigrant Racism in the U.S."* and *"A World on the Move: A Report from the UN World Conference Against Racism."* She is a Steering Committee member of the Committee on Women, Population, and the Environment. A Korean American hailing from Arizona, she drums and chants with Jamaesori: Sister Sound, a Korean women's drumming group. She is a graduate of Yale University with a degree in American Studies and Ethnicity, Race, and Migration Studies.

Sasha Khokha is the former Communications Direct at NNIRR, where she co-produced the documentary film *Uprooted: Refugees of the Global Economy*. She is now completing her masters at the UC Berkeley School of Journalism, and sits on the national board of Working Films, an organization linking documentary films to social change campaigns. Sasha co-authored *"Hate Unleashed: Los Angeles in the Wake of Proposition 187."* Sasha was recognized as one of 25 "Next Generation Leaders" through a fellowship awarded by the Rockefeller Foundation in 1998, and is active with Trikone, a network of lesbian and gay activists of South Asian origin.

Miriam Ching Yoon Louie's books, *Sweatshop Warriors: Immigrant Women Workers Take on the Global Factory* (South End Press, 2001) and *Women's Education in the Global Economy: A Workbook* (with Linda Burnham, WCRC, 2000) are dedicated to the "women without whose labor, love, sweat, and tears we would not even exist on this planet." Louie works on the BRIDGE Project with NNIRR, runs with her Women of Color Resource Center (WCRC) Board sisters, and formerly served as national campaign media coordinator of Asian Immigrant Women Advocates in Oakland, CA, and Fuerza Unida in San Antonio. Of Korean and Chinese descent, Miriam clangs lion cymbals in *XicKorea: Poems, Rants and Words Together* (with Beth Ching and Arnoldo García, Xingao Productions, 2002), and jams with Jamaesori/Sister Sound, a drumming group of Korean American women community activists.

BRIDGE Project Staff

Eunice Hyunhye Cho, *BRIDGE Project Coordinator*

Francisco Argüelles Paz y Puente, *BRIDGE Project Consultant*

Miriam Ching Yoon Louie, *BRIDGE Project Consultant*

Sasha Khokha, *BRIDGE Project Consultant*

BRIDGE Project Interns:

Diana Bernal, Tzong Chang, Christina Charuhas, Evonne Lai, David Menninger, Betty Marín, Shea Rao, and Michelle Yamashita.

BRIDGE Advisory Committee:

Tomás Aguilar

Jennifer Allen, *Border Action Network*

Susan Alva, *Migration Policy and Resource Center, Occidental College*

Pablo Alvarado, *National Day Labor Organizing Network*

Sung E Bai, *CAAAV: Organizing Asian Communities*

Amy Casso, *National Organizers Alliance*

Jung Hee Choi, *Women of Color Resource Center*

Trishala Deb, *Audre Lorde Project*

Eman Desouky, *Arab Women's Solidarity Association*

Leah Grundy, *UC Berkeley Labor Center*

Mónica Hernández, *Highlander Center*

Stacy Kono, *Asian Immigrant Women Advocates*

Alma Maquitico, *Border Network for Human Rights*

Víctor Narro, *UCLA Labor Center*

Lisa Moore, *Mujeres Unidas y Activas*

Rosa Perea, *Centro Juan Diego*

Katie Quan, *UC Berkeley Center for Labor Research and Education*

Tarso Ramos, *Western States Center*

Ninaj Raoul, *Haitian Women for Haitian Refugees*

Loretta Ross, *National Center for Human Rights Education*

Jerome Scott, *Project South, Atlanta, GA*

Mangala Sharma, *Refugee Women's Network*

NNIRR Staff:

Eunice Cho, *BRIDGE Project*

Arnoldo García, *Enforcement Project*

Claudia Gómez-Arteaga, *Immigrant Rights Project*

Colin Rajah, *International Project*

Catherine Tactaquin, *Executive Director*

NNIRR Board:

Susan Alva, *Migration Policy and Resource Center, Occidental College, Los Angeles*

Francisco Argüelles Paz Y Puente, *Houston*

Sung E Bai, *CAAAV: Organizing Asian Communities, New York*

Eduardo Canales, *Mountain West Regional Council, United Brotherhood of Carpenters, Denver*

Brad Erickson, *Oakland*

Lillian Galedo, *Filipinos for Affirmative Action, Oakland*

Isabel García, *Coalición de Derechos Humanos, Tucson*

Maricela García, *Chicago*

María Jiménez, *Houston*

Dan Kesselbrenner, *NLG/National Immigration Project, Boston*

Stan Mark, *Asian American Legal Defense and Education Fund (AALDEF), New York*

Rogelio T. Núñez, *Casa de Proyecto Libertad, Harlingen*

Ramón Ramírez, *Pineros y Campesinos Unidos del Noroeste (PCUN), Woodburn, OR*

Juan Manuel Sandoval, *Seminario Permanente de Estudios Chicanos y de Fronteras, México*

Reneé Saucedo, *La Raza Centro Legal, San Francisco*

Catherine Tactaquin, *NNIRR Director*

Join the National Network!

As a member of the National Network for Immigrant and Refugee Rights, you'll receive periodic updates, fax or email action alerts, and be part of our electronic mailing list. Most importantly, you'll become a part of a vibrant and innovative network of activists, organizations, and communities working for the rights of all immigrants and refugees. In addition, you'll also receive Network News, our cutting-edge newsmagazine published three times a year. You'll also receive invitations to Network educational events, including BRIDGE train-the-trainers in your area!

Join the National Network!

Please print clearly: mail this form with your check or money order payable to "NNIRR," and send to: NNIRR, 310 8th St. Suite 303, Oakland, CA 94607

Annual membership dues:

Individual membership:
- ❏ $25 (regular)
- ❏ $15 (low income)
- ❏ $5 (unemployed, fixed income)

Organizational membership:
- ❏ $35 (annual budget below $50,000)
- ❏ $50 ($50,000-$99,999)
- ❏ $100 ($100,000-$199,999)
- ❏ $150 ($200,000-$349,999)
- ❏ $250 ($350,000 +)

Amount Enclosed$_____

Name _____
Organization _____
Address _____
City/State/Zip _____
Phone _____ Fax _____ Email _____

The National Network for Immigrant and Refugee Rights (NNIRR) is a national organization composed of local coalitions and immigrant, refugee, community, religious, civil rights and labor organizations and activists. It serves as a forum to share information and analysis, to educate communities and the general public, and to develop and coordinate plans of action on important immigrant and refugee issues.

We work to promote a just immigration and refugee policy in the United States and to defend and expand the rights of all immigrants and refugees, regardless of immigration status. The National Network bases its efforts in the principles of equality and justice, and seeks the enfranchisement of all immigrant and refugee communities in the United States through organizing and advocating for their full labor, environmental, civil and human rights. We further recognize the unparalleled change in global, political and economic structures which has exacerbated regional, national and international patterns of migration, and emphasize the need to build international support and cooperation to strengthen the rights, welfare and safety of migrants and refugees.

Uprooted order form
Order the award-winning video produced by NNIRR!

Uprooted: Refugees of the Global Economy

Uprooted is a compelling tale of how the global economy, including U.S. corporations and the International Monetary Fund, has forced people to leave their home countries.

Uprooted presents three stories of immigrants who left their homes in Haiti, Bolivia, and the Philippines after global economic powers devastated their countries, only to face new challenges in the United States.

Maricel is one of thousands of women encouraged by the Philippine government to work abroad as a domestic in order to pay for its international debt. Her employer, a top New York corporate executive, refused to pay her the minimum wage. Free trade destroyed Jessy and Jaime's family business in Bolivia. They came to the U.S. and worked as janitors despite their engineering degrees. Luckner left Haiti after working for 14 cents an hour in a U.S.-owned baseball factory that moved to China in search of cheaper labor costs.

Uprooted weaves these stories into a penetrating film, raising critical questions about U.S. immigration policy in an era when corporations cross borders at will.

Uprooted is available in a bilingual version, subtitled in English and Spanish. 26 minutes.
Uprooted is $20.00, plus $3.50 shipping and handling for each copy.

Yes! I'd like to order ____ video(s). Please send it to:

Name _____
Organization _____
Address _____
City/State/Zip _____
Phone _____ Fax _____ Email _____

To order, send this completed order form with a check or money order payable to "NNIRR," and mail to: NNIRR, 310 8th St. Suite 303, Oakland, CA 94607. For more information, call 510-465-1984 or visit www.nnirr.org.

Order your copy of

BRIDGE: Building a Race and Immigration Dialogue in the Global Economy
A Popular Education Resource for Immigrant and Refugee Community Organizers

"In all of my years since the 1960's as an activist for peace and justice, I have never come across such an important and exciting book that offers us the tools essential for effective organizing on the issues of immigrant rights and building viable social movement coalitions."
— Dr. Carlos Muñoz, Jr.,
Award winning author and Professor Emeritus, University of California, Berkeley.

"BRIDGE is an important and exciting collection of educational tools that any organizer can use to build the connections between immigration, worker and civil rights, and justice. "
— Maria Elena Durazo,
National Chair, Immigrant Worker Freedom Rides and Vice-President, Hotel Employees and Restaurant Employees Union

BRIDGE is a popular education resource of exercises and tools for immigrant and refugee community organizations, and other allies of immigrants and refugees. It features workshop modules that include activities, discussion questions, fact sheets, and other resources to help build dialogue, engagement, and shared action within and between communities. BRIDGE also includes educational material on NNIRR's award-winning video, Uprooted: Refugees of the Global Economy!

Topics covered in BRIDGE include:
- Immigration History 101
- Building Common Ground With Other Communities
- The Human Rights of Migrants and Refugees
- Intersection of Race, Migration, and Multiple Oppression
- Immigration and Globalization
- LGBT Immigrant Rights
- Immigrant Women's Leadership
- Conflict Transformation in Community Organizing

To order, send a check or money order payable to NNIRR. BRIDGE is $30 + $4 shipping and handling; or order BRIDGE and a copy of Uprooted: Refugees of the Global Economy for $40 + $5 shipping and handling (a $10 savings!).

Please send me _____ **copies of BRIDGE/ Uprooted**   **Amount Enclosed $**_____

Send your order to: National Network for Immigrant and Refugee Rights
310 8th St. Suite 303, Oakland, CA 94607 USA
www.nnirr.org | nnirr@nnirr.org
tel: 510-465-1984 | fax: 510-465-1885

Name

Organization

Address

City/State/Zip

Phone   Fax   Email

___Yes! I would like to be placed on the BRIDGE e-mail list serve, which will give me updates on BRIDGE workshops and trainings around the country!